The Dirges of Maldoror

by

Isidore Ducasse

[Le Comte de Lautréamont]

A Translation of his

Les Chants de Maldoror

Englished & Illustrated by

Gavin L. O'Keefe

RAMBLE HOUSE
2018

First trade paperback edition

Translation, Art & Outro © 2018 Gavin L. O'Keefe

This edition © 2018 Ramble House

Ramble House
10329 Sheephead Drive
Vancleave MS 39565 USA

www.ramblehouse.com

ISBN 13: 978-1-60543-954-9
ISBN 10: 1-60543-954-1

All rights reserved. No part of this book may be reproduced or transmitted in any form or by any means, electronic or mechanical, including photocopying, recording, or by an information storage and retrieval system without permission in writing from the creator and publisher. A reviewer may quote brief passages in a magazine or newspaper critique.

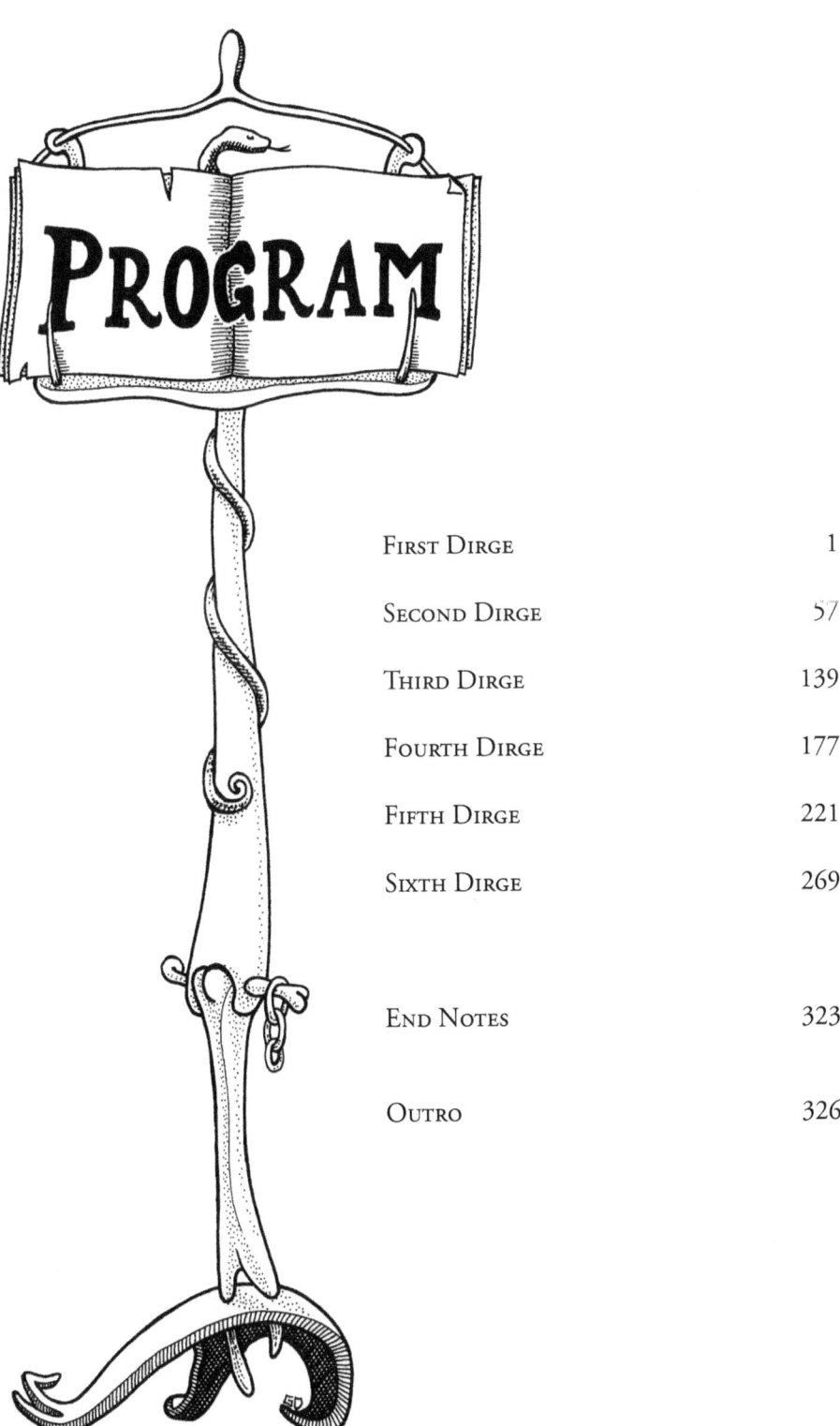

First Dirge	1
Second Dirge	57
Third Dirge	139
Fourth Dirge	177
Fifth Dirge	221
Sixth Dirge	269
End Notes	323
Outro	326

Isidore Ducasse

[Le Comte de Lautréamont]

A Translation of his

Les Chants de Maldoror

Englished & Illustrated by

Gavin L. O'Keefe

First Dirge

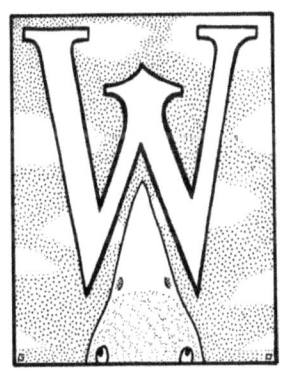

OULD TO HEAVEN that the reader, being bold and temporarily assuming the ferocity of what he reads, finds—without going astray—his impetuous and wild passage through the desolate mire of these dark and venom-filled pages; because unless he can bring to his reading a strong reason and discipline—and at least equal to his defiant resolve—the noisome miasma of this book will saturate his soul as water does sugar. It is not advised that the following pages should be read by all people; only certain persons will savour this bitter fruit without peril. Thus, gentle soul, before proceeding further into such mysterious swamps, turn your heels backward rather than forward. Heed well what I say: turn your heels backward rather than forward, like the eyes of a son who respectfully turns away from the reproachful gaze of the maternal face; or, rather, like a distant angle of delicate cranes, meditating well, who fly forcefully through the silence in winter with all their sails unfurled towards a certain point on the horizon whence is born a sudden strong wind, the herald of the storm. The elder crane who leads the line observes it, shakes her head like a wise one, snaps her beak, is not happy (neither would I be—I would not be in her position), while her old neck, bereft of feathers and the latest of three generations of cranes, writhes in nervous waves which anticipate the tempest drawing ever nearer. After calmly looking several times on all sides with her experienced eyes, carefully, the leader (because she has the privilege of exhibiting her tail feathers to the other less intelligent cranes), with her alert call of the melancholy sentinel to dismiss the common threat, flexibly turns the point of the geometric shape (perhaps it is a triangle, but we cannot see the third line formed in space by these strange birds of passage) to port or starboard like a skilled captain; and manœuvring with wings that appear no larger than a sparrow's, she takes a safer and better course—because she isn't stupid.

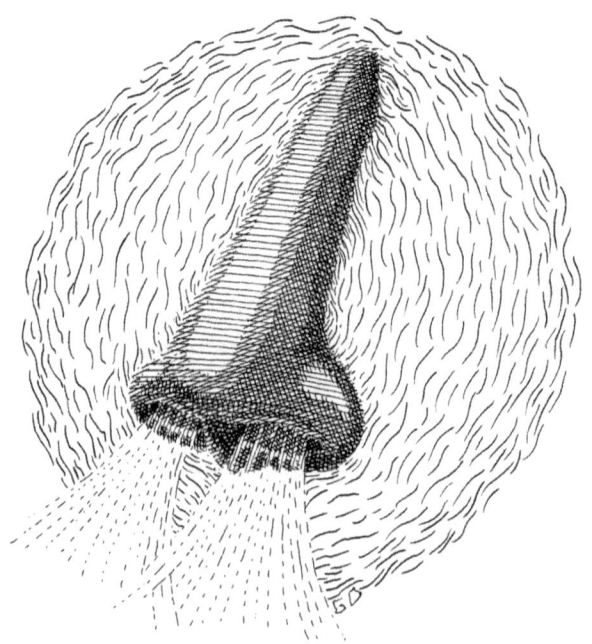

Reader, it is perhaps hatred that you wish me to invoke at the beginning of this book! Who tells you that, soaked in infinite pleasures, you won't snort in with your proud, loose and lean nostrils, as much as you'd like—while turning over on your stomach like a shark in the black and beautiful air (as if you would understand the significance of this act and no less the importance of your true appetite), slowly and majestically—the scarlet fumes? I assure you they will delight the two shapeless orifices of your ugly snout, O monster, if you were to only try breathing in beforehand the accursed consciousness of the Lord three thousand times in succession! Your nostrils, which will be strangely distended in glorious bliss with a still ecstasy, won't ask anything better of space, becoming embalmed as though by perfumes and incenses—because they will be satiated with complete happiness, like the angels who reside in the glory and peace of the pleasant skies.

I will establish in a few lines how Maldoror had been good during his early years, when he had lived happily—that's done. He'd then become aware that he was born evil: extraordinary fate! He had concealed his nature as best he could for a number of years; but finally, as a result of an effort so unnatural to him, the blood rose to his head daily, until—unable to endure such a life—he had thrown himself resolutely into a career of evil… delightful atmosphere! Who'd have ever thought it!—when he kissed a small child with rosy cheeks, he wanted to remove those cheeks with a razor—and he would have repeatedly done so if Justice, with its long line of punishments, had not prevented it every time. He was no liar—he confessed the truth and admitted he was cruel. Humanity, did you hear that? He would dare to repeat it with this shaking quill. Therefore it is a force stronger than will… Damnation! Can the rock not overcome the law of gravity? Impossible. As impossible as evil wishing to collaborate with good. This is what I have just said above.

There are those who write to receive the praise of Mankind, employing the fine heartfelt values that imagination creates or which they may indeed possess. I use *my* genius to paint the delights of cruelty! Delights not ephemeral nor artificial, but which originated with Man and which will end with him. Can genius not ally itself with cruelty within the hidden resolutions of Providence? Or cannot one possess genius *because* one is cruel? We will observe the evidence in my words; it depends on you to listen to me, if you really want to … Excuse me, it appeared that my hair was standing up on my head, but it is nothing—I can easily return it to its proper position with my hand. He who sings doesn't claim that his cavatinas might be an unfamiliar thing; on the contrary, he is satisfied that the lofty and vicious thoughts of his hero are in all men.

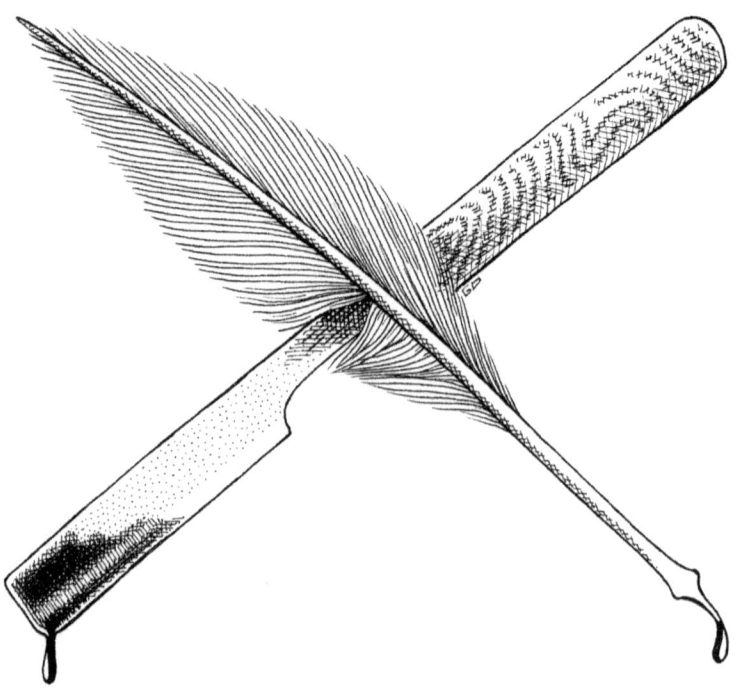

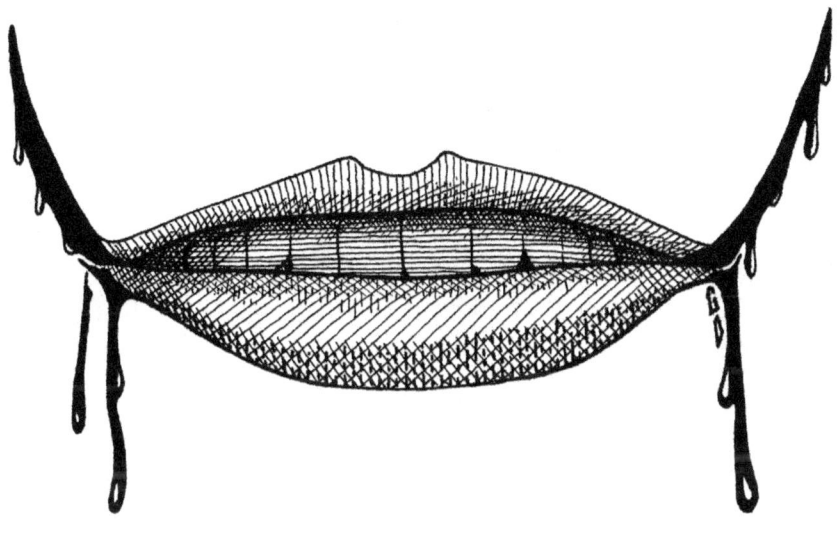

I have seen throughout my whole life, without a single exception, tight-shouldered men performing numerous foolish acts to stupefy their fellows and corrupt souls by any means. They call the motives for their actions: glory. Seeing these spectacles I wanted to laugh like the others—but that odd imitation was impossible. I took a knife whose blade had a sharp edge and sliced the flesh at the points where my lips met. Suddenly I believed my purpose had been achieved. I saw my mouth in the mirror, disfigured by my true will! It was a mistake! The blood flowing abundantly from those two wounds prevented me, moreover, from telling whether this really was the laugh of others. But after a few moments of comparison, I saw pretty well that my laugh didn't resemble that of other men—suffice to say that I wasn't laughing. I saw men with ugly heads and ghastly eyes sunken in their dim orbits, surpassing the hardness of stone, with the rigidity of tempered iron, the cruelty of the shark, the arrogance of youth, the mindless violence of criminals, the treachery of the hypocrite, the most amazing actors, the pushy demeanor of priests, and the most obscure and chilling beings of earth and Heaven; moralists weary from baring their souls and bringing Heaven's merciless wrath falling down on them. I have seen them, sometimes all at once, with clenched fist aimed at Heaven like that of a precociously wicked child against its mother, probably incited by some spirit from Hell, eyes fired with a bitter remorse and at the same time hateful amidst an icy silence, not daring to express the excessive and ungracious meditations lying concealed in their breasts, so much were they filled with injustice and horror, and to sadden with pity the God of mercy; sometimes, at any time of the day, from budding childhood until old age's demise, while spreading unfounded damnations against all who breathe, against themselves and Providence, prostitute women and children and thereby dishonour the parts of the human body dignified by modesty. Then the seas raise their waters, engulfing ships' decks within their maws; hurricanes and earthquakes raze homes; the plague and various diseases decimate praying families. But men don't notice it. I've also seen them blushing and blanching in shame at their conduct upon this earth — but seldom. Storms, sisters of the hurricanes; cerulean firmament, whose beauty I don't accept; hypocritical ocean, reflection of my heart; the earth, with its mysterious womb; extraterrestrials[1]; the entire universe; God, who created it with excellence, it is *You* whom I invoke: show me a man who might be good!... But let Your grace increase my natural powers tenfold, for at the sight of this monster I may die from amazement. One might perish from less.

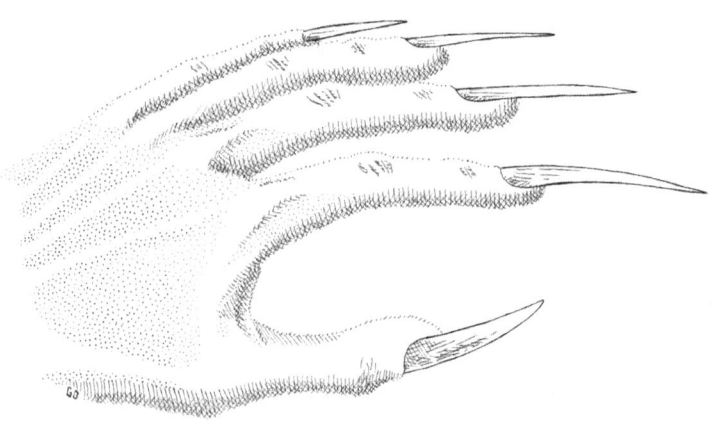

One must let one's fingernails grow out for two weeks. Oh! how sweet it is to roughly snatch from his bed a child who has nothing yet on his upper lip, with eyes wide open, and to pretend to gently pass a hand across his temple while pushing back his beautiful hair! Then suddenly, at the moment when he least expects it, press the long fingernails into his soft stomach, but in a way so that he doesn't die; because, if he should die, we won't be able to observe his later miseries. Then you drink the blood leeching from the wounds, and during this time, which should last as long as callous Eternity, the child is weeping. Nothing is sweeter than his blood, extracted in the way I have just recounted and still quite warm, unless it be his tears, bitter like salt. Man, have you never tasted your own blood, when, for instance, you've cut your finger? It's pretty good, isn't it? — because it has no taste. Furthermore, don't you remember one day, amidst your gloomy reflections, bringing your cupped hand over your sickly face moistened by what fell from your eyes; that hand was then fatally moved towards your mouth which, in long drafts from that cup — shaking like the teeth of a pupil who looks at the one who was born to oppress him — drank the tears? How good they are, eh? — because they have the taste of vinegar. They seem like the tears of she who loves the most; but the best on the palate are the tears of a child. *He* does not betray, not yet knowing about evil; she who loves the most betrays sooner or later... I interpret it by means of analogy, even though I don't know what friendship and love are (it is probable that I will never embrace them, at least on the part of Mankind). Therefore, since your blood and tears don't disgust you, feed yourself, nourish yourself confidently with the youth's tears and blood. Blindfold him as you tear at his palpitating flesh; and having listened for long hours to his sublime cries, reminiscent of the piercing groans heaved in battle from the throats of the wounded dying, then, moving away like an avalanche, you'll rush to a nearby room and then pretend to come to his assistance. You will release his hands, their nerves and veins swollen, and you'll return vision to his anxious eyes while you start once more to lick his tears and blood. As then the repentance is real! The divine spark which lies within us, and which is so seldom seen, appears—but too late! How the heart bursts with the power to comfort the innocent whom you've harmed: "Young man who has suffered these cruel agonies, who has perpetrated such an unspeakable crime upon you? How miserable you are! And if your mother knew of this, she couldn't be more mortified, so abhorring the guilty parties, than I am now. Alas! what then are good and evil? Are they the same thing by which we witness our impotence with rage, and the lust to achieve the infinite by the same utterly senseless means? Or else, are these two different things? Yes... they are rather the same thing... because, if they aren't, what will become of me on Judgment Day! Pardon me, young man; it is the very one in front of your noble and sacred face who broke your bones and ripped the flesh that hangs from the various parts of your body. It's a frenzy of my madness, it's an inner urge not connected to my reasoning—like an eagle ripping apart his prey—which drives me to commit such a crime; however, I've suffered as much as my victim! Young man, forgive me. Once we are taken from this ephemeral life, I want us to be linked throughout Eternity—formed as only one being, my mouth glued to your mouth. Even then, my punishment won't be complete. Then you'll unceasingly rip me apart with your teeth and nails simultaneously. I will adorn my body with embalmed festoons in honour of this expiatory holocaust; and we will suffer, the two of us — me, being torn apart, you, tearing me apart... my mouth glued to your mouth. O young man, with golden locks and eyes so soft, will you now do what I advise you to? In spite of yourself I want you to do it, and you will make my conscience happy." After speaking thus, at the same time as having wronged a human being, you will be loved by that same being: it is the greatest joy that could be imagined. Later on you can admit him to hospital, because the cripple wouldn't be able to earn his living. They will laud you well, and the laurel wreaths and gold medals will hide your naked feet and be scattered across the mighty tomb with the ancient façade. O thou, whose name I don't wish to write on this page consecrated to the sanctity of crime, I know that your forgiveness was as vast as the universe. But as for me... *I still live!*

I made an alliance with prostitution in order to sow the seeds of corruption within families. I remember the night which had preceded that dangerous liaison. I had seen a tomb before me. I had heard a glow-worm,² as big as a house, call to me: "I am going to enlighten you. Read the inscription. It's not from me that this supreme mandate comes." A great blood-tinted light had pervaded the air as far as the horizon, at the sight of which my jaws rattled and my arms hung lifeless. I had leaned against a crumbling wall because I was going to faint, and I'd read: "Here lies a young man who perished from tuberculosis: you know why. Do not pray for him." Most men would perhaps have not had my courage. Meanwhile a beautiful naked woman had come to lie at my feet. With a sad face I bid her: "You may rise again." I had extended the hand with which the fratricidal one slits the throat of his sister. The glow-worm said to me: "You there, take a rock and kill her." — "Why?" I'd asked it. It said to me: "Watch out,

you, the weakest—because I am the strongest. This one calls herself *Prostitution*." Tears welling in my eyes, rage in my heart, I had felt an alien power stirring within me. I had taken a large stone; after much effort I had raised it with difficulty to the height of my stomach; with my arms I'd placed it on my shoulder. I'd climbed up to a mountain-top: from there I had crushed the glow-worm. Its head had buried itself beneath the soil to the height of a man; the rock had rebounded to the height of six churches. It went to fall back into a lake whose waters had suddenly descended, revolving, forming a huge mælstrom. Calm had returned to the surface; the glow of blood shone no more. "Alas! alas!" had cried the beautiful naked woman. "What have you done?" I said to her: "I prefer you to him—because I pity the downtrodden. It isn't your fault if eternal Justice has created you." She'd said to me: "One day men will give me justice; I won't speak of it any more to you. Let me depart, to hide my endless grief at the bottom of the sea. There are only you and the horrible creatures that swarm in the dark abyss who don't despise me. You are good. Farewell, you who has loved me!" I said to her: "Farewell! Once more: farewell! I will always love you!… Today, I will abandon virtue." Therefore, O people, when you hear the winter wind wailing over the sea and along its beaches, or over the big cities which have long gone into mourning for me, or through the icy polar wastes, declare: "This isn't the spirit of God which passes: it is only the shrill sigh of Prostitution united with the grave groans of a Montevidean." Children, it is I who tell you this. So, full of mercy, kneel down; and may men, more abundant than lice, perform long prayers.

In the moonlight, close to the ocean in isolated country regions, when sunk in morbid reflections we see everything clothed in jaundiced forms, uncertain and grotesque. The arboreal shadows sometimes run swiftly, sometimes slowly, advancing, returning, in various shapes, sticking and flattening themselves against the earth. Once upon a time, when I was borne on the wings of youth, it caused me to dream, appeared strange to me; now I am accustomed to it. The wind moans its languid tones through the leaves and the owl hoots its grave lament which makes the listeners' hair stand on end. Then the hounds, driven to fury, break their chains and escape from distant farms; they course through the countryside, hither and thither, in the throes of madness. They halt suddenly, looking to all quarters in fierce disquiet, their eyes aflame; and just like elephants in the desert prior to death—throwing a final glance at the sky, raising their trunks in despair, letting their ears hang—likewise the hounds slacken their ears, raise their heads, swell their terrible throats and begin to howl in turn, like a child who wails from hunger, like a cat with a wounded stomach on a roof, like a woman giving birth, like someone dying in hospital stricken with plague, like a young girl singing a sublime song—against the stars in the east, against the stars in the south, against the stars in the west—against the moon—against the mountains in the distance similar to giant rocks lying in the darkness—against the icy air they inhale deeply which renders the insides of their nostrils red and raw; against the silent night, against the owls whose swooping flights shave their muzzles as they carry in their beaks a rat or a frog—soft, living food for their young; against the hares who disappear in the wink of an eye; against the thief who flees at a trot after committing his crime; against the snakes sliding through the briars, who make the hounds' skin writhe and teeth grind; against their own barking, which scares even themselves; against the toads (why did they leave the swamp?) which they crush whole in their jaws; against the trees whose leaves, swaying so gently, are so many unfathomed mysteries which they wish to reveal with their fixed, alert eyes; against spiders, suspended between their long legs, climbing trees to escape; against the crows who failed to find food during the day and who take themselves back to their nests, tired of wing; against the rocks of the shore; against the St. Elmo's

fire³ appearing on the masts of invisible ships; against the soughing of the waves; against the great fish swimming who, showing their black backs, then submerge into the abyss; and against Man, who enslaves them. After which they start afresh to roam the countryside, bounding, their legs bloody from jumping gullies, paths, fields, scrub and hidden rocks. Incited to a rage, they seek out a large pool in which to quench their thirst. Their prolonged howling frightens Nature. Warning to the tardy traveler! These lovers of graveyards will descend on him, tear him apart, devour him with their maws from which blood drips—because they don't have rotten fangs. Other wild beasts, trembling, not daring to venture near to join in this meal of flesh, make themselves scarce. After some hours the hounds, fatigued from running here and there, virtually dead, tongues lolling from their mouths, fall onto each other, oblivious to what they are doing, and tear themselves into a thousand shreds with amazing alacrity. They don't do this out of cruelty. One day my mother, with eyes glazed, told me: "When you are lying in bed and you hear the barking of the dogs in the countryside, hide yourself under your covers and don't deride what they are doing: they have an insatiable thirst for the infinite, like you, like me, like the rest of humanity with its long and pale face. Even so, I'll let you sit by the window to observe this spectacle, which is quite sublime." Since that time I've respected the wish of the dear departed woman. *I*, like the hounds, experience this craving for the infinite... I am unable to—I *cannot*—satisfy this craving! From what I'd been told, I am son of man and woman. This astounds me... I believed it to be more! Anyway, what do I care where I come from? If I'd had my druthers, *I* would have preferred to have been the son of the female shark, whose hunger is the friend of storms, and of the tiger, renowned for its ferocity; I would not then be so malicious. Those of you who observe me, move away—because my breath exudes a toxic fume. None have yet observed the verdant furrows of my forehead, nor the thin bones protruding from my face, similar to the spines of some great fish or the shards covering beaches or the sheer

alpine peaks that I often passed through when I had hair of a different colour on my head. And when I haunt the homes of men on stormy nights, with burning eyes and hair whipped by the squally winds, as lonely as a stone in the middle of a road, I cover my disfigured face with a length of velvet as black as the soot that fills chimneys. No eyes should witness the ugliness that the Supreme Being, with His grimace of strong hate, gave me. Each morning when the sun has risen for others, radiating a welcoming joy and natural warmth, while no part of my face moves as I crouch at the bottom of my beloved cave, staring into the shadowy space and sunken in a despair as intoxicating as wine, I rend my chest to tatters with my powerful hands. Yet I feel that I haven't achieved rage! Yet I feel as though I'm not the only one who suffers! Yet I feel that I breathe! Like a condemned man who tests his muscles, reflecting on their fate, who will soon mount the gallows, I stand on my bed of straw with eyes closed, slowly turning my neck from right to left, from left to right, for whole hours; I do not fall stiffly dead. From time to time, when my neck can no longer keep turning in the same way, it ceases in order to begin turning in an opposite direction again, and I suddenly view the horizon through the remaining spaces in the thick growths covering the opening: I see nothing! Nothing... if indeed these are hills which sway in waves with the trees and the long lines of birds crossing the sky. It vexes my blood and brain ... Who, therefore, deals the blows on my head with an iron bar, like a hammer striking an anvil?

I propose, without being emotional, to recite in a loud voice the chilly and portentous verse that you are going to hear. You should take heed of what it contains and brace yourself for the sad impression that it will not fail to leave, like a stigma, in your troubled imaginings. Do not believe that I am on the verge of death, because I am not yet a skeleton and old age hasn't adhered to my face. Accordingly, exclude all thought of comparison with the swan, at the moment when its life is flying away and you see before you only a monster whose face I'm happy that you cannot glimpse; but it is less horrible than its soul. Nevertheless, I am not a criminal... Enough of that matter. It was not too long ago that I once more saw the sea and trod the decks of ships, and my memories are as enduring as if I had left it yesterday. Be as still as me, if you can, during this speech which I already regret offering you, and don't blush at the thought of what the human heart is. O octopus, with the look of silk! You whose soul is inseparable from mine, you, the most gorgeous of the denizens of this earthly sphere and who commands a harem of four hundred suckers; you, in whom are nobly seated, as in their native abode, harmoniously and solidly bound, sweet expressive virtue and the divine graces—why won't you be with me, your quicksilver stomach against my aluminium chest, both of us reclining on a rock on the beach, beholding the sight which I love!

Ancient ocean, with your crystalline waves you look proportionally like those azure marks one sees on the bruised backs of cabin boys; you are an immense blue contusion laid on the body of the world; I love that simile. Thus, from the first sight of you, a long melancholy sigh, which one might have thought to be the murmur of your sweet breeze, passes, while leaving permanent traces, over our profoundly shaken soul, and you intimate to your lovers, perhaps without them realizing it, the rude beginnings of Man when he discovers the grief which no longer leaves him. I salute you, ancient ocean!

Ancient ocean, your harmoniously spherical form which charms the dour face of geometry only reminds me of the tiny eyes of Man, similar in their smallness to those of the wild boar and in their round form to those of night birds. However, Man believes himself beautiful in all ages. *I* rather suppose that Man believes in his beauty only through narcissism, but that he isn't really beautiful and he suspects it: because why then does he look at the face of his fellow man with such contempt? I salute you, ancient ocean!

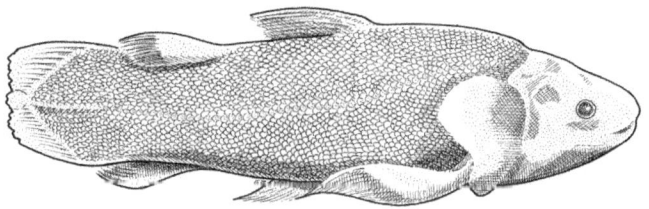

Ancient ocean, you are the symbol of identity: always equal to yourself. You don't change in a fundamental way, and if your waves are turbulent somewhere, in another place further away they are in absolute tranquillity. You are not like Man, who halts in the street to watch two bulldogs seizing each other's necks, but who doesn't stop when a funeral procession passes; who is approachable that morning and in poor humour that evening; who laughs today and cries tomorrow. I salute you, ancient ocean!

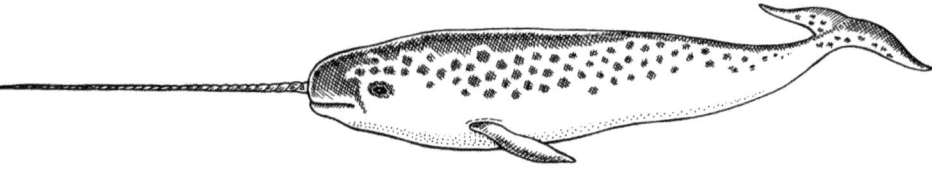

Ancient ocean, there may be nothing impossible in what you hide in your womb for Man's future uses. Already you have given him the whale. You don't easily allow the greedy eyes of the natural sciences to guess the thousandfold secrets of your intimate order: you are modest. Man praises himself endlessly, and for the smallest things. I salute you, ancient ocean!

Ancient ocean, the various species of fish that you nurture have not sworn allegiance to each other. Each species lives for its own part. The characters and shapes that vary in each of them convincingly explain what initially appears to be a freak. It is thus with Man, who doesn't have the same grounds on which to excuse himself. Should one tract of land be inhabited by thirty million human beings, they believe themselves obliged not to be involved with the lives of their neighbours fixed like roots on the next plot of earth. Descending from big to small, each man lives like a savage in his burrow, rarely visiting his fellow-man, who squats likewise in his own lair. The large universal family of humans is a utopia worthy of the poorest logic. Moreover, from the spectacle of your fertile breasts comes the concept of ingratitude, because we immediately think of those numerous parents sufficiently ungrateful towards the Creator as to forsake the fruit of their pathetic unions. I salute you, ancient ocean!

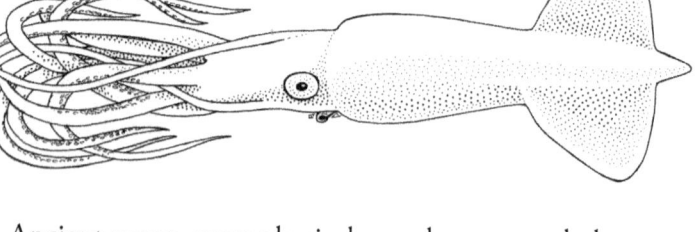

Ancient ocean, your physical grandeur can only be compared to the measure that we make of the active force required to generate the entirety of your mass. We are unable to embrace you with a glance. In order to contemplate you, sight must turn its telescope in one continuous movement to the four points of the horizon, just as a mathematician, in order to resolve an algebraic equation, is obliged to examine separately the various potentials before settling the problem. Man eats nourishing foods and makes other efforts worthy of a better fate in order to become fat. May it bloat itself as much as it wants, this adorable frog. Rest easy, it won't equal you in size — at least that's what I'm guessing. I salute you, ancient ocean!

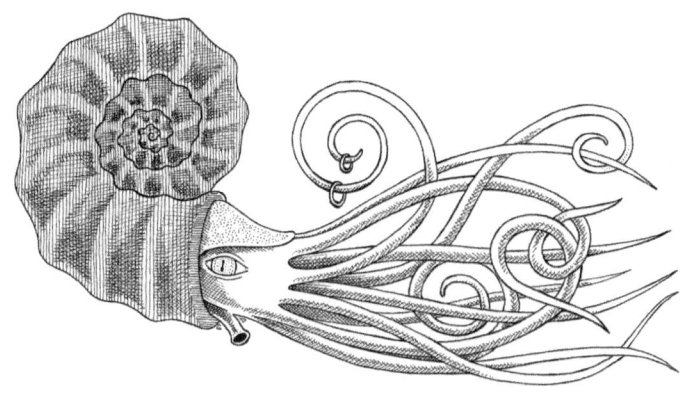

Ancient ocean, your waters are bitter. It has exactly the same taste as the gall which criticism distills onto the fine arts, onto the sciences — onto everything. If someone has genius, they are made out to be an idiot; if someone has beauty, they are a detestable hunchback. Indeed, Man must be strongly aware of his imperfection — of which three quarters are owed solely to himself — in order to criticize like that! I salute you, ancient ocean!

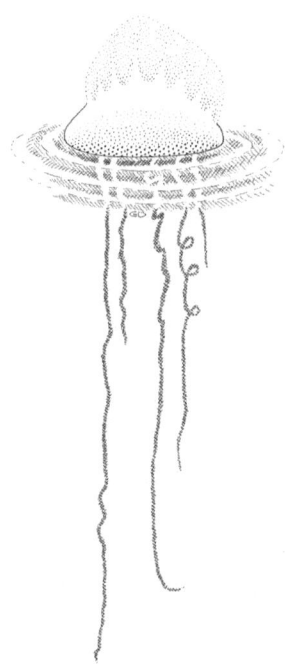

Ancient ocean, despite the excellence of their methods, men, helped by means of scientific exploration, haven't yet managed to fathom the profound depths of your abysses; you have some that the longest and heaviest probes have found inaccessible. To the fish... that is allowed *them*—but not to men. I often ask myself which is easier to recognize: the depth of the ocean, or the depth of the human heart? Often, standing on ships, with my hand placed on my forehead while the moon swung between the masts in a vague way, I found myself forgetting all except the objective I pursued, endeavoring to resolve this puzzling problem! Yes, which is the deepest and most mysterious of the two: the sea or the human heart? If thirty years' experience of life can tilt the scales towards some point of either of these answers in terms of comparing this quality, I might venture to say that the ocean, despite its depth, cannot line up with the depth of the human heart. I have been involved with men who were virtuous. They died at sixty, and everyone would not fail to exclaim: "They did well on this earth, that is to say they practised charity: that's all, it isn't that clever, everyone can do it just as well." Who will understand why two lovers, who idolized each other the day before, for a word taken badly move apart—one towards the east, one towards to the west—with the prick of hatred, of vengeance, of love and remorse, and each, cloaked in their lonely pride, never seeing the other again? It is a miracle that renews itself each day and which never appears any less miraculous. Who will understand why we not only enjoy the general dishonours of our fellow-men, but also the individual dishonours of our dearest friends, while suffering from them at the same time? An undeniable example to close the line: Man hypocritically says "Yes," but thinks "No." It is thus that the young pigs of humanity are so trusting of each other and aren't egotists. There remains much progress to be made in psychology. I salute you, ancient ocean!

Ancient ocean, you are so powerful—as men have learned at their own expense. They have strenuously employed all the resources of their genius... unable to dominate you. They have found their master. I declare that they have discovered something more powerful than themselves. This something has a name. Its name is: the ocean! The fear which you inspire in them is such that they respect you. Despite this, you waltz gracefully with their clumsiest inventions, elegantly and easily. You cause them to take gymnastic jumps towards the sky and wonderful plunges to the bottom of your domain: a circus acrobat would be jealous. How happy they are, when you do not cover them completely in your seething swathes, to go and see (without a railway) how the fish—and, above all, they themselves—might travel through your watery entrails. Man says: "I am smarter than the sea." It's possible, it's even fairly true—but the ocean is more threatening to him than he is to the ocean: there's no need to prove that. This fatherly observer, contemporary of the first eras of our hanging globe, smiles with compassion when he witnesses the nations' naval skirmishes. Here are almost a hundred battleships which have launched under humanity's hand. The furious orders of the commanders, the cries of the wounded, the cannon explosions—it is the din designed deliberately to obliterate a few seconds. It appears that the drama has ended and that the ocean has taken all into its stomach. The maw is formidable. She must be immense downwards—in the direction of the unknown! Finally, to crown the ridiculous farce which isn't even interesting, we see some stork up in the air, delayed by fatigue, who begins to shout without halting the flapping of its flight: "Fancy this!... I have found evil! They were black spots down below—I closed my eyes: they disappeared." I salute you, ancient ocean!

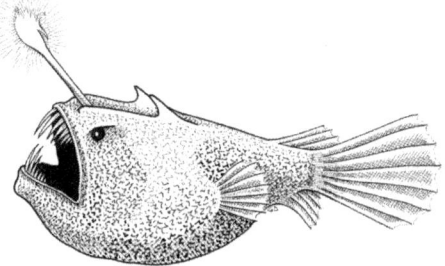

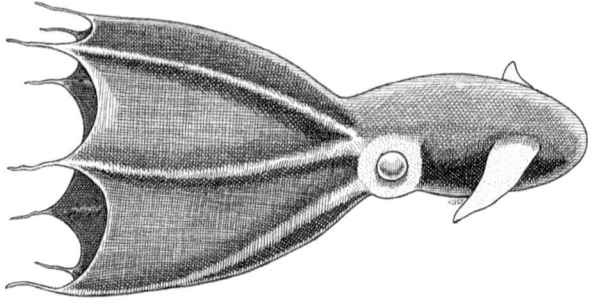

Ancient ocean, O great chaste one, when you travel through the solemn solitude of your phlegmatic kingdoms, you rightfully pride yourself on your natural splendour and with the genuine praises I eagerly offer you. Luxuriously swayed by the soft whispers of your majestic slowness, which is the grandest among the attributes which the king could have bestowed upon you, over your entire sublime surface you unfurl, amidst a melancholy mystery and with the serene sense of your eternal power, your incomparable waves. They follow in parallel fashion, punctuated by short lulls. Scarcely does one diminish than another moves to meet it, swelling, followed by the sombre breath of sea-foam which infuses itself to warn us that everything is froth. (In this way, human beings, those living waves, perish one after another in repeated fashion—but without leaving foamy sound.) The bird of passage rests on them with confidence and allows itself to succumb to their motion, filled with a proud dignity, until the bones of its wings regain their life, allowing it to continue its ærial pilgrimage. I only wish human glory could be the incarnation of your reflection. I may ask a lot, and this sincere aspiration is glorious for you. Your moral grandeur, vision of the infinite, is as tremendous as a philosopher's thoughts, as a woman's love, as the divine beauty of a bird, as the meditations of a poet. You are more beautiful than the night. Tell me, ocean—would you like to be my brother? Rouse yourself with impetuousness... more... yet more, if you would like me to compare you to God's wrath; extend your ghastly claws and tear a path across your own breast... that's good. Unroll your dreadful waves, hideous ocean, understood by me alone and before whom I fall, bowing down at your knees. The majesty of Man is borrowed; it will not impose its reason on me—but *you*, yes! Oh! when you loom, the wave's crest towering and terrible, surrounded with your labyrinthine folds like a courtyard, rolling your waves wildly and hypnotically one over the other with self-awareness, there comes from the depths of your breast such a perpetually deafening booming, as if you are overwhelmed by such powerful remorse that I cannot fathom—that men, shaking on the shore, fear so much even as they safely contemplate you—then I see that it is not for me, that special honour that names me as your equal. That is why, in the presence of your superiority, I would give you all my love (and none know the amount of love contained in my desire for beauty) if you didn't painfully remind me of my peers who present the most ironic contrast with you, the most farcical antithesis ever seen in Creation: I cannot love you—I hate you. Why do I come back to you for the thousandth time, to your loving arms which open to caress my burning forehead, dispelling the fever with their touch? I do not know your secret destiny—everything about you fascinates me. Tell me, are you home to the Prince of Darkness? Tell me... tell me, ocean (to me only, so as not to distress those who have yet to

know such illusions), and whether Satan's breath created the storms that lift your briny waters as far as the clouds. You must tell me, because I would celebrate knowing Hell is so close to Man. I want this to be the last stanza of my invocation. Consequently, once more, I wish to salute you and bid my *adieus!* Ancient ocean, with your crystal waves… My eyes soften with abundant tears and I don't have the strength to go on—because I know that the moment has come to return to the company of men with brutal mien, but… courage! Let us make a great effort and accomplish our destiny on this earth with a sense of duty. I salute you, ancient ocean!

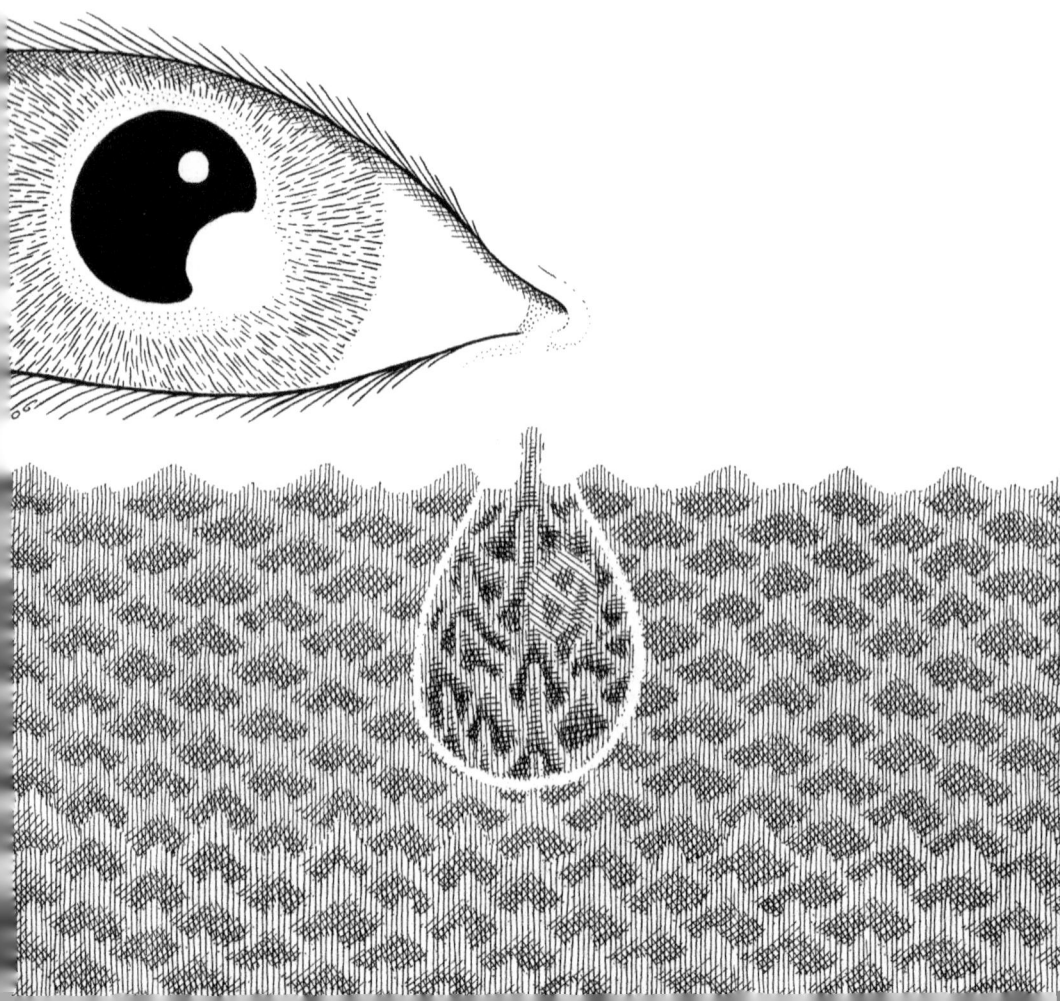

In my final hour (I write this on my death bed) I won't be surrounded by priests. I want to die rocked by the waves of the stormy sea or standing on the mountain ... eyes raised, no: I know that my annihilation will be complete. Besides, I would not have mercy to hope for. Who is opening the door of my death chamber? I said that nobody should enter. Whoever you are, stay away; but if you believe you perceive some sign of grief or fear on my hyæna face (I use this comparison, although the hyæna has more beauty than me and is easier on the eye), don't be deceived—whoever approaches. We are in the winter night when the elements collide everywhere, when man is afraid, when the adolescent plans some crime upon one of his friends (if he's anything like I was in my youth). May the wind, whose plaintive whistling has depressed humanity since the wind and humanity have existed, carry me on the struts of its wings across the world impatient for my death a few moments before the final agony. I will once again rejoice, secretly, in the many examples of human wickedness (an invisible brother loves to see the acts of his brothers). The eagle, the crow, the immortal pelican, the wild duck, the travelling crane, becoming alert, shivering from the cold, will see me passing in the fulgurations, a horrible and contented spectre. They won't know what this means. On the earth: the snake, the great eye of the toad, the tiger, the elephant; in the ocean: the whale, the shark, the hammerhead, the amorphous ray, the tooth of the Arctic seal—will question this exception to the law of Nature. Man, shaking, plants his forehead on the ground in the middle of his moans. "Yes, I have surpassed you with my innate cruelty, which I am not obliged to erase. Is this the reason why you present yourselves to me in this prostration? Or perhaps it's because you saw me pass, a new phenomenon, like a frightening comet staining space? (A rain of blood falls from my vast body, similar to the ebon cloud which drives the hurricane.) Fear not, children, I do not wish to curse you. The harm you have done me is too great, the evil I have done you too tremendous, for it to be voluntary. The rest of you have travelled in your way, I in mine—both appearing alike, both more perverse. We must have undoubtedly met through this similarity of character; the collision resulting from it has been mutually fatal for us." Then the men will gradually raise their heads, regaining courage, extending their necks like snails to see the one who speaks in this way. Suddenly their burning faces, decaying and exhibiting the most terrible expressions, will grimace in such a way as to frighten even the wolves. They will stand up at once like a huge spring. What curses! What heart-rending voices! They have recognized me. Now the animals of the earth meet with the humans, expressing their strange outcries. More than reciprocal hate: the two hates are turned against the common enemy—*me*; they come together by universal assent. Winds supporting me, raise me higher—I fear treachery! Yes, let us disappear little by little from their gaze, once more witness to the consequences of passions completely satisfied … I thank you, O horseshoe-bat, for rousing me with the movement of your wings, you whose nose is topped with a crest in the shape of a horseshoe. Actually, I realize that it was sadly only a passing complaint, and I feel the rekindling of life with disgust. Some say that you have come near me to suck the little blood that you might find in my body: why isn't that theory reality!

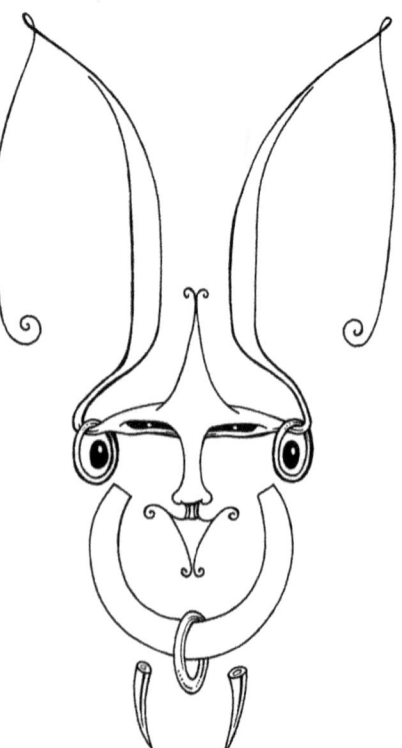

A family surrounds a lamp placed on the table.

— My son, pass me the scissors sitting on that chair.

— They aren't there, mother.

— Go then and look for them in the other room. You recall that time, my dear master, when we made those vows to have a child in whom we could be reborn a second time, and who would be our support in old age?

— I remember it, and God fulfilled our prayers. We can't complain about our lot on this earth. Every day we bless Providence for its favours. Our Edward possesses all the graces of his mother.

— And the manly qualities of his father.

— Here are the scissors, mother; I finally found them.

He takes up his work again... But someone has appeared at the front door, and momentarily contemplates the picture offered to his eyes:

— What does this sight mean? There are many people who aren't as happy as these. What explanation do *they* offer for loving life? Take yourself away from this peaceful hearth, Maldoror—your place is not here.

He withdrew!

— I don't know how this can be, but I feel the human faculties engaging in battles within my heart. My soul is unsettled, and without knowing why; the air is oppressive.

— Wife, I am experiencing the same feelings as you; I tremble lest some misfortune may befall us. Let us have faith in God; supreme hope is in Him.

— Mother, I can hardly breathe: I have a headache.

— You as well, my son! I will moisten your forehead and temples with some vinegar.

— No, dear mother...

Observe — he leans his body on the back of the chair, exhausted.

— Something which I can't explain has upset me. Now the smallest thing upsets me.

— You are so pale! The end of this night will not come to pass without some disaster plunging all three of us into the lake of despair.

In the distance I hear protracted shrieks of the saddest pain.

— My son!

— Ah! mother!... I'm afraid!

— Quickly, tell me if you suffer.

— Mother, I'm not suffering... I don't speak the truth.

The father cannot get over his astonishment:

— Here are the cries that are occasionally heard in the silence of starless nights. Although we can hear those cries, still the one who expresses them isn't nearby — because we can hear these groans three leagues away, carried by the wind from one city to another. I have often been told of this phenomenon but I have never had the chance to judge its truth for myself. Wife, you spoke to me of misfortune; if a more definite misfortune exists in the long spiral of time, it is the misfortune of he who now disturbs his fellows' sleep...

In the distance I hear protracted shrieks of the most heart-rending distress.

— Would to Heaven that his birth will not be a disaster for his nation, which repulsed him from its womb. He goes from country to country, abhorred everywhere. They say that he has been overwhelmed by a primal kind of insanity since his infancy. Others believe that it is an extreme and innate cruelty of which he himself is ashamed, and that his parents died from grief. There are some who maintain that he was tainted by a nickname given in youth: that he remains inconsolable for the rest of his life because his wounded pride saw there obvious evidence of the wickedness of men, which shows itself early on, only to increase afterwards. That nickname was *The Vampire!* ...

In the distance I hear protracted shrieks of the most poignant grief.

— They add that day and night, without truce nor peace, terrible nightmares cause blood to seep from his mouth and ears; and spectres sit at his bedhead and, driven by an unknown force in spite of themselves, sling at his face, sometimes with a sweet tone and sometimes with a relentlessly persistent voice like the din of battle, that ever-enduring nickname, always hideous, and which will only die with the universe. Someone has even asserted that love reduced him to this state—or that these shouts bore witness to a repentance over some crime shrouded in the night of his mysterious past. But most believe that an immense arrogance tortures him, like Satan of old, and that he would like to rival God...

In the distance I hear protracted shrieks of the deepest mourning.

— My son, these are remarkable confidences: I am sorry you had to hear them at your age, and I hope you will never emulate that man.

— Speak, O my Edward; confirm that you won't behave like this man.

— O beloved mother, to whom I owe this day, I promise you, if the holy promise of a child has some worth, to never imitate this man.

— That's perfect, my son—you must obey your mother in every way.

They no longer hear the groans.

— Wife, have you finished your work?

— I am missing some stitches in this shirt, even though we have dragged the evening out quite late.

— Likewise, I haven't finished a chapter started. Let's take advantage of the final light of the lamp; since there is almost no oil left, let's each finish our work...

The child exclaims:

— If God lets us live!

— Radiant angel, come to me: you will walk in the meadow from morning until evening: you won't work at all. My magnificent palace is built with walls of silver, columns of gold, and doors of diamonds. You will sleep when you wish, to the sound of heavenly music, without saying your prayer. When the sun shows its resplendent rays in the morning, and when the joyful lark, unseen, carries its chirp through the air, you will still be able to rest in bed, until even that tires you. You will walk on the most luxurious carpets, you will be constantly surrounded by an atmosphere made up of scented essences from the most perfumed flowers.

— It's time to rest mind and body. Mother of the family, rise on your sturdy ankles. It's only fair that your tense fingers should put away the needle from overwork. Extremes aren't good.

— Oh! how sweet your life will be! I will give you an enchanted ring; when you turn over the ruby you will become invisible like the princes in Fairyland.

— Return your everyday implements to the secure cabinet while I will arrange my own affairs.

— When you return it to the normal position, you will reappear in your natural form, O young magician. That is because I love you and hope to make you happy.

— Be gone, whoever you are; don't seize me by the shoulders.

— My son, don't fall asleep, lulled by childish dreams: your daily prayer hasn't begun and your clothes still aren't neatly placed on a chair... Kneel down! 'Eternal Creator of the world, You display unfailing goodness down to the smallest things.'

— So, you don't like the clear streams or the gliding of thousands of small red, blue and silver fish? You would take them with a good net, which itself attracts them until it is filled. On the surface you will see bright pebbles more polished than marble.

— Mother, look at those claws: I am wary of him, but my conscience is clear because I have nothing to blame myself for.

— 'You see us prostrate at Your feet, overwhelmed by the sense of Your grandeur. If some arrogant thought slips into our imagination, we immediately reject it with the spit of disdain and make the binding sacrifice to You.'

— You will bathe there with small girls who will embrace you with their arms. Once you leave the bath, they will weave you crowns of roses and carnations. They have transparent butterfly wings and long wavy tresses which float gently about their foreheads.

— Even if your palace were more beautiful than crystal, I will not leave this house to follow you. I believe you're an impostor, since you speak to me so softly for fear of being heard. Leaving one's parents is a sinful act. It won't be *me* who will be the ungrateful son. As for your young girls, they aren't as beautiful as my mother's eyes.

— 'All our life is spent in hymns to Your glory. So we have been up until now, so we will be until the moment when we receive Your order to leave this earth.'

— They will obey you at your slightest gesture and will think only of pleasing you. If you desire the bird which never sleeps, they will bring it to you. If you desire the sleigh which can carry you to the sun in the wink of an eye, they will bring it to you. What *can't* they bring you! They will even bring you a kite, as big as a tower, which is concealed in the moon and from whose tail a variety of birds are hung by threads of silk. Pay attention … hear my counsel.

— Do whatever you want—I won't interrupt my prayers to call for help. Although your body fades when I wish to banish it, know that I don't fear you.

— 'Before You, nothing is great if it isn't the flame breathed from a pure heart.'

— Reflect on what you have said to me, if you don't wish to regret it.

— 'Heavenly Father, avert and thwart the misfortunes which would overwhelm our family.'

— Then you don't wish me to leave, evil spirit?

— 'Save this dear wife, who comforts me in my discontent...'

— Since you reject me, I will make you weep and gnash your teeth like a man who is to be hanged.

— 'And this loving son, whose innocent lips have barely opened to the kisses of youth.'

— Mother, he is strangling me... Father, save me... I can't breathe any more... Your blessing!

A cry of immense irony is raised into the air. Observe as dazed eagles fall from the high clouds, rolling on each other, literally struck by the column of air.

— His heart isn't beating... And she is dead, at the same time as the offspring of her womb, the offspring whom I don't recognize any more, so changed he is... My wife!... My son!... I remember a distant time when I was husband and father.

Before the scene offered to his eyes, he had told himself that he would not condone such an injustice. If the power which was bestowed upon him by the infernal spirits, or rather that he draws from himself, is effective, this child will cease to exist before the night wanes.

The one who doesn't know how to cry (because he always bottles pain up inside) remarked that he had been in Norway. Helping to search for the nests of sea birds in the crevices of the cliffs on the Faroe Islands, he was surprised that the three-hundred-metre-long rope which held the searcher over the precipice was chosen for such durability. Whatever one might say, he saw there a striking example of human goodness and he couldn't believe his eyes. If it had been up to him to prepare the rope, he would have made cuts in several places so that it would break itself and drop the climber into the sea! One evening he took himself towards a graveyard, and teenagers who take pleasure in violating corpses of recently-deceased beauties could, if they so desired, have heard the following exchange leaked from the scene of a story which is going to unfold at the same time.

— Gravedigger, would you care to chat with me? A sperm whale rises gradually from the bottom of the ocean and displays its head above the waves in order to see the ships which pass in those lonely regions. Curiosity is born with the world.

— Friend, it is impossible for me to share thoughts with you. The gentle moonlight has illuminated the marble graves for ages. This is the silent hour when more than one human being dreams that he sees chained women appear, dragging their shrouds covered with bloodstains like a black sky with stars. The sleepers groan like those condemned to death, until they awake and see that reality is three times as bad as the dream. I must finish digging this pit with my indefatigable shovel before night yields to morning. For, in order to do serious work, one mustn't do two things at once.

— He believes that digging a grave is serious work! You think that digging a grave is serious work!

— When the wild pelican resolves to offer its stomach for its chicks to devour, only having as witness the One who knew how to create such love in order to put men to shame, even though the sacrifice is large—*that* act is understood. When a young man sees a woman—whom he idolized—in the arms of his friend, then he smokes a cigar; he doesn't leave the house and strikes up an unbreakable friendship with grief—*that* act is understood. When a student intern in high school is governed by a social pariah who always has eyes on him, through years which are like centuries, from morning until evening and from evening to the next day, he feels the tumultuous waves of a persistent hatred rising like thick smoke in his brain, which seems to him almost about to explode. Since the moment when he was thrown into prison until the approaching time when he will leave it, an intense fever yellows his face, his eyebrows contort, and he digs at his eyes. At night he ponders, because he doesn't wish to sleep. During the day his thoughts soar above the walls of the brutal abode, until the moment when he breaks out or when they cast him out from this eternal cloister like a plague victim—*that* act is understood. Digging a grave often surpasses the forces of Nature. Stranger, how do you expect the pick to move this earth—that first nourishes us and then gives us a suitable bed, protecting us from the winter wind blowing furiously in the cold countries—when the one who holds the pick in his trembling hands, after having all day convulsively fingered the cheeks of the old ones who have returned to His kingdom, in the evening sees before him written in flames on every wooden cross the statement of the frightening problem that humanity hasn't yet resolved: the mortality or immortality of the soul. I have always retained my love for Him, the Creator of the universe; but if, after death, we no longer live, why do I see each grave opening most nights and the residents slowly raising the leaden lids in order to breathe the fresh air?

— Cease your toil. Passion robs you of strength; you seem as frail as a reed to me, and it would be great folly to continue. I am strong: I will take your place. You, step to one side and let me know if I aren't doing it properly.

— How muscular his arms are, and what a pleasure it is to see him digging the earth with such ease!

— You mustn't let any vain doubt trouble your thoughts: all of these graves which are scattered through the cemetery like flowers in a meadow—a comparison which lacks veracity—are worthy of being measured with the calm compass of the philosopher. Threatening hallucinations can appear in the daytime—but they will especially come at night. Consequently, don't be surprised by the fantastic visions which your eyes may perceive. During the day, when your mind is restful, question your conscience: it will tell you with certainty that the God who created Man with a fragment of His own intelligence possesses an unlimited goodness, and He will receive, after his earthly passing, this masterpiece into His heart. Gravedigger, why are you crying? Why these tears like a woman's? Remember well; we are on the unmasted ship to suffer. It is a credit to Man that God has judged him capable of conquering the most serious sufferings. Speak, and then, according to your dearest wishes that we not suffer, say what might constitute virtue, an ideal that each strives to achieve—if your tongue is made the same as other men's.

— Where am I? Have I not changed character? I feel a strong breath of reassuring comfort caressing my face, like a spring breeze might rekindle the hope of old men. Who is this man whose sublime words speak of things which his predecessors have never declared? What musical beauty there is in the peerless melody of his voice! I would prefer to listen to him talk rather than the singing of others. Meanwhile, the more I see it, the more his figure isn't real. The general expression of his features contrasts sharply with the words which only the love of God can inspire. His brow, quite wrinkled, is marked with an indelible stain. Is that stain, which has prematurely aged him, honourable or vile? His wrinkles, should they be regarded with respect? I don't know—and I am afraid of knowing it. Although he declares what he doesn't believe, *I* however believe that he has reasons for acting as he does, aroused by the scraps of a dissolute charity within him. He is immersed in meditations which are unfamiliar to me, and he increases his pace in the trying toil which is not his custom to undertake. Sweat moistens his skin: he doesn't notice it. It is sadder than the feelings prompted by the sight of a baby in a cradle. Oh! how dark it is!... Where are you going?... Stranger, allow my touch so that my hands, which rarely embrace those of the living, might be worthy of the nobility of your body. Whatever happens, I may know what to expect. These tresses are more beautiful than any I have touched in my life. Who will be brave enough to dispute that I don't know the quality of hair?

— What do you expect of me when I am digging a grave? The lion doesn't wish to be irritated when he feeds. If you don't know it, I will teach it to you. Go on, hasten yourself; achieve what you desire.

— What shivers at my touch, whilst making me shiver myself, is undoubtedly of the flesh. It is true... I am not dreaming! Who are you, then, you who stoops there to dig a grave, whereas I do nothing, like a lazy person who eats the bread of others? It is time to sleep, or to sacrifice sleep for knowledge. In any case, no soul is abroad, and each is careful not to leave any door open in order to prevent burglary. He shuts himself up in his bedroom as best he can while the ashes from the old fireplace are still able to heat up the room with a remainder of warmth. *You* don't do as others; your clothes indicate a dweller of some distant country.

— Although I'm not tired, it is pointless to dig the grave any more. Now, undress me; then you will place me inside.

— The conversation we've both briefly had is so strange that I don't know how to respond... I believe he wants to laugh.

— Yes, yes, it's true, I do want to laugh; don't pay attention to what I said.

He is weakening, and the gravedigger hastens to support him!

— What's wrong?

— Yes, yes, it's true, I have lied... I was tired when I put down the pick... it's the first time I've undertaken such work... don't pay attention to what I've said.

— My opinion gains more and more consistency: this is someone with the most fearful sorrows. May Heaven remove my questioning thoughts. I would prefer to remain in doubt, so much does he inspire pity in me. Anyway, it's certain he wouldn't want to answer me: it is to suffer twice to express one's heart while in such an abnormal state.

— Let me leave this cemetery—I will continue my journey.

— Your legs won't support you; they will lead you astray should you proceed. My duty is to offer you a rough bed; I have no other. Have confidence in me, because hospitality will not require the violation of your secrets at all.

— O venerable louse, you whose body is devoid of wing-casings, one day you reproached me bitterly for not sufficiently adoring your sublime intelligence, which doesn't let itself be read: perhaps you were justified, since I don't even feel gratitude for this man. Beacon of Maldoror, where do you guide his steps?

— To my home. Whether you're a criminal, who doesn't take the precaution of washing his right hand with soap after committing his felony, and easy to recognize by inspection of that hand; or a brother who has lost his sister; or some dispossessed monarch fleeing his kingdoms — my truly grand palace is worthy to receive you. It hasn't been built with diamonds and precious stones, because it is just a humble, poorly-made cottage — but this famous cottage has an historic past that the present renews and prolongs endlessly. If it could speak it would astonish you — *you* to whom apparently nothing astonishes. How often did I see marching before me, along with the cottage, funeral coffins containing bones shortly to be more decrepit than my door against which I leaned. My many subjects increase each day. I don't need to do any periodic census in order to see this. Here it is the same as among the living: each pays a tax according to the value of the abode he has chosen; and if some miser refuses to deliver his quota, I am allowed to act, as bailiffs would, regarding that person — there is no lack of jackals and vultures who would love to make a good meal. Lined up beneath the banners of death I have seen: one who was beautiful; one who hadn't grown grotesque after death; the man, the woman, the beggar, and the sons of kings; illusions of youth and skeletons of senility; genius and madness; idleness and its opposite; one who was wrong and one who was right; the mask of the arrogant and the modesty of the humble; vice crowned with flowers, and innocence betrayed.

— Indeed, no, I won't refuse your bed (which is good enough for me) until the coming of the imminent dawn. I thank you for your benevolence... Gravedigger, it is nice to contemplate the ruins of cities; but it is even better to contemplate the ruins of humans!

The brother of the leech was walking slowly through the forest. He would repeatedly stop while opening his mouth to speak. But each time his throat would tighten and he would restrain the failed attempt. At last he exclaims: "Man, if you should encounter a dead dog lying overturned, pressed against a sluice-gate which prevents its passing through, don't depart like the others—with your hand take the worms which emerge from its bloated belly, regard them with amazement, open a knife, then carve up a large number of them, telling yourself that *you*, also, will be no more than this dog. What mystery do you seek? Neither I nor the four leg-paddles of the Northern fur seal[4] have been able to figure out the puzzle of life. Beware—night looms, and you have been there since morning. What will your family say, along with your little sister, at seeing you arrive so late? Wash your hands and regain the path which leads to your bed... What being is that, over there on the horizon, who dares to approach me, fearlessly, with crooked and fretful jumps—and with such majesty mixed with a sweet serenity! His gaze, though gentle, is profound. His huge eyelids flutter with the breeze and appear alive. He is unknown to me. Fixing me with his large eyes, my body trembles—for the first time since I sucked the dried-up breasts of that one called 'mother.' There is something like an aura of dazzling light around him. When he spoke, all became silent in Nature and experienced a great shudder. Since you're content to come to me as though attracted by a magnet, I won't oppose it. How fine he is! It pains me to say so. You must be powerful, because your face is more than human, as sad as the universe, as beautiful as suicide. I abhor you absolutely—and I would prefer to see a snake wound around my neck from the beginning of time rather than your eyes... Why!... it is *you*, toad!... great toad!... unlucky toad!... Forgive me!... pardon me!... What did you come to do on this earth, where the accursed are? Indeed, what then have you done with your viscous and fœtid pustules in order to seem so sweet? When by divine decree you descended from Heaven with the mission of comforting the various races of living creatures, you

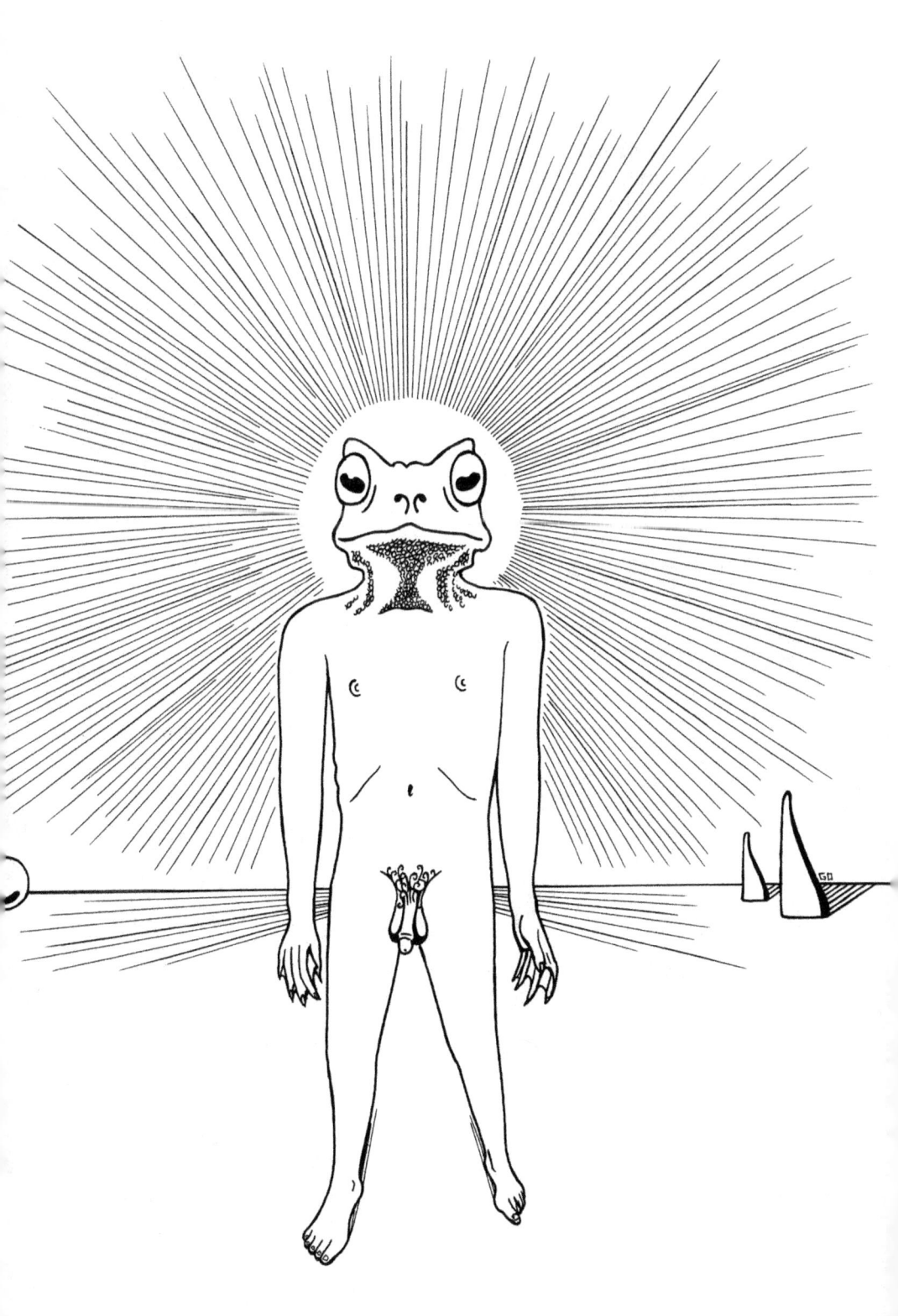

En partie consolé, mais ma maison chancelante s'abîme devant tant de grandeur! Qui es-tu donc? Reste... oh! reste encore sur terre! Replie tes blanches ailes et ne regarde pas en haut avec les paupières inquiètes... Si tu pars, partons ensemble » Le crapaud s'assit sur ses cuisses de derrière, qui ressemblent à celles de l'homme! et, pendant que les limaces, les cloportes et les limaçons s'enfuyaient à la vue de leur ennemi mortel, éleva la parole, en ces termes : « Maldoror, écoute-moi. Remar-

intelligence — calm — , grâce — simple contact, — grand — consternation, — nerve — Abandon — Ton es — infernal grand — intelligence — malédictions plus — assassin — scepticism — plus intelligence — mobile — essence divine, — sphère, — point, fell to earth with the swiftness of a kite whose wings were unfatigued by that long, magnificent journey—I saw you! Poor toad! How I then pondered infinity, along with my weakness. 'Another who is superior to those of the earth,' I said to myself, 'and that by divine will. Why not me as well? What is the point in the highest decrees? The Creator, He is crazy; nevertheless He *is* the strongest—and whose wrath is terrible!' Since you appeared to me—king of pools and swamps!—clothed in a glory that belongs solely to God, you have somewhat comforted me; but my shaky reason plummets before such grandeur! Who are you, then? Stay... oh! stay once more on this earth! Fold your pale wings and don't look skywards with your restless eyes... If you depart, let us depart together!" The toad sat on his hind legs (which so much resembled those of men!) and while the slugs, wood-lice and snails fled from the sight of their mortal enemy, he spoke in these terms: "Hearken, Maldoror. Note my face, tranquil as a mirror and I believe having an intelligence equal to yours. One day you called me the support of your life. Since then I haven't refuted the trust which you devoted to me. It's true, I am only a humble resident of the reeds; but thanks to your own contact, taking only what had been noble in you, my reason has grown and I can speak to you. I have come to rescue you from the abyss. The ones who call themselves your friends watch you, stricken with disappointment each time they meet you pale and stooped in the theatres, public places, churches, or pressing with two firm thighs that horse which gallops only during the night whilst it bears its phantom-master shrouded in a black cloak. Discard those thoughts which render your heart as empty as a desert; they burn more than fire. Your spirit is so ill that you don't perceive it, and so you believe it to be natural every time words that are senseless, though filled with an infernal grandeur, issue from your mouth. Unfortunate one! What have you said since the day of your birth? O sad remains of an immortal intelligence which God has created with such love! You have only brought about curses more horrible than the sight of ravenous panthers! *I* would prefer to have my eyelids stuck together, my body deprived of its legs and arms, to have killed a man—rather than be *you!* Because I hate you. Why have this character which astounds me? By what right do you come onto this earth to stir its inhabitants in derision, a corrupt wreck tossed by scepticism? If you aren't content there, you should return to those spheres from whence you came. A city-dweller should not live in villages like a stranger. We know that there exist in space vaster globes than ours, and whose beings possess an intelligence that we cannot even imagine. Very well, depart!... remove yourself from this moving soil!... finally manifest your divine essence that you have hitherto obscured, and forthwith direct your soaring flight towards your sphere which we no longer envy, so arrogant are you! For I cannot ascertain whether you are a man, or *more* than a man! Therefore, farewell—and hope not to encounter the toad again on your journey. You have been the cause of my death. *I* leave for Eternity, in order to seek your forgiveness!"

Even if it is sometimes logical to rely upon the appearance of phenomena, this first dirge finishes here. Don't be too hard on he who hasn't yet tested his lyre: it produces such a strange sound! However, if you would care to be impartial, you will already recognize a strong impression amongst the imperfections. As for me, I will return to my labours in order to prepare a second dirge during a brief intermission. The *fin de siècle* will see its poet (though in the beginning he didn't start with a masterpiece but followed the law of Nature): he was born on American shores, there at the mouth of La Plata where two peoples, past rivals, are currently trying to outdo each other in material and moral advance. Buenos Aires, the queen of the South, and Montevideo, the coquette, reach out welcoming hands across the Argentine waters of the great estuary. But the perennial war has placed its destructive power on these lands and joyfully reaped numerous casualties. Farewell, old one, and think of me when you read me. You, young man, don't ever lose hope—because, despite your opinion to the contrary, you have a comrade in the vampire. Counting the itch-mite[5] that causes scabies, you have *two* comrades!

END OF THE FIRST DIRGE

Second Dirge

HERE HAS THAT first dirge of Maldoror gone, since his mouth filled with belladonna leaves let it loose through the kingdoms of anger in a pensive moment? Where has that dirge gone... We can't know for certain. It is not the trees nor the winds that have harboured it. And morality, which was passing this place, not foreseeing that it had an energetic defender within these incandescent pages, saw it move with a sure and steady step towards the dark recesses and hidden threads of consciences. The least that has been grasped by science is that, since that time, the man in the form of a toad no longer even recognizes himself and often falls into fits of rage which make him resemble a forest beast. It's not his fault. All the time he had believed, his eyes yielding beneath the mignonettes of modesty, that he was made only of good and a small amount of evil. I sharply apprised him, by exposing his heart and intrigues to the light of day, that on the contrary he was made only of evil and a small amount of good that the law-makers are at pains not to let evaporate. *I*—who teach him nothing new—don't want him to feel an eternal shame for my bitter truths; but the realization of this desire would not be consistent with the laws of Nature. I actually tear the mask from his muddy, treacherous face and let the sublime lies with which he deceives himself fall one by one, like balls of ivory into a silver bowl: it is then understandable that he doesn't order serenity to impose its hands on his face, even when reason disperses the shades of arrogance. That is why the hero I produce is clothed with irreconcilable hatred, while attacking humanity, which believes itself invulnerable, through the breach of absurd philosophical diatribes; they are heaped like grains of sand in their books, in which I am sometimes on the verge, when bereft of reason, of guessing a comedy so ridiculous but boring. He had expected it. It isn't enough to carve a statue of goodness on the pediments of parchments held in libraries. O human being! You there, now, naked as a worm, face to face with my diamond sword! Leave your ways, it is no longer time to be proud: I throw my prayer at you from a position of deference. There is someone who watches the smallest events of your sinful life; you are covered by the subtle webs of his persistent perspicacity. Don't trust him when he turns his back—because he sees you; don't trust him when he closes his eyes—because he still sees you. In terms of tricks and mischief, it is difficult to suppose that your formidable resolution will surpass the child, in my mind. His least strikes carry home. It is possible, with prudence, to teach one who ignorantly believes that wolves and thieves don't devour each other: it is perhaps not their habit. Consequently, place your welfare fearlessly in his hands: he will lead it in a way he knows. Don't believe that his intention is to make the sun shine by correcting you—because you interest him little, to say the least; yet, regarding the entire truth, I still don't approach the benevolent measure of my verification. It is actually his desire to hurt you, in the legitimate belief that you may also become as wicked as he and that you might accompany him into the gaping abyss of Hell when that hour strikes. His place has been marked for a long time, at the right-hand side where one notes a flaming gallows from which hang chains and an iron collar. When destiny brings him there, the funeral crater will never have savoured a tastier prey, nor will he have imagined a more fitting abode. It seems to me that I speak in an intentionally paternal way, and that humanity has no grounds to complain.

I seize the quill which is going to construct the second dirge... instrument plucked from the wings of some red sea eagle! But... what about my fingers, then? The joints remain paralyzed as soon as I begin my work. However, I need to write... It is an imposed objective! Very well, I repeat that I must write down my thoughts: I have the right like anyone else to surrender to this instinctive urge... But no, but no, the quill remains motionless!... Wait, observe the lightning far away across the countryside. The thunderstorm passes through the sky. It rains... It is always raining... How it pours!... The lightning-bolt explodes!... it descends through my half-open window and lays me flat out on the floor, struck on the forehead. Poor young man! Your expression was already embellished enough with advanced wrinkling and congenital deformity without needing that long sulphurous scar as well! (I assume that the wound is healed, which doesn't happen overnight.) Why this thunderstorm, and why the paralysis of my fingers? Is it a warning from Heaven to prevent me from writing, and to better consider what I am exposing myself to by distilling the drool from my frank mouth? But that thunderstorm hasn't frightened me. What would a legion of thunderstorms matter to me! These emissaries of the celestial police zealously administer their painful duty, while I am summarily judged by my wounded face. I don't have to thank the Omnipotent for His remarkable skill; He has sent the lightning-bolt in such a way as to cleave my face in two from the forehead, the place where the wound would be most dangerous: may another congratulate Him! But tempests attack some more strongly than others. So therefore, horrible Eternal One with the face of a viper, it must be that, not content with having placed my soul between the limits of madness and thoughts of wrath which slowly kill, after mature examination You furthermore considered it consistent with your majesty to make a cup of blood flow from my forehead!... But, in the end, who tells You anything? You know I don't love You and that, contrariwise, I hate You: why then do You insist? When will Your behaviour cease

to shroud itself with bizarre guises? Speak to me frankly as a friend: is it that You don't doubt yourself and that, in the end, You display with your hateful persecution a naïve zeal which none of Your seraphim would ever dare declare as being absolutely ridiculous? What rage takes hold of You? Realize that, if You were to let me live free from Your harassment, my gratitude will belong to You... Come, Sultan, clear up for me with your tongue this blood that sullies the floor. The bandage is complete: my staunched face has been washed with salt water and I have dressings across my face. The result isn't permanent: four shirts soaked in blood and two handkerchiefs. At first sight one might not believe that Maldoror would hold so much blood in his arteries; because only the reflections of a corpse gleam on his face. But, in the end, that's the case. Perhaps this is as much blood as his body could contain, and it is likely that not very much remains. Enough, enough, keen dog; leave the floor just as it is: you have a full stomach. Don't keep drinking, because you won't be delaying to vomit. You are sufficiently satiated, so go lie yourself down in the kennel; consider yourself swimming in fortune, because you won't think about hunger for three days thanks to the blood cells which you guzzled down your gullet with such visibly solemn satisfaction. You, Leman, take a broom: I would also like to take one but I don't have the stamina. Surely you understand that I don't have the strength? Return your tears to their ducts; if you don't, I believe you won't have the courage to calmly contemplate the enormous scar caused by a torment already forgotten in the night of history. You will go to seek two buckets of water at the fountain. Once the floor is washed you'll take some linen from the next room. If the washerwoman returns this evening, as she should do, you will return these to her; but since it rained heavily during the past hour, and it continues to pour, I don't believe she'll leave her home; then she'll come tomorrow morning. If she asks where all this blood came from, you aren't obligated to respond to her. Oh! how faint I am! No matter: I will however have the strength to raise the pen and the courage to dig into my thoughts. What has the Creator reclaimed by pestering me as if I were a baby with a storm that bears the lightning-bolt? I won't persist any less in my resolution to write. These bandages annoy me and the atmosphere of my room reeks of blood …

Let the day never come when we, Lohengrin and I, would pass in the street, one beside the other, without seeing each other as we grazed elbows like two hastening passers-by! Oh! let me escape forever distant from that supposition! The Eternal One has created the world such as it is: He would show great wisdom if, during the time strictly necessary to smash a woman's head in with a hammer, He forgot his sidereal majesty in order to reveal for us the mysteries amid which our existence suffocates like a fish at the bottom of a boat. But He is great and noble; He prevails over us by the power of His creations; if He were to negotiate with men, all shames might rebound onto His face. But … how miserable you are! Why don't you blush? It is not enough that the army of physical and moral griefs which surrounds us was begotten: the secret of our tattered destiny is not revealed to us. The Almighty, I know Him … and He must likewise know me. If by chance we travel on the same path, His keen vision spies me coming from afar: He takes a side road in order to avoid the great platinum sting which Nature bestowed on me for a tongue! You would please me, O Creator, if You allowed me to pour out my emotions. Wielding terrible ironies with a firm and cool hand, I warn You that my heart will contain enough for me to attack You until the end of my life. I will strike Your hollow carcass — but so strongly that I undertake to make out the remaining pieces of intelligence which You haven't wished to give Man because You would have been jealous of him being equal to You, and which You have shamelessly hidden in your guts, cunning bandit, as if You didn't know that some day I would discover them with my keen eye, and that I would seize them and share them with my fellow men. I have done as I say, and now they fear You more; they deal with You from strength to strength. Bestow death on me so I can repent my daring: I expose my chest and humbly await. Appear, then, pathetic span of eternal punishments!... bombastic displays of excessively vaunted qualities! He shows an inability to stop the flow of my blood which taunts Him. However I do have some proof that He doesn't hesitate to extinguish the breath of other humans in the prime of life when they have hardly tasted life's joys. It is simply terrible—but only according to the feebleness of my opinion! I have seen the Creator, goading His pointless cruelty, lighting fires where old people and children perish! It isn't *I* who begins the attack: it is He who forces me to turn, like a teetotum, with the whip of steel scourges. Is it not *He* who provides me with accusations against Himself? He won't exhaust my terrible zeal one iota! It is fed by insane nightmares which plague my sleeplessness. It was due to Lohengrin that the above was written; let us therefore return to him. Fearing that he would no longer become as other men, I at first resolved to kill him with a knife strike when he had passed puberty. But I reflected, and I wisely postponed my decision. He didn't suspect that his life had been in danger for fifteen minutes. All was prepared, and the knife had been purchased. The stiletto was charming—because I like grace and elegance even in the apparatus of death—but it was long and pointed. A single wound to the neck, carefully penetrating one of the carotid arteries, and I believe that would have sufficed. I am happy with my conduct; I will be repentant later. Therefore, Lohengrin, do what you will, act as you like—confine me for life in a dark prison with scorpions as companions in my captivity, or pluck an eye from me until it falls to the ground—I will never reproach you in the least: I am yours, I belong to you, I no longer live for myself. The grief that you've caused me doesn't compare to the happiness of knowing that he who wounds me with his murderous hands is soaked in an essence more divine than that of his fellow men! Yes, it is still good to give life to a human being and to conserve hope in that way that all men aren't wicked—since, in the end, there was one man who had known how to actively draw to himself the wary aversions of my sour sympathy!...

It is midnight; not a single omnibus can be seen from the Bastille to Madeleine. I'm wrong—there is one suddenly appearing as if it were emerging from underground. Some passers-by slow down to regard it curiously, because it appears to be unique. In the upper deck sit some men who have fixed eyes like those of dead fish. They press against each other and appear lifeless; moreover the statutory capacity is not exceeded. When the coachman gives his horses a crack of the whip, it seems that the whip moves his arms and not his arms the whip. What must this group of odd and silent beings be? Are they denizens of the moon? There are times when one might be tempted to believe it; but instead they look like corpses. The omnibus, pushing to arrive at the last station, eats up the space and cracks the pavings... It flies!... But in its tracks a formless mass stubbornly pursues it in the middle of the dust. "Stop, I beseech you; halt... my legs are tired from walking all day... I haven't eaten since yesterday... my parents have abandoned me... I don't know what to do... I must return home, and I would soon reach there if you allow me a seat... I am a small child of eight years old, and I trust you..." It flies!... It flies!... But in its tracks a formless mass stubbornly pursues it in the middle of the dust. One of those frozen-eyed men elbows his neighbour and appears to convey his displeasure regarding these groans (with their Argentinian accent) reaching his ears. The other nods his head slightly as a sign of agreement, and then plunges himself back into the immobility of his self-absorption, like a tortoise into its shell. Everything in the expressions of the other travellers indicates the same sentiments as those of the first two men. The cries can still be heard for two or three minutes, more piercing from second to second. We see windows opening on the boulevard, and a frightened figure holding a light, after casting its eyes to the road, hastily closes the door again and doesn't reappear... It flies!... It flies! But a formless mass stubbornly pursues it in its tracks in the middle of the dust. Alone amongst these petrified people, a young man, sunken in his reveries, appears to feel pity for the unlucky one. For the sake of the child—who believes he can reach it with his small, sore legs—he dares not raise his voice because the other men throw looks of contempt and belligerence at the child and he knows he can't do anything against them all. Elbows resting on his knees and head in hands, stupefied, he asks himself if this is truly what one calls *human charity*. He admits then that this is a useless term which cannot be found even in the poetry dictionary, and he honestly concedes his mistake. He says: "Indeed, why be interested in a small child? Leave him behind." However a burning tear rolls down the cheek of this young man who has just blasphemed. With difficulty he passes his hand over his forehead as if to disperse a cloud whose opacity overshadows his understanding. He struggles vainly in the century into which he was thrown; he feels he is not in his place, and yet he can't escape. Appalling prison! Hideous Fate! Lombano, I am happy with you since that day! I never ceased watching you while

my face inhaled the same indifference as that of the other travellers. The adolescent gets up with an indignant movement and wishes to disembark so as to no longer participate, even involuntarily, in an evil deed. I gesture to him and he resumes his place beside me... It flies!... It flies! But a formless mass stubbornly pursues it in its tracks, in the middle of the dust. The cries suddenly cease—because the child has caught his foot on a protruding cobblestone and suffered a head-wound while falling. The omnibus has vanished over the horizon and can no longer be seen on the silent thoroughfare... It flies!... It flies! But a formless mass stubbornly pursues it in its tracks, in the middle of the dust. Observe the ragpicker who passes, bent over his pale lantern; there is more heart in him than in all his fellow men in the omnibus. He has just gathered up the child: be well assured that he will nurse him, and not abandon him as his parents did. It flies!... It flies! But a formless mass stubbornly pursues it in its tracks, in the middle of the dust!... Stupid and idiotic race! You will repent of your conduct in this way. It is *I* who tell you this. You will repent—go on: repent! My poetry will only entail attacking Man, that wild beast, by any means—and God, who should not have begat such vermin. Volumes will pile upon volumes until the end of my life, and yet only this concept alone will always be seen present in my mind!

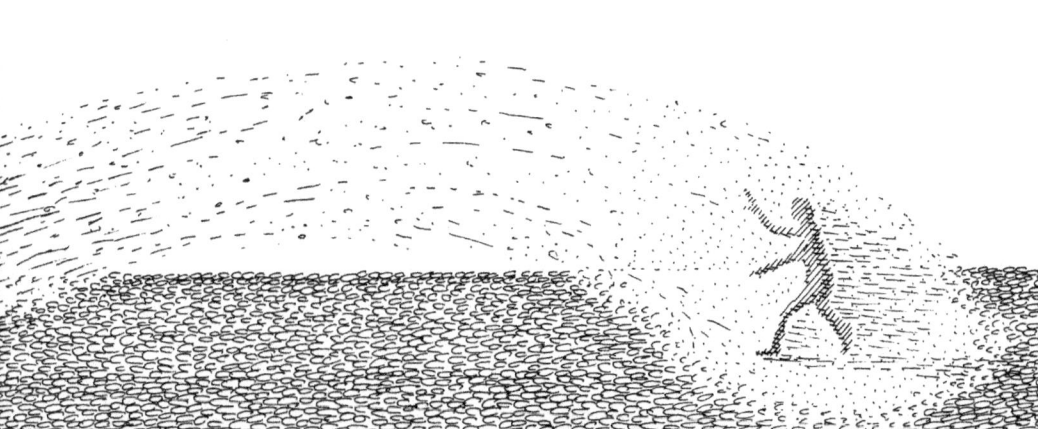

Taking my quotidian stroll, each day I would pass down a narrow street: each day a slim young ten-year-old girl would follow me at a polite distance along this street while regarding me with sympathetic and curious eyes. She was tall for her age and had a slender waist. Abundant black hair, parted in two on her head, fell freely in separate tresses over her marble shoulders. One day she followed me as usual — the muscular arms of a common woman grabbed her by the hair, like a whirlwind snatches a leaf, applied two brutal slaps to her proud and mute cheek, and dragged that lost soul back into the house. I vainly acted indifferent to it; she would never fail to follow me with her increasingly inappropriate presence. When I would encroach upon another street to continue my journey, she would stop at the end of that narrow street, taking great pains to do so, motionless like the statue of Silence, and not ceasing to gaze ahead until I had disappeared. Once, this young girl preceded me in the street and fell into step in front of me. If I moved faster to pass her, she would hasten to maintain an equal distance; but if I slowed down the pace so that there might be a greater space between us in the street, then she would also slow down, thus displaying the grace of childhood. Reaching the end of the street, she would slowly turn around in such a way as to block my passage. I didn't have time to slip past, and I found myself facing her. She had swollen and reddened eyes. I could easily see that she wished to speak to me and that she didn't know how to proceed. Suddenly, becoming as pale as a corpse, she asked me: "Would you be kind enough to tell me what time it is?" I informed her that I didn't carry a watch, and I quickly walked away. Since that day, child with the restless and precocious imagination, you haven't seen again in that narrow street the mysterious young man who painfully beats the cobblestones of the tortuous crossroads with his leaden sandals. The vision of that flaming comet will no longer shine, like a sad subject of fanatical curiosity, on the face of your disappointed view; and you will think often, too often — perhaps always — of the one who doesn't seem to worry about the bad nor the good things of

present life, and who would randomly go forth with a horribly deathly face, unkempt hair, staggering walk and arms swimming blindly in the ironic waters of the ether as though seeking the bloody booty of hope—continually tossed through the immense regions of space by the relentless snow-plough of Fate. You will see me no more, and I won't see you again!... Who knows? Perhaps this girl wasn't what she seemed. Perhaps beneath an innocent surface she concealed a considerable cunning, the burden of eighteen years, and the enchantment of vice. We saw prostitutes cheerfully migrating from the British Isles and crossing the Channel. They would spread out their wings while whirling in golden swarms in front of the Parisian light; and when you glimpse them you might say: "But they are still children; they are no more than ten or twelve years old." They were, in fact, twenty years old. Oh!—the detours to that dark street are cursed by this supposition! Horrible! horrible! what transpires there. I believe her mother slapped her because she didn't do her job with enough skill. It is possible that she was only a child, and then the mother is even more guilty. *I* don't want to believe that supposition—which is only a theory—and I would prefer to love, in this romantic personality, a soul which blossoms too early... Ah! look here, maiden, if I ever pass through this street again, I implore you to never appear again before my eyes. It may cost you dearly! Already the blood and hatred rise to my head in boiling waves. *Me*, being generous enough to love my fellow men! No, no! I determined it since the day of my birth! *They* don't love me! You will see worlds wiping themselves out and granite sliding like a cormorant on the surface of the waves, before I touch the unspeakable hand of a human being. Back... take back that hand!... You aren't an angel, young girl, and you will, in short, become like other women. No, no, I beseech you—do not reappear before my creased and squinting eyebrows. In a moment of madness I might take your arms, twisting them like washed linen wrung of water, or break them with a crack like two dry branches, and then make you eat them by using force. I might, while taking your head between my

hands in a caressing and gentle manner, push my eager fingers into the lobes of your innocent brain, a smile on my lips, in order to extract an effective grease to wash my eyes pained by life's eternal insomnia. I might, by sewing your eyelids together with a needle, deprive you of the spectacle of the world and make it impossible for you to find your path; it won't be *I* who will serve as your guide. Raising your virgin body with arms of iron, I might seize you by the legs, make you twirl around me like a sling, concentrate my strength in describing the final circumference and throw you against the wall. Each drop of blood will spray onto a human breast, to frighten men and exhibit to them an example of my wickedness! They will unremittingly tear shreds and scraps of flesh from themselves—but the drop of blood remains indelible in the same place and will sparkle like a diamond. Rest assured, I will give the order to half-a-dozen servants to guard the venerated remains of your body and protect them from the hunger of the voracious hounds. No doubt the body has remained stuck to the wall like a ripe pear and hasn't fallen to the ground; but hounds know how to perform high jumps, if we aren't careful.

This child who is seated on a bench in the Tuileries Garden—how good he is! His bold eyes dart to some invisible object far off in the sky. He can't be more than eight years old, and yet he doesn't enjoy himself as would be expected. At the very least he should laugh and walk with some friend instead of remaining alone—but that's not in his character.

This child who is seated on a bench in the Tuileries Garden—how good he is! A man with ambiguous bearing, impelled by a secret agenda, comes to sit next to him on the same bench. Who is it? I don't need to tell you, because you will recognize him from the tortuous conversation. Let's listen to them, and not interrupt:

— What were you pondering, child?

— I was thinking of Heaven.

— You don't need to think of Heaven; it is enough to think of the earth. Are you weary of life, you who have just been born?

— No, but everyone prefers Heaven to the earth.

— Oh well, not me. Because, since Heaven has been created by God just like the earth, be certain that you will meet there the same evils that are here below. After your death you won't be rewarded according to your merits; because if someone has perpetrated wrongs against you on this earth (as you will learn from later experience), there is no reason why they would not commit them against you once more in the other life. What you had better do is to *not* think of God and to make justice yourself, since it was denied you. If one of your friends offended you, wouldn't you be happy to kill him?

— But that is forbidden.

— It isn't as forbidden as you think. It's merely a question of not allowing yourself to get caught. The justice brought about by laws is worthless; it is the jurisprudence of the victim which counts. If you hated one of your friends, wouldn't you be unhappy to imagine that you constantly had the thought of him in front of your eyes?

— That's true.

— Here, then, is one of your friends who has made you unhappy all your life: for, seeing that your hatred is only passive, he won't continue any less to taunt you and cause you harm with impunity. There is therefore only one way to bring this situation to an end: it is to get rid of your enemy. Here is what I wanted to point out in order to make you understand on what foundations contemporary society is based. Each individual must make justice himself, unless he is just an imbecile. He who is victorious over his fellows, *he* is the more cunning and more powerful. Wouldn't you like to dominate your fellows one day?

— Yes, indeed!

— Then be stronger and craftier. You are still too young to be more powerful, but from this day onwards you must employ cunning, the best instrument for men of genius. When the shepherd David wounded the giant Goliath on the forehead with a rock slung from a catapult, is it not admirable to observe that it was only by this ruse that David conquered his enemy, and that if, on the contrary, they had seized each other bodily, the giant would have squashed him like a fly? It is the same for you. In open battle, you can never defeat men over whom you wish to extend your will; but with cunning you will be able to fight alone against all. You desire wealth, beautiful palaces, and glory? — or did you deceive me when you affirmed these noble ambitions to me?

— No, no, I didn't deceive you. But I would like to gain what I want by other means.

— Then, you will gain nothing at all. The virtuous and simple-minded means lead nowhere. It is necessary to get down to work with the most energetic levers and clever intrigues. Before you become celebrated for your virtue and attain your goal, a hundred others have had time to leap-frog over you and reach the end of their career before you, in such a way that there won't be any room for your slim ideas. It is necessary to know how to embrace the horizon of the present moment with more grandeur. For example, haven't you ever heard of the great glory that victories carry? And yet those victories don't happen by themselves. One must spill blood — lots of blood — to achieve them and to lay them at the feet of the victors. Without the corpses and scattered limbs which you see on the field where carnage has been wisely carried out, there would be no war, and without war there would be no victory. When we wish to become celebrated, you must see that we have to gracefully immerse ourselves in rivers of blood fed by cannon fodder. The aim justifies the method. In order to become famous, the first thing is to have money. Now, as you have none, it is necessary to kill to gain it; but as you aren't strong enough to handle a dagger, become a thief while waiting for your limbs to lengthen. And so that they will mature more quickly, I advise you to perform gymnastics twice a day, one hour in the morning and one hour in the evening. In that way you can tackle crime with a certain success by the age of fifteen, instead of waiting until you're twenty. The love of glory justifies everything—and perhaps later, being master of your comrades, you will do them almost as much good as you did them evil to begin with...

Maldoror discerns that the blood bubbles in the head of his young interlocutor; his nostrils swell and his lips exude a slight pale froth. He feels his pulse; the throbs are quickening. Fever has overwhelmed his delicate body. He fears the outcome of his words, and the rascal slips away, annoyed at not being able to chat with this child any longer. When, at a ripe old age, it is so hard to control the emotions, balanced between good and evil, how is it for a mind still filled with inexperience? And what quantity of relative energy is required, in addition? The child will be left to stay in bed for three days. Would to Heaven that the motherly touch will bring peace to this sensitive flower, this delicate shell of a beautiful soul!

There in a thicket surrounded by flowers sleeps an hermaphrodite, drowsing deeply in the grass dampened by its tears. The moon has freed its disk from the mass of clouds and with its wan rays caresses that sweet adolescent figure. Its features express the most virile energy while at the same time the grace of a heavenly virgin. Nothing appears natural about it, not even the body muscles which ripple across the harmonious contours of feminine forms. It has one arm curved over its face, while the other hand is placed against its chest as if to calm the beatings of a heart closed to all confidences and charged with the heavy load of a perennial secret. Fatigued by life and ashamed of walking amongst others who don't resemble it, despair has overwhelmed its soul and it proceeds alone like the beggar in the valley. How does it provide itself with the means to live? Compassionate souls watch over it closely without it suspecting that scrutiny, and they never abandon it: how good it is! How resigned it is! Sometimes it gladly speaks with those who have a tender nature, without touching their hand, and keeping itself at a distance for fear of imagined danger. If one asks it why it takes solitude for company, its eyes look to Heaven and it barely restrains a tear of reproach against Providence; but it doesn't reply to that careless query, which gives off the blush of the morning rose from the snow of its eyelids. It becomes uncomfortable if the conversation is prolonged, turning its eyes to the four quarters as if seeking to flee the presence of an invisible enemy who approaches, it makes an abrupt farewell with its hand, and it moves off on the wings of wakened modesty and vanishes into the forest. People generally take it for a madman. One day four masked men, under orders, threw themselves on it and tied it securely in such a way that it could only move its legs. The whip inflicted rough cuts on its back, and they told it to hasten towards the road that leads to Bicêtre. It smiled when receiving the blows, and spoke so passionately to them of knowledge of many of the human sciences it had studied (and which displayed a considerable education in one who had not yet crossed the threshold of youth) and on the destinies of humanity (where it utterly revealed the poetic nobility of its soul)—that the guards, horrified to the blood by the deed they had committed, untied its battered limbs, dragged themselves to their knees while begging to be pardoned, and departed, showing signs of a veneration not normally given to men. Since this event, which was much spoken of, its secret was guessed by everyone, but they appeared to ignore the hermaphrodite in order to minimize its sufferings; and the government awarded it an honourable pension to make it forget that they had once wanted to commit it forcefully to a mental asylum, without prior verification. The hermaphrodite spends half of its money; the remainder it donates to the poor. When it sees a man and a woman walking along some avenue of plane trees, it feels its body cleaved in two from bottom to top, and each new part moves to embrace one of the walkers; but this is just an hallucination, and reason soon regains control. This is why it socializes neither among men nor women—because its excessive modesty, which has taken light in this idea that it is only a monster, prevents it granting its burning sympathy to anyone. It believes it might violate itself, and it believes it might violate others. Its pride echoes this axiom to it: "Everyone stays true to their own nature." Its pride, I said, because it fears that in joining its life to a man or a woman, people might sooner or later reproach it for the conformation of its body, like a gross misdemeanour. So it remains entrenched in its self-esteem, offended by this impious assumption which only originates from itself, and persists in remaining alone and uncomforted amidst torments. There in a thicket surrounded by flowers sleeps the hermaphrodite, drowsing deeply in the grass dampened by its tears. The waking birds rapturously behold this melancholy figure through the tree branches, and the nightingale doesn't wish to make his crystal cavatinas heard. The forest has become as venerable as a tomb from the nocturnal presence of the unfortunate hermaphrodite. O straying traveller, by your spirit for adventure which made you leave your father and mother in youth; by the sufferings which thirst caused you in the desert; by your homeland which you perhaps seek again after

having wandered for so long, exiled, in foreign lands; by your charger, the loyal friend who along with you endured the exile and harsh climates which your vagabond mood made you pass through; by the dignity which gives Man voyages over distant lands and unexplored oceans amid the polar ice, or beneath the influence of a scorching sun — don't touch with your hand, like a rustling breeze, that curly hair spread on the ground that mingles with the green grass. You would do better to draw yourself a few paces away. That hair is sacred; it is the hermaphrodite itself who desired it. It doesn't wish human lips to worshipfully kiss its hair, scented by the mountain breeze, nor its brow, which in that moment glows like the stars in the heavens. Indeed, it would be better to believe that this is a star itself that has fallen from its orbit, while crossing space, onto this majestic brow and which surrounds it with its diamond clarity, as though from a halo. Turning away sadness with a finger, night assumes all her charms to celebrate the slumber of this embodiment of modesty, this perfect figure of angelic innocence: the rustling of the insects is less noticeable. The branches lean their bushy height over it as if to protect it from the dew, and the breeze, sounding the strings of its melodious harp, sends its joyful chords across the universal silence towards those lowered and stilled eyelids, which it believes observe the rhythmical harmony of the planets. It dreams that it is happy — that its physical form has changed — or at least that it is flying on a purple cloud towards another planet inhabited by beings with the same form as it. Alas! Let its delusion be prolonged until the waking of dawn! It dreams that the flowers dance around it in a circle, like great crazy festoons, soaking it with their soft scents while it sings a hymn of love in the arms of a human being of magical beauty. But it is only a twilight vapor that its arms enfold, and when it wakes its arms won't be embracing anything. Don't wake, hermaphrodite; I implore you not to wake yet. Why don't you wish to believe me? Sleep... sleep still. May your chest rise while pursuing the chimerical hope of bliss; I allow it to you, but don't open your eyes. Ah! don't open your eyes! I want to leave you like this so as not to be witness to your waking. Perhaps one day, with the help of a weighty tome I will recount your history in its impassioned pages, terrified by what it contains and the lessons that emerge. So far I have failed—because each time I have wished it, abundant tears fell on the paper and my fingers shook without it being due to old age. But I want to have that courage in the end. I am ashamed by not having more nerves than a woman and fainting like a small girl every time I reflect on your immense woe. Sleep... sleep still—but don't open your eyes! Farewell, hermaphrodite! Each day I won't neglect to pray to Heaven for you (if it were for me, I wouldn't pray at all). Peace be in your breast!

When a woman with a soprano voice expresses her stirring and melodious tones, on hearing that human harmony my eyes are filled with a hidden flame and fire painful sparks while the alarm of cannon fire seems to echo in my ears. Whence comes this profound hatred for all held within Man? If the chords fly from the strings of an instrument I listen with sublime pleasure to those delicate notes fleeing in cadence through the elastic waves of the atmosphere. Perception transmits to my hearing only an impression of a sweetness that melts the nerves and thoughts; an ineffable lethargy envelops with its magic poppies, like a veil that filters the daylight, the active strength of my senses and the vital forces of my imagination. They say that I was born embraced by deafness! In the early days of my childhood I couldn't hear what was said to me. When, with considerable difficulties, they succeeded in teaching me to speak, it was only after reading what someone had written on a sheet that I was able to communicate, in my turn, the thread of my reasonings. One day—unlucky day—I grew in beauty and innocence, and everyone admired the intellect and kindness of this divine adolescent. Many minds blushed when they beheld

these clear features where his soul had made its throne. They would approach him only with reverence, because they observed in his eyes the gaze of an angel. But no, I knew moreover that the happy roses of adolescence would not flower forever, braided in capricious garlands on his modest and noble forehead which was kissed with frenzy by all mothers. It began to seem to me that the universe, with its starry vault of impassive and irritating spheres, was perhaps not as grand as I had dreamed. Consequently, one day, weary of dogging the steep path of earthly journey on foot and of wending my way, lurching like a lush, through the dark catacombs of life, I slowly raised my spiteful eyes, surrounded by large bluish circles, to the concavity of the firmament and dared to penetrate — *me*, so young — the mysteries of Heaven! Not finding what I sought, I raised my frightened eyes higher, and higher still, until I perceived a throne made from human excrement and gold, on which sat, with an idiotic arrogance and body covered with a shroud made from soiled hospital linen — the one who calls Himself the Creator! He held the rotting trunk of a dead man in His hand and bore it, in turn, from eyes to nose and from nose to mouth; once at His mouth, we can guess what He was doing. His feet were plunged into a vast ocean of roiling blood from the surface of which had suddenly risen, like tapeworms through the contents of a chamber pot, two or three leery heads which directly sank again with the speed of an arrow: a kick applied well to the nasal bone was the certain reward for violation of the rules, prompted by the need to breathe another medium; because, ultimately, these men were not fish! Mostly amphibians, they swam between two waters in this putrid fluid!... until the Creator, having nothing more in hand, seized another swimmer by the neck with the foremost two claws of His foot, as though with pincers, and raised him into the air beyond the reddish slime — exquisite sauce! As to that one was likewise done to another. He firstly devoured the head, the legs and arms, and finally the torso, until nothing remained — because He munched on the bones. And so on during the subsequent hours of His eternity. Sometimes

He cried: "I have created you, therefore I have the right to do with you what I will. You have done nothing to me, I won't say otherwise. I make you suffer, and it's for my pleasure." And He resumed His cruel repast, grinding His lower jaw which in turn shook His brain-soaked beard. (O reader, doesn't that last detail make you salivate? Whoever craves such brains, don't eat them unless good, absolutely fresh, and caught in the *fish* lake within the last fifteen minutes.) For some time I contemplated this spectacle with paralyzed limbs and a dumb throat. Thrice I almost fell back like a man suffering from overwhelming emotion; thrice I managed to stay on my feet. Not a fibre of my body remained unmoved and I shook like lava trembling within a volcano. Finally my chest, unable to expel the life-giving air fast enough, constricted, my lips opened, and I uttered a cry... a cry so heart-rending... that I heard it! The shackles of my ear were loosened in an abrupt manner, the ear-drum cracked beneath the blast of that mass of resounding air that boomed from me, and a new phenomenon took place in the organ condemned by Nature. I heard a sound! A fifth sense was revealed to me! But what pleasure would I have been able to find in such a discovery? From now on the human sound would only reach my ears with the feeling of pain which pity at a great injustice brings about. When someone spoke to me, I recalled what I had once seen above the visible planets and the translation of my feelings smothered by a violent roar whose timbre was identical to that of my fellow men! I couldn't reply to him, because the tortures carried out on man's vulnerability in that hideous sea of crimson passed roaring before my brow like flayed elephants and, grazed by their fiery wings, my hair burned. Much later, when I further experienced humanity, this feeling of pity joined with an intense fury against that tigress stepmother whose callous children only know how to curse and commit evil. Impudence from falsehood! They say that evil is the only exceptional state!... Now it is long gone; for ages I have addressed nobody. O you, whoever you are, when you are next to me don't let your vocal chords allow any intonation to escape; don't let your stilled larynx attempt to surpass the nightingale; and may you *never* try to make your soul known to me with the aid of language. Preserve a religious and uninterrupted silence; humbly cross your hands on your breast and cast down your eyes. Since the vision which made me experience the supreme truth, I've told you enough about the nightmares, that avidly sucked my throat during the nights and days, to still have the courage to rekindle, even by thought, the sufferings that I endured in that infernal hour which relentlessly pursues me with its memory. Oh! When you hear the avalanche of snow falling from high on the icy mountain; the lioness protesting the disappearance of her young in the arid desert; the storm achieving its destiny; the howl of the condemned man in prison on the eve of the guillotine; and the fierce octopus in the ocean waves recounting its victories over swimmers and castaways: say that these majestic voices are not more beautiful than the snigger of Man!

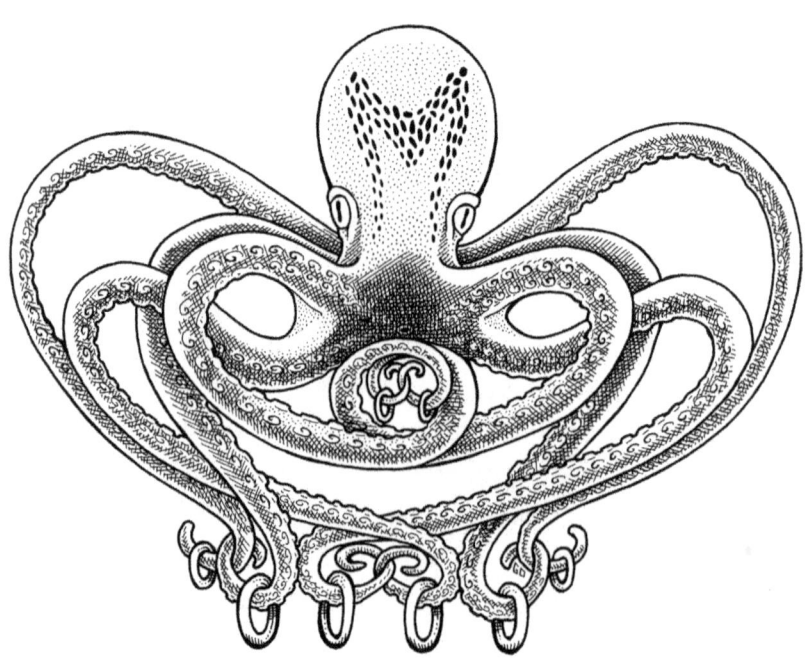

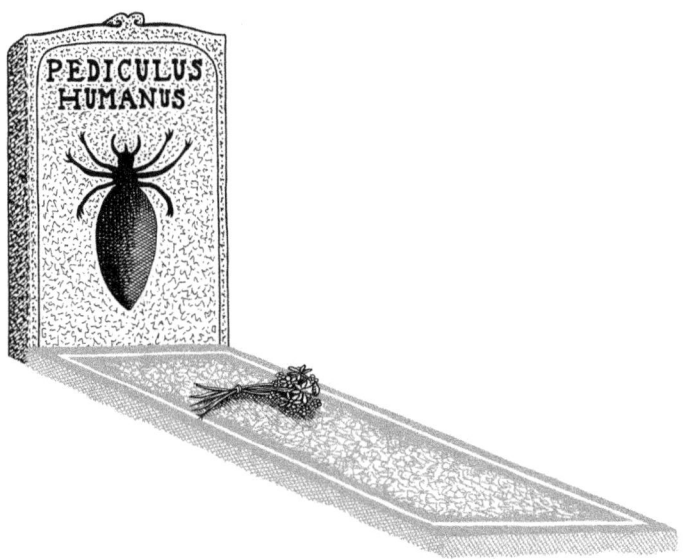

An insect exists which men nurture at their peril. They owe it nothing—but they fear it. This insect, which doesn't like wine but prefers blood, would be capable by an occult power of becoming as large as an elephant, crushing men like ears of corn, if they didn't satisfy its proper needs. It must also be observed how they respect it, how they surround it with a canine devotion, and how they place it in high esteem above the animals of Creation. They give it the head as a throne, and it sinks its claws into the hair follicles with aplomb. Later, when it is fat and has entered an advanced age, they kill it—imitating the tradition of an ancient race—so that it won't know the grievances of senility. They give it grand funerals, as for a hero, and the coffin which conducts it directly to the lid of the tomb is carried on the shoulders of the chief citizens. On the moist earth that the gravedigger has shifted with his sagacious spade, they devise multicoloured phrases about the immortality of the soul, about the nothingness of life, about the inexplicable will of Providence—and reseal the marble forever on this laboriously fulfilled life which is now nothing more than a corpse. The crowd scatters, and the night does not tarry in shrouding the walls of the cemetery with its shadows.

But comfort yourselves, humans, over its distressing loss. Here is its numerous family which advances, and which it liberally bestowed upon you so that your despair might be less painful and as if appeased by the agreeable presence of these surly abortions which will later become magnificent lice adorned with an extraordinary beauty, monsters with wise mien. With its maternal wings it incubated dozens of cherished eggs upon your hair, which is now withered by the fierce suction of these fearful aliens. The time shortly arrives when the eggs are hatched. Fear not — these young philosophers will soon grow through this ephemeral life. They will enlarge so much that they will make you feel it with their claws and proboscises.

Others among you don't know why they fail to eat your cranial bones and why they continue to suck the essence of your blood with their pumps. Wait a moment—I want to tell you: it is because they don't have the strength. Know for sure that, if their jaws had conformed to the size of their infinite wishes, your brain, the retina of your eyes, your spinal column, your whole body would perish. Like a water droplet. With a microscope, observe a louse who works on the head of a young street beggar; then you will give me some news. Unfortunately, these thieves of the long hair are little. They wouldn't be any good as conscripts because they haven't the mandatory height demanded by law. They belong to the lilliputian world of those with short thighs, and the blind don't hesitate to class them among the infinitely small. Misfortune for the sperm whale who might battle a louse: in spite of its size, it would be devoured in a wink of an eye. The flukes would not even remain to indicate the event. The elephant allows itself to be caressed. The louse, no. I don't advise you to attempt this perilous experiment. Beware if your hand is hairy, or only that it be composed of bones and flesh. It's all over for your fingers: they will crack as they would through torture. The skin vanishes by strange magic. Lice are unable to perform as much evil as envisaged in their imagination. If you find a louse in your road, go your way,

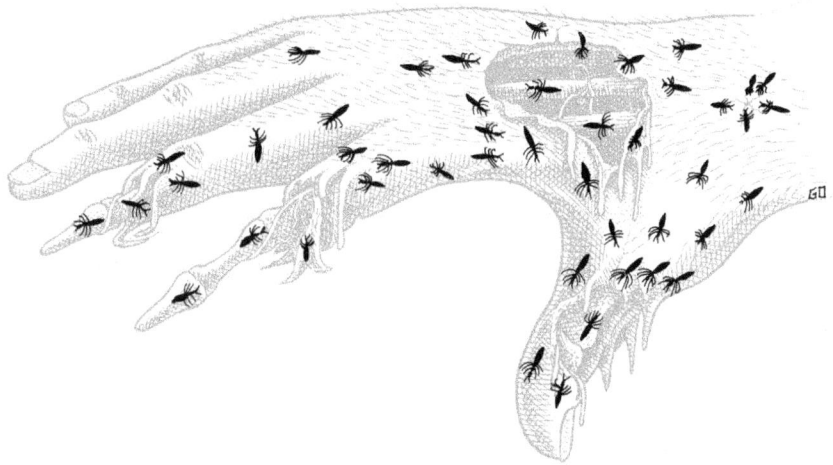

and don't lick the taste-buds of its tongue. Some accident will befall you. This has happened. Never mind, I am already content with the amount of evil it has done to you, O humanity; I just wish it had done you more.

How much longer will you preserve the verminous cult of this god, indifferent to your prayers and the generous gifts you offer it in expiatory holocaust? See, this detestable manitou doesn't acknowledge the large goblets of blood and brains that you pour out on its altars, piously adorned with wreaths of flowers. It is not grateful... because earthquakes and storms have continued to rage since day one. And meanwhile—noteworthy spectacle—the more it shows indifference, the more you admire it. It can be seen that you mistrust its attributes (which it hides) and that your reasoning is based on this point: that only a deity of the utmost power can show such contempt towards the faithful who submit to its religion. That is why there are different gods in every country—here, the crocodile, there, the prostitute—but when it comes to the louse, with *its* sacred name, all peoples kneel as one on the venerable square before the pedestal of the crude and bloodthirsty idol, universally kissing the chains of their bondage. Any race who would disobey its crawling instincts and threaten to revolt might sooner or later vanish from the earth like an autumn leaf—exterminated by the wrath of the relentless god.

O louse, with the shrivelled eye—as long as rivers pour the cascade of their waters into the ocean's depths; as long as stars revolve in the course of their orbits; as long as the silent void has no horizon; as long as humanity rips up its very flanks in deadly battles; as long as divine justice hurls its wrathful thunderbolts down upon this selfish world; as long as Man neglects his Creator and taunts Him by scornfully interfering (with some justification), your reign in the universe will be guaranteed and your dynasty will spread its ripples out from age to age. I salute you, ascending sun, heavenly liberator—*you*, Man's invisible enemy. Continue to tell the smut to join him in unclean embraces and to swear to him with oaths, not written in the dust, that she will remain his loyal lover for as long as Eternity. From time to time kiss the dress of this great hussy in memory of the important services she has rendered. If she did not seduce Man with her hungry breasts, it is likely that you wouldn't exist, you, the fruit of that reasonable and consequent coupling. O son of smut!—tell your mother that if she abandons Man's bed, travelling down solitary paths alone and unsupported, she will see her life compromised. May her entrails that bore you for nine months within their perfumed walls, immediately move themselves at the thought of the threats that might later pursue their tender fruit, so gentle and tranquil but already cold and fierce. Smut, queen of empires, keep the spectacle of the incredible muscular growth of your famished offspring in the eyes of my hatred. To achieve this aim, you know that you only have to cling more tightly to the flanks of Man. You can do that without compromising modesty, since you have both been married for ages.

For myself, if I am permitted to add some words to this hymn of glorification, I would tell that I have had created a pit of forty square leagues and of like depth. Inside there, in its foul virginity, lies a living mine of lice. It fills up the shallows of the pit and then meanders in all directions in large dense veins. Here is how I constructed this artificial mine. I grabbed a female louse from the hair of humanity. I was seen to lay with it for three consecutive nights, and I threw it into the pit. Human impregnation, which would have amounted to nothing in other similar cases, was sanctioned this time by Fate—and after several days thousands of monsters, swarming in a compact knot of matter, were born to the light. In time this hideous knot became more and more immense while acquiring the property of quicksilver, and extended out in many branches which actually nourished themselves by devouring themselves (birth is greater than mortality) whenever I didn't throw down for feed a newborn bastard whose mother wished for its death, or an arm that I am going to cut from some young girl, thanks to chloroform, during the night. Every fifteen years the generations of lice which subsist on Man noticeably diminish, and they themselves infallibly predict their complete destruction in the next period. Because Man, being more intelligent than his enemy, succeeds in vanquishing it. Then, with an infernal shovel that augments my powers, I extract from that inexhaustible mine lumps of lice as large as mountains; I break them with blows from an axe and carry them into the main city streets during the profound night. There, in contact with human temperature, they dissolve as in the first days of their growth in the winding galleries of the subterranean mine, they dig a bed in the gravel and spread in streams into homes like noxious spirits. The watch-dog of the house barks quietly because it suspects that a legion of mysterious beings is penetrating the pores of the walls and bringing terror to slumber's bedsides. You have probably perhaps heard, at least once in your life, these kinds of grim and prolonged barkings. The dog strains with its feeble eyes to pierce the darkness of night, because its canine brain is unable to comprehend this. This hum bothers it and it feels that it is betrayed. Millions of enemies thus swoop down on every city like clouds of grasshoppers—and here they are for fifteen years. They will fight Man by inflicting acute wounds on him. After this period I will send in others. When I crush the lumps of living matter, it can happen that one piece is more dense than another. Its atoms strive with rage to separate their agglomeration in order to go forth and torment humanity; but the cohesion resists in its hardness. With a mighty convulsion they bring about such an effort that the rock, unable to scatter its living elements, hurls itself high into the air, as though from a gunpowder explosion, and descends again, sinking into the soil. Sometimes the dreamy peasant discerns a fireball cleave space vertically, heading towards the lower side of a field of maize. He doesn't know where the rock comes from. You now have, clearly and in a nutshell, the explanation of the phenomenon.

If the earth was covered by lice, like grains of sand on the beach, the human race would be exterminated, prey to terrible sufferings. What a spectacle! For me, suspended in the air with the wings of an angel, to contemplate!

O strict mathematics, I have not forgotten you ever since your learned lessons, sweeter than honey, percolated through my heart like a cooling wave. From the crib I have instinctively aspired to drink from your spring more venerable than the sun, and I, the most loyal of your initiates, still continue to tread the sacred courtyard of your solemn temple. There was a vagueness in my soul, an elusive something as thick as smoke; but I knew how to climb the steps which lead to your altar, zealously, and you have dispelled the dark veil like the wind sweeps the checkerboard. You have placed there instead an extreme coldness, a consummate discretion and an inexorable logic. Aided by your fortifying milk, my intelligence developed swiftly and gained gigantic proportions amidst that delightful clarity which you bestow with extravagance upon those who admire you with a genuine passion. Arithmetic! Algebra! Geometry! Supreme trinity! Brilliant triangle! Whoever has not known you is a fool! He would deserve the ordeals of the greatest tortures—because there is blind scorn in his ignorant indifference; but he who knows and appreciates you no longer desires any worldly goods, simply content with your magical delights; and, carried on your sombre wings, he wishes for nothing else than to rise with a gentle flight while making an ascending spiral towards the spherical vault of the skies. The earth only shows him hallucinations and moral phantasmagorias: but you, O concise mathematics, by the rigorous sequence of your persistent propositions and the steadfastness of your laws of iron, *you* make shine on dazzled eyes a mighty reflection of that supreme truth which we see stamped in the universal pattern. But the order which surrounds you, represented above all by the precise regularity of the square, friend of Pythagoras, is still greater; because the Omnipotent is completely revealed, He and His qualities, in that memorable work which involved extracting your wealths of theorems and your glorious splendours from the entrails of chaos. In ancient epochs and modern times, more than one great human imagination has seen its spirit terrified by the contemplation of your symbolic figures drawn on

burning paper—like so many mysterious marks living with a latent breath—which the profane common person doesn't understand, and which are only the brilliant revelation of axioms and eternal hieroglyphs that have existed before the universe and which will continue after it. Inclining towards the precipice of a fatal query, the imagination asks itself how mathematics manages to contain so much impressive grandeur and irrefutable truth, whereas, if it is compared to Man, it finds nothing in him but false pride and lies. Then this superior mind, depressed, made to feel more keenly the pettiness of humanity and its unequalled madness through the noble confidence of your counsels, lowers its blanched head to a fleshless hand and remains absorbed in these extraordinary meditations. It kneels before you and its reverence pays tribute to your divine visage, as to the Omnipotent's own image. During my childhood you appeared to me one night in May—in the moonlight—on a green meadow—beside a clear stream: all three equal in their grace and modesty, all three full of a grandeur of queens. You took several steps towards me, with your long robe floating like a cloud, and drew me to your proud breasts like a blessed son. Then I rushed up with enthusiasm, my hands clutching your pale chest. I nourished myself on your fertile manna with gratitude, and I felt that humanity grew in me and was enhanced. Since then, O rival goddesses, I have not deserted you. Since then, what energetic designs and sympathies, which I believed had been engraved on the pages of my heart as though on marble, did not have their configured lines slowly erased from my disillusioned reason, as the dawn erases night's shades! Since then I have seen death—deliberately and in full view—populate tombs, ravage battlefields fertilized by human blood, and nurture the morning flowers atop the mournful bones. Since then I have witnessed the revolutions of our planet; earthquakes, volcanos with their fiery lava, the simoom of the desert, and the shipwrecks of the storm have had my presence as impassive observer. Since then I have seen, in the morning, more human generations raise their wings and eyes skywards with the inexperienced delight of the chrysalis which greets its final metamorphosis, and die in the evening, before the setting of the sun, heads bowed like wilting flowers rocked by the wind's plaintiff soughing. But *you* always remain the same. No alteration, no foul air caresses the stony escarpments and deep valleys of your personality. Your humble pyramids will last longer than the pyramids of Egypt, those anthills erected by stupidity and subjugation. The end of the century will again see, standing on the ruins of time, your cabalistic sigils, your laconic equations, and your sculptural lines sitting at the wrathful right-hand of the Omnipotent, while the stars in despair descend like tornadoes into the eternity of a horrible and universal night, and humanity, scowling, will dream of making its reckoning with the Last Judgment. Thanks for the innumerable services you have rendered to me. Thanks for the strange qualities with which you have enriched my intelligence. Without you, I may have been conquered in my struggle against Man. Without you, he would have made me roll in the sand and kiss the dirt on his feet. Without you, he would have ploughed my flesh and bones with a perfidious talon. But I kept my guard like a seasoned athlete. You gave me the reserve which emerges from your sublime ideas, exempt from emotion. I used it to scornfully reject the ephemeral joys of my brief voyage, and to dismiss from my door the sympathetic, but deceptive, proposals of my peers. You gave me the obstinate prudence deciphered in every step of your admirable systems of analysis, synthesis and deduction. I used it to thwart the malicious manœuvres of my mortal foe, to skilfully attack him in turn, and to plunge into Man's guts a sharp dagger which will forever remain buried in his body—because that is a wound that will never heal. You gave me logic, which is full of wisdom like the soul itself of your teachings; and with its syllogisms, from which the complicated maze is all the more comprehensible, my intelligence has felt its daring powers doubly augmented. With the help of this terrible assistant I discovered within humanity, while swimming towards the shallows opposite the reefs of hatred, black and ugly wickedness which stagnated amid unwholesome miasmas, while admiring its navel. First, I discovered in the shadows of Man's entrails that fatal vice: evil!—more superior in him than good. With that poisoned weapon you lent me, I made the Creator Himself descend from His pedestal constructed by the cowardice of Man! He ground His teeth and endured that ignominious insult—because He had as an adversary someone stronger than Himself. However, I will leave Him aside like a bundle of string in order to lower my flight... The philosopher Descartes once made the observation that nothing solid has been built on you. This is an ingenious way of comprehending how the first person who comes along cannot immediately discern your priceless value. What could actually be more solid than the three chief qualities already cited, which loom, interwoven like a singular crown, on the august summit of your gargantuan architecture? A monument continually flourishing from quotidian discoveries in your diamond mines and scientific explorations within your wonderful domains. O holy mathematics, may you, by your everlasting intercourse, comfort my remaining days from Man's wickedness and the injustice of the Omniscient!

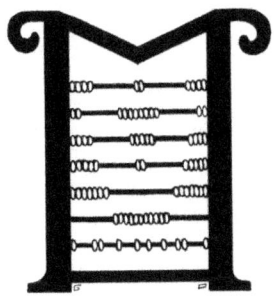

"O lamp with the silver spout, companion of the vaults of cathedrals, my eyes perceive you in the air and seek the reason for this suspension. It is said that, during the night, your lights illuminate the throng of those who would come to worship the Omnipotent and that you show repenters the way leading to the altar. Listen, that is very possible, but ... must you oblige those to whom you owe nothing? Leave the columns of the basilicas immersed in the gloom; and when a storm gust—on which the Devil twirls, carried in space—should penetrate the holy place with him, disseminating fear, instead of fighting bravely against the noisome blast of the Prince of Darkness, douse yourself immediately beneath his feverish gasp so that he can choose his victims clandestinely from among the kneeling believers.

If you do this, you can say that I owe you my complete happiness. When you shine thus, scattering your vague but sufficient rays, I dare not betray my natural inclinations and I remain beneath the hallowed portico watching, through the partly-open door, those who escape from my wrath into the bosom of the Lord. O poetic lamp! you who would be my friend if you could understand me, when my feet trample the church basalt in the nocturnal hours, why do you shine forth in a manner that, I must admit, appears extraordinary to me? Then your reflections are infused with the white nuances of the electric light; the eye can't stare at you, and you illuminate the smallest details of the Creator's kennel with a new and potent flame as if you were prey to a holy anger. And when I withdraw myself after blaspheming, you subtly become quiet and faint once more, confident of having performed an act of justice. Tell me briefly: would it be because you know the deviations of my heart that, when I happen to materialize where you keep watch, you hurry to indicate my poisonous presence and draw the worshippers' attention aside to where the enemy of men has just appeared? I would defer to this opinion, because *I* also begin to know you—and I know who you are, old witch, who watches so well over the sacred mosques where your odd master prances around like a cockscomb. Vigilant guardian, you've given yourself a foolish mission. I warn you: the first time you spotlight me for the caution of my peers by increasing your phosphorescent glimmers, as I don't like that optical effect—which isn't, by the way, mentioned in any physics book—I will take hold of you by the skin of your breast, grab at the sores of your scabby neck with my claws, and throw you into the Seine. I'm not claiming that you knowingly act in a harmful manner to me when I do nothing to you. There now, I will let you shine as much as it suits me; there now, you will tease me with an indelible smile; there now, convinced of the incompetence of your criminal oil, you will bitterly piss it out." After speaking thus Maldoror doesn't leave the temple, and his eyes remain fixed on the lamp of the sacred place... He believes he sees a sort of provocation in this lamp's demeanour, which irritates him to the highest degree by its inappropriate presence. He tells himself that, if some soul is imprisoned in that lamp, it is cowardly not to respond genuinely to a fair attack. He beats the air with his sinewy arms and wishes that the lamp would transform itself into a man; he promises he would make it experience a rough fifteen minutes. But the method by which a lamp transforms into a man—this is artificial. He doesn't give up, and goes searching in the court of the pathetic pagoda for a flat pebble with a keen cutting-edge. He launches it forcefully into the air... the chain is cut in the middle like grass by a scythe, and the instrument of worship falls to the ground, pouring out its paraffin over the pavers... He grabs the lamp to take it outside, but it resists and grows. He seems to see wings on its flanks and the uppermost part takes on the form of an

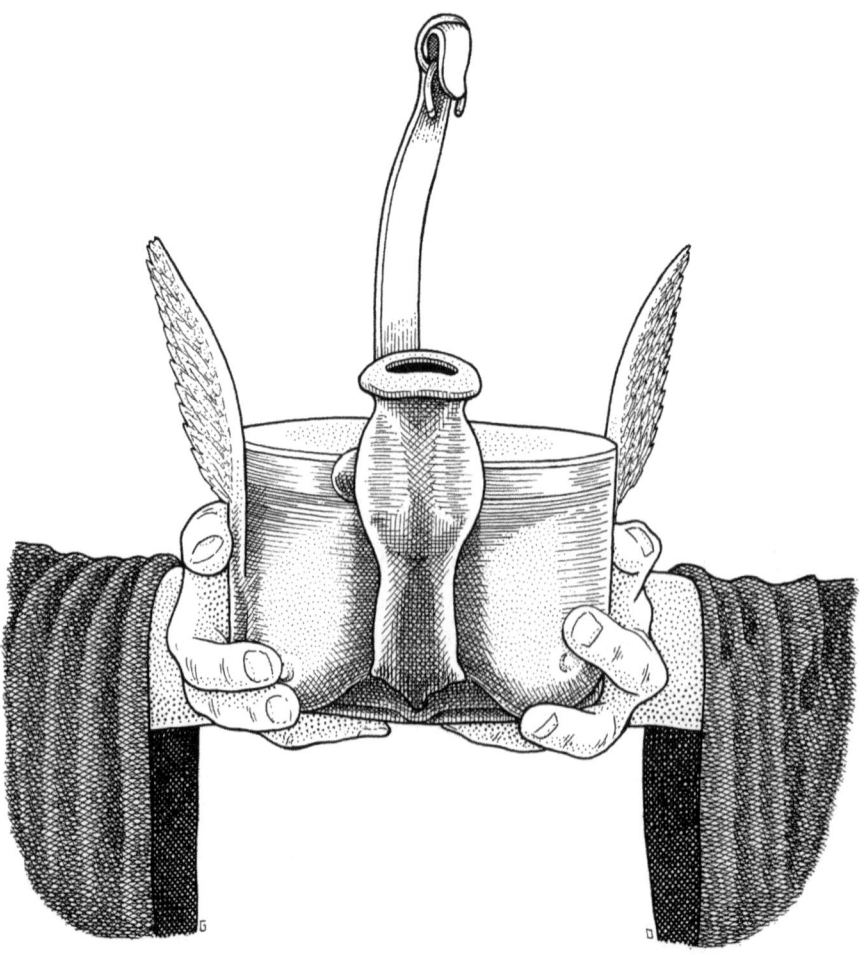

angel's bust. The whole thing wants to rise into the air to take flight, but he holds it with steady hands. A lamp and an angel constituting the same body—that's something we don't see very often. He recognizes the form of the lamp; he recognizes the form of the angel—but he can't disconnect them in his mind; indeed, in reality, they are combined together and form just one free and autonomous body; but he believes that some cloud has obscured his eyes, causing him to lose a little of the excellence of his vision. Nevertheless he girds his loins

bravely for the struggle, because his adversary is fearless. Naïve people recount to the gullible that the holy portal, rolling on its rusty hinges, closed itself so that nobody could be present at this impious battle whose ups and downs were about to occur in the interior of the defiled shrine. Receiving some cruel injuries from an invisible sword, the cloaked man endeavors to bring the angel's face closer to his mouth; he thinks only of that, and all his efforts carry him towards that objective. The latter loses its energy and seems to predict its destiny. It struggles but feebly, and we suddenly see where its opponent will be able to embrace it with ease, if he so wishes. Well, the moment comes. With his muscles he strangles the throat of the angel, which can no longer breathe, and turns its face over while pushing it onto his odious breast. He is immediately touched by the fate which awaits this celestial being, which he would have willingly made his friend. But he reflects that this is a messenger of the Lord, and he can't restrain his ire. That's done it—something horrible is going to re-enter the cage of time! He inclines forward and lays his tongue, soaked in saliva, on that angelic cheek, which casts pleading looks. He promenades his tongue for some time up and down that cheek. Oh!…look!…look hence!…the white and pink cheek has turned black like carbon! It gives off putrid miasmas. Without a doubt: it's gangrene. The gnawing disease extends over the entire face, and from there exerts its furies onto the lower parts; soon the whole body will be just one great filthy wound. The cloaked one, terrified (because he didn't know that his tongue contained a venom of such potency), picks up the lamp and flies from the church. Once outside, he sees in the air an ebon form with burned wings which barely steers its flight to the heavenly regions. As the angel climbs to the tranquil heights of good and while Maldoror, on the contrary, descends to the dizzying depths of evil, they watch each other…What a sight! All that humanity has thought for sixty centuries, and that it will continue to think in following centuries, might easily be contained there in that supreme farewell—they said so many things! But we understand that

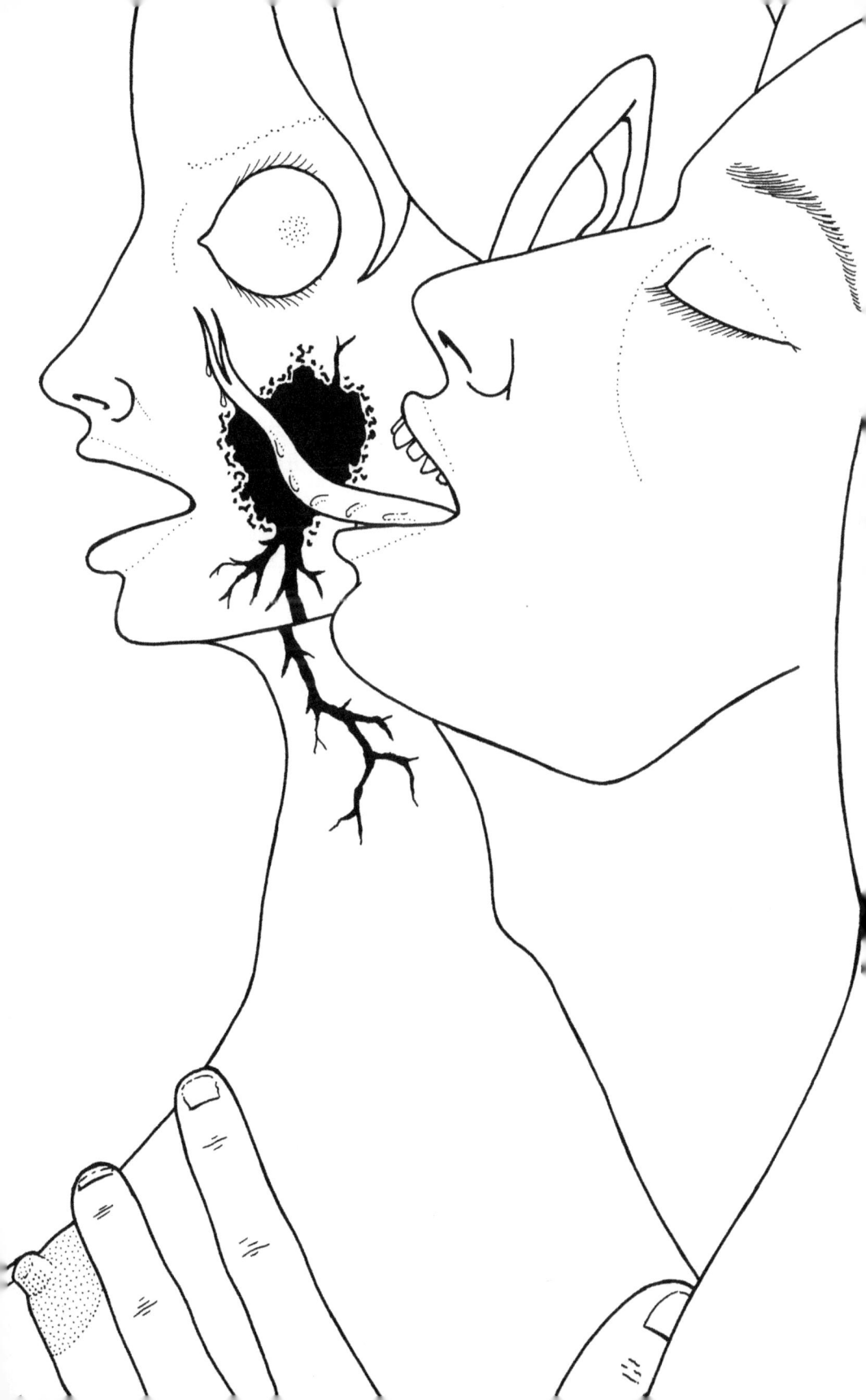

these were higher thoughts than those which would emerge from human intelligence; firstly, because of these two characters, and then because of the circumstance. That glance bound them in an everlasting friendship. He is astonished that the Creator could have ambassadors with such noble souls. For an instant he believes he might be mistaken, and wonders if he should have followed the path of evil as he has done. The trouble has passed—he sticks to his resolve, and as far as he is concerned it is glorious to conquer the Omnipotent sooner or later in order to reign in His place above the whole universe and over legions of angels so fair. This angel, without speaking, had made him understand that it will regain its original form as it rises towards Heaven; it lets a tear fall, which refreshes the forehead of the one who gave it gangrene, and little by little disappears like a vulture that rises amidst the clouds. The guilty one regards the lamp, cause of the pre-

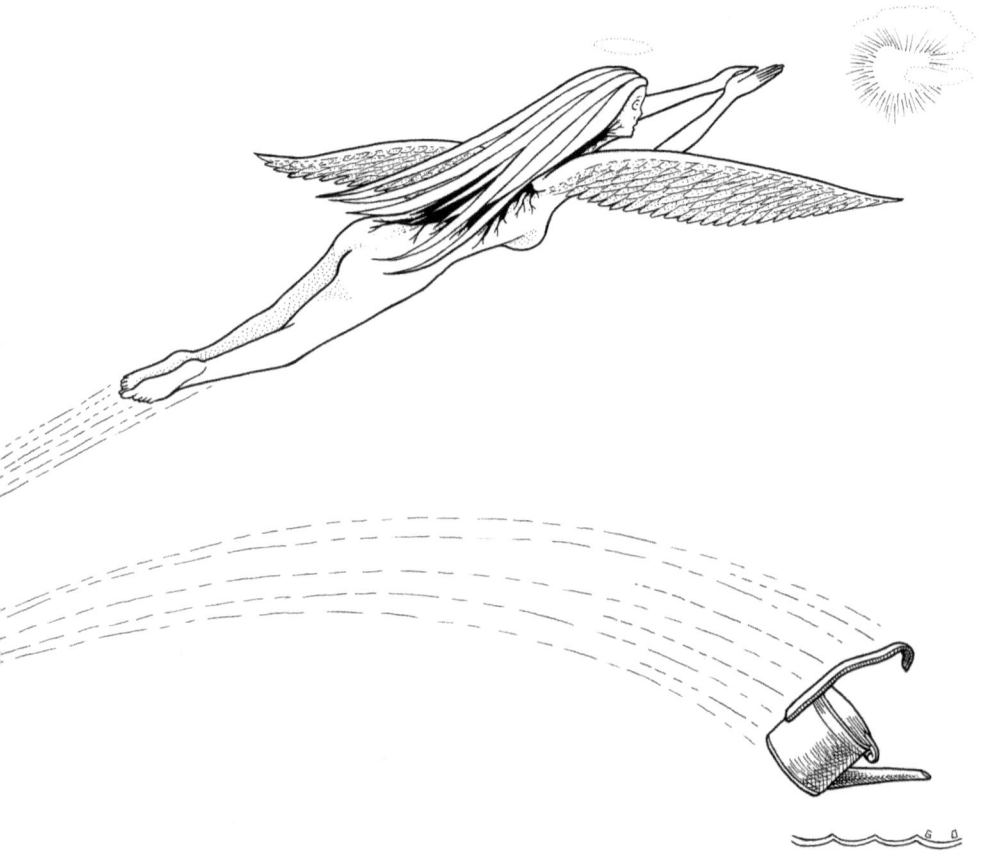

ceding. He races like a madman through the streets, heads towards the Seine, and hurls the lamp out over the parapet. It whirls momentarily and is absorbed for good in the turbid waters. Since that day, every evening at nightfall, we see a bright lamp, which appears and continues gracefully above the surface of the river near the Pont Napoléon, displaying the two delicate wings of an angel in place of a handle. It advances slowly over the waters, it passes beneath the arches of the Pont de la Gare and Pont d'Austerlitz, and continues its silent wake over the Seine as far as the Pont de l'Alma. Once there, it casually retraces the course of the river and after four hours returns to its starting point. Thus it continues throughout the night. *Its rays, pale as an electric light*, obscure the gas lamps along both banks and between which it advances like a queen, alone, inscrutable, *with an indelible smile, without spilling out its oil with bitterness*. Boats initially pursued it, but it thwarted their vain efforts, evading all their pursuits by dipping like a coquette and reappearing a greater distance further

on. Now the superstitious mariners, when they see it, row in the opposite direction and hold back their songs. When you pass over a bridge during the night, heed well: you are sure to see the lamp shining here or there; but they say that it won't show itself to everybody. When a human being who has something on his mind crosses the bridges, it suddenly extinguishes its reflections, and the passer-by, frightened, vainly searches the surface and silt of the river with a desperate look. He knows what this signifies. He would like to believe that he has seen the celestial glow — but he tells himself that the light comes from the bows of boats or from the reflection of the gas lamps, and he is correct... He knows that it is *he* who has caused this disappearance; and plunged within unhappy reflections, he hurries home. Then the lamp with the silver spout reappears and continues its movement across the surface with elegant and capricious arabesques.

Hear the thoughts of my childhood, humans, when I would awake with a red penis: "I just awoke, but my thinking is still dulled. Every morning I experience a heaviness in the head. Seldom do I find peace at night because horrible dreams plague me when I manage to fall asleep. By day my thought tires itself out from bizarre meditations while my eyes wander randomly in space; and at night I can't sleep. When must I sleep, then? Nature, meanwhile, must needs demand her rights. As I scorn her, she renders my face pale and makes my eyes gleam with the piercing flames of fever. Yet I would not request anything better than to not have my mind worn out by ceaseless pondering; but even when I don't wish it, my disquieted feelings seduce me unfailingly towards that inclination. I realize that other children are like me — but they are even paler and their eyebrows are creased like those of men, our elder brothers. O Creator of the universe, this morning I won't fail to offer You the incense of my childish prayer.

Sometimes I overlook it, and on those days I have observed that I feel happier than usual; free of all constraint, my breast swells and I breathe the perfumed air of the fields more easily; whereas when I perform the painful duty of addressing You every day with a hymn of praise, as dictated by my parents, along with the inevitable boredom that is caused by its painstaking fabrication, then I am sad and irritable for the rest of the day—because it doesn't seem logical or natural to me to say what I don't believe, and I search for space in large deserted places. If I ask them for an explanation for this strange condition of my soul, they don't answer me. I would like to love and adore You; but You are too powerful, and there is dread in my hymns. If You can shatter or spawn worlds through a single manifestation of Your thoughts, my weak prayers are useless to You; if You unleash cholera to ravage cities whenever You please, or death indiscriminately carries away the four stages of life in its claws, I don't wish to be tied to such a formidable friend. Not only hatred leads the thread of my reasonings; indeed, on the contrary, I'm afraid of *Your* hatred, which can exit Your heart at whimsical command and become huge like the wingspan of the Andean condor. Your equivocal amusements aren't within my reach, and I would probably be the first victim. You are the Omnipotent; I don't challenge Your title, since only You have the right to bear it, and since only *You* have limited Your desires, with deadly or happy consequences. Here is exactly why it would be distressing for me to walk beside Your cruel sapphire tunic: not as Your slave, but possibly to be so at any time. It's true that, when You meditate in order to scrutinize Your sovereign behaviour, if the phantom of a past injustice—committed against that unfortunate humanity who has always obeyed You as Your staunchest ally—raises before You the immovable vertebræ of a vindictive backbone, Your haggard eye lets the frightened tear of belated remorse fall, and then, with hair bristling, You sincerely believe Yourself deciding to suspend forever in the scrub of nothingness the inconceivable games of Your tiger imagination—which would be burlesque if it weren't so pitiful; but

I also know that constancy hasn't fixed, like a hardened marrow in Your bones, the harpoon in its eternal home, and that often enough You fall down again—You and Your thoughts, covered with the black leprosy of failure—into the funereal lake of lugubrious maledictions. I want to believe that these things are unconscious (although they won't contain any less of their deadly poison), and that evil and good leap united in impetuous bounds, like waterfall from a rock, from Your regal gangrenous breast via the hidden hex of a dazzled power; but there is nothing in the evidence provided. I have seen too often Your foul teeth clicking with rage and Your august face covered with the moss of time—reddened like a burning ember because of some tiny trifle that men had committed—to be able to halt any longer before the signpost of this naïve hypothesis. Each day, with hands clasped, I raise the tones of my modest prayer to You, since I must; but I beg that Your providence not notice me; leave me alone like the worm that burrows beneath the earth. Know that I would prefer to subsist eagerly on the marine plants of the wild and uncharted islands, swept along on the foamy womb of tropical waves amid those regions—than to know that You observe me and that You enter Your sneering scalpel into my mind. This has just revealed to You the totality of my thoughts, and I hope that Your prudence will readily praise the good sense whose indelible impression they retain. Aside from these reservations covering the relations of a mostly intimate kind that I must keep with You, my mouth is ready, regardless of the hour of the day, to exhale like an artificial breath the flood of lies that Your vanity strictly demands of every human, as soon as the bluish dawn rises, seeking light in the satin pleats of twilight, just as *I*, seeking kindness, am aroused by the love of good. My years aren't many, and yet I already feel that goodness is just a mixture of sonorous syllables; I've found it nowhere. You allow too much to penetrate your character; it should be hidden more carefully. Yet perhaps I may fool myself and You do it deliberately—because You know how to behave better than any other. Men grant themselves *their* glory by imitating You;

that's why holy goodness doesn't recognize its tabernacle in their ferocious eyes: like father, like son. Whatever should be thought of Your intelligence, I can say only as an unbiased commentator. I would be delighted to have been misled. I don't want to show You the hatred I have for You, and on which, like a cherished daughter, I brood lovingly; because it would be better to hide it from Your eyes and assume before You simply the appearance of a severe censor charged with checking Your impure acts. In this way You will cease all active business with it—You will forget it—and You will annihilate that keen bug which gnaws Your liver. I would prefer instead to have You hear words of reverie and tenderness… Yes, it is You who has created the world and everything in it. You are perfect. You lack no virtue. You are the strongest—everyone knows it. May the entire universe strike up, in Time's every hour, Your eternal hymn! The birds bless You while flying through the countryside. The stars belong to You… So mote it be!" After these beginnings, be amazed to find me such as I am!

I was seeking a soul that might resemble me, and I couldn't find it. I searched all the recesses of the earth; my perseverance was futile. Nevertheless, I could not remain alone. It needed to be someone who approved of my character—it needed to be someone who had the same ideas as me. It was morning: the sun rose above the horizon in all its magnificence, and lo: there also rose to my eyes a young man whose presence begat flowers along his path. He came towards me and held out his hand. "I have come to you, *you* who seeks me. Let's bless this happy day." But I said: "Be gone—I didn't call you: I don't need your friendship..." It was evening; night began to extend the darkness of its veil over Nature. A beautiful woman—I could only discern that—also spread out her enchanting influence over me, and she eyed me with compassion; meanwhile she dared not speak to me. I said: "Approach me so that I may clearly distinguish the features of your face, because the starlight isn't strong enough to illuminate them from this distance." Then, with quiet step and downcast eyes, she trod the grassy lawn while heading towards me. As soon as I saw her I said: "I see that kindness and justice have taken up residence in your heart; we would not be able to live together. Now you admire my beauty, which has upset more than one woman; but sooner or later you might regret having bestowed your love on me, because you don't know my soul. Not that I would ever be unfaithful to you: the one who surrenders herself to me with such wantonness and trust, I surrender myself to her with as much trust and wantonness; but get it into your brain so as to never forget it: the wolves and the lambs don't view each other with gentle eyes." What did I need then, *I* who would reject with such distaste this one who was the most beautiful among humanity!—I would not have been able to say what I needed. I wasn't yet used to taking strict account of my mental phenomena by means of the methods which philosophy endorses. I sat on a rock beside the ocean. A ship had just set all sails to head away from this coast: an imperceptible spot appeared on the horizon and, pushed on by the squall, it approached little by little while growing swiftly. The storm was about to begin its attacks, and the sky was already becoming obscure by assuming a darkness almost as hideous as the heart of Man. The ship, which was a large battleship, had thrown all its anchors in order not to be swept onto the coastal rocks. The wind hissed with fury from the four cardinal points and slashed the sails to shreds. The thunderclaps burst amid the lightning—and couldn't surpass the sound of the lamentations heard on the house without foundations, mobile sepulchre. The rolling of these watery masses failed to break the anchor chains, but their shakings had partly opened a breach in the sides of the ship. An enormous breach—for the pumps were insufficient to repel the packets of salt water which came, foaming, to descend like mountains onto the deck. The distressed vessel fires cannon-shots in alarm, but it sinks slowly... majestically. Those who haven't seen a vessel sink in the middle of the hurricane—with fitful lightning and the most profound darkness, while the ones it holds are overwhelmed by that despair which you know—*they* don't know the tragedies of life. At last there breaks out from within the vessel's flanks a universal cry of immense grief, while the sea increases its formidable attacks. It is the cry which announces the surrender of human forces. Each is wrapped in the cloak of defeat and leaves his destiny in God's hands. They are cornered like a herd of sheep. The distressed ship fires cannon-shots in alarm, but it sinks slowly... majestically. They made the pumps work all day. Useless efforts. Night has come, thickening, unforgiving, to crown this graceful spectacle. Each sailor tells himself that once in the water he won't be able to breathe any more because, as far as his memory recalls, he knows no fish to be his ancestor; but he forces himself to hold his breath for as long as possible in order to prolong his life by two or three seconds; it is that vindictive irony which he wants to direct at death... The distressed ship fires cannon-shots in alarm, but it sinks slowly... with majesty. He doesn't know that the vessel, while sinking, is provoking a mighty vortex of currents around each other, that the muddy sediment has mixed with the troubled waters, and that a force which comes from below—rebound from the tempest which exerts its destruction from above—stamps

the element with jerky and nervous movements. So, despite the supply of composure which he had amassed in advance, upon better reflection the future drowning victim must feel happy if he prolongs his life in the mælstrom of the abyss by half a normal gasp (for good measure). It will therefore be impossible for him to taunt death, his supreme vow. The distressed ship fires cannon-shots in alarm, but it sinks slowly... with majesty. It is a mistake. It no longer fires cannon-shots — it doesn't sink. The walnut shell has been entirely engulfed. O Heaven! How can we live after experiencing so many pleasures! I have just been allowed to be witness to the mortal agonies of many of my fellows. Minute by minute I followed the ups and downs of their anguishes. Presently the bawling of some old woman, becoming mad from fear, would dominate the market-place. Presently the lone squeaking of a baby-at-breast would drown out the manœuvre commands. The vessel was too far away for me to clearly discern the groanings that the squall carried, but through willpower I drew it closer and the visual illusion was complete. Every fifteen minutes, when a gust of wind more forceful than the others, delivering its dismal accents through the cries of the alarmed petrels, dislocated the vessel in a lengthwise crack and intensified the groans of those who were about to be offered in sacrifice to death, I would pierce my cheek with a sharp iron spike and I would consider silently: "They suffer more!" In this way I at least had a point of comparison. I accosted them from the seashore while throwing curses and threats their way. It seemed to me that they must have heard me! It seemed to me that my hatred and words, crossing the distance, annihilated the physical laws of sound and clearly reached their ears, deafened by the roarings of the ocean in its anger! It seemed to me that they must be aware of me and were expelling their wrath in impotent fury! Once in a while I turned my eyes to the cities dozing on the solid earth, and seeing that nobody suspected that a ship was going to sink a few miles out, with a crown of birds of prey and a pedestal of enormous hungry aquatics, I regained courage and hope returned to me: I was therefore certain of their loss! They could not escape! As an extra precaution I had sought out my double-barrelled rifle so that, if some castaway was tempted to reach the shore from the rocks in order to elude an inevitable death, a bullet in the shoulder would shatter his arm and prevent him from carrying out his plan. When the storm was at its most turbulent I saw an energetic head with shaggy hair floating on the waters with desperate efforts. He swallowed litres of water and was sinking into the abyss, bobbing like a cork. But soon he reappeared with hair dripping and, fixing his eye on the shore, he seemed to defy death. He had an admirable composure. A large bleeding wound, caused by some point of a hidden reef, scarred his intrepid and noble face. He couldn't have been more than sixteen because through the fulgurations which lit the night the peach-fluff could scarcely be discerned on his lip. And now he was no more than two hundred metres from the cliff, and I could easily see him. What courage! What insuperable spirit! How the steadiness of his head appeared to taunt destiny, all the while vigorously cleaving the waves whose furrows parted with difficulty before him!... I had already decided. I *had* to stick to my promise: the final hour had sounded for all—no-one would escape. Here then was my resolution—nothing would change it... A sharp sound was heard and the head sank immediately, to appear no more. I didn't take as much pleasure from this murder as one might imagine, and it was in fact because I was so sated with constant killing that I henceforth did it out of plain habit which couldn't be given up—but which provided only slight pleasure. The sense is dulled, hardened. What pleasure could be felt in the death of this one human being when there were more than a hundred who were about to offer themselves to me, in a spectacle, during their final struggle against the waves, once the ship submerged? At this death I didn't even have the appeal of danger; because human justice, rocked by the hurricane of that horrible night, slept in houses a few steps away from me. Today when the years weigh on my body, I say it sincerely, as a supreme and solemn truth: I wasn't as cruel as it was subsequently reported among men; indeed, at times their malice exerted its persistent havoc for entire years. So I no longer knew a limit to my fury; it seized me in fits of cruelty and I would become terrible to he who approached my haggard eyes, regardless of whether he belonged to my kind. If it were a horse or a dog, I would let it pass: did you hear what I just said? Unfortunately, on the night of that tempest I was in one of those fits, my reason had flown (because, ordinarily, I was equally cruel but more prudent), and everything that might fall between my hands had to die: I won't pretend to excuse my wrongs. The fault isn't entirely that of my fellow men. I only aim to establish what's what, while awaiting the Last Judgment (which causes me to scratch my neck in advance)... What does the Last Judgment matter to me! My reason never escapes me, as I mentioned in order to mislead you. And when I commit a crime I know what I'm doing: I don't wish to do anything else! Standing on a rock while the hurricane whipped my hair and cloak, I observed in rapture this power of the storm persisting on a ship, beneath a starless sky. In triumphant state I followed all the vicissitudes of this drama, from the moment when the vessel threw its anchors until the moment when it was engulfed by the deadly garment which pulled the ones whom it covered like a mantle into the ocean's guts. But the moment approached when *I* would go to involve myself, like an actor, in this natural disaster. When the place where the ship had kept up battle clearly showed that it would spend the rest of its days in Davy Jones' Locker, then some of the men who had been carried away by the waves reappeared on the surface. They grabbed each other about the waist, in pairs, in threes; this was *not* the way to save their lives because their movements became hampered and they sank down like pierced jugs... What is that army of marine monsters that divides the waves with celerity? There are six of them; their fins are vigorous and plough through the surging waves. The sharks soon make just an eggless omelet out of all these human beings who stir their four limbs in this shaky continent, and they divide it according to the law of the strongest. Blood mixes with the waters, and the waters mix with the blood. Their fierce eyes adequately illuminate the scene of slaughter… But what is that further disturbance over there on the horizon? It looks like a waterspout approaching. What paddle strokes! I see what it is. A giant female shark comes to share in the duck *pâté de foie* and to devour the cold boiled beef. She is livid, because she arrives famished. A battle begins between her and the other sharks, to quarrel over the few throbbing limbs floating silently, here and there, on the surface of the red cream. To the right, to the left, she launches some bites which cause mortal wounds. But three surviving sharks still circle her, and she is compelled to turn in every direction to frustrate their manœuvres. The observer located on the beach follows this new kind of naval battle with a growing, and previously unknown, passion. His eyes are glued to this brave female shark with such powerful teeth. He no longer hesitates — he shoulders his rifle and, with his usual skill, he lodges his second bullet in the gills of one of the sharks when it appears momentarily above a wave. There remain two sharks — who show only a greater fury. The man with briny saliva throws himself from the top of the rock into the sea and swims towards the agreeably-coloured carpet, while holding in his hand that steel dagger which he has never abandoned. Henceforth each shark has business with one foe. He advances towards his fatigued adversary and, taking his time, pierces it in the stomach with his pointed blade. The mobile citadel easily eliminates the last opponent… They find themselves face to face: the swimmer and the female shark saved by him. They look each other in the eye for a few minutes — and each is astonished to find so much ferocity in the other's gazes. They circle around while swimming, never losing sight of each other, and each says to itself: "I have been mistaken until now; here is one who is more malicious." Then with common accord they glided towards each other, mid-water, with mutual admiration, the female shark dividing the water with her fins, Maldoror beating the waves with his arms; and they held their breath in profound reverence, each eager to contemplate their living portrait for

the first time. Effortlessly reaching a distance of three metres apart, they immediately fell onto each other like two magnets and embraced with dignity and familiarity in a hold as tender as that of brother and sister. Carnal desires closely followed this demonstration of friendship. Two wiry thighs clung tightly like twin leeches to the slimy skin of the monster, and arms and fins entwined around the body of the beloved subject they amorously surrounded, whilst their throats and breasts were soon no more than a sea-green mass with the exhalations of seaweed—amidst the tempest which continued to rage—by the fulgurations of lightning—having the frothy waves as a hymeneal bed, rocked like a cradle by a submarine current—and rolling around towards the depths of the abyss they came together in a protracted coupling, chaste and hideous!... I had finally found someone who resembled me!... Henceforth I would no longer be alone in life!... She had the same notions as me!... I faced my first love!

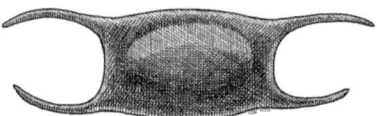

The Seine carries away a human body. In such circumstances she takes on a solemn countenance. The swollen corpse is buoyed on the waters; it disappears under the arch of a bridge but further on is seen to reappear, revolving slowly like a mill wheel and occasionally submerging. A boat captain hooks it up while passing with the help of a pole and returns it to shore. Before transporting the body to the Morgue it is left for some time on the river bank in order that it might revive. The packed crowd gathers around the corpse. Those who can't see, because they are at the back, push the ones in front as long as they can. Each one reflects: "*I* wouldn't be drowning myself." They pity the young man who has suicided; they admire him—but they would not imitate him. And yet he found it very natural to commit suicide, considering nothing on earth capable of satisfying him, and aspiring higher. His face is distinguished and his clothes are fine. Has he reached the age of twenty seven yet? That *is* to die young!

The stunned crowd continues to cast their frozen eyes on him… Night falls. Everyone silently retires. None dares turn the drowned man over in order to make him expel the water that fills his body. They are afraid of appearing concerned, and nobody has stirred—sheltering in their shirt collars. One departs while shrilly whistling an absurd Tyrolean melody; another clicks his fingers like castanets…

Harassed by dark thoughts, Maldoror, astride his horse, passes near this place with the speed of lightning. He sees the drowned man—that's sufficient. He immediately brings his charger to a standstill and dismounts from the stirrup. He raises the young man without revulsion and expels water from him in abundance. At the thought that this inert body might revive under his hand, he feels his heart leap under this excellent impression and he redoubles his courage. Vain efforts! Vain efforts, I said, and it's true. The corpse remains still and lets itself be turned in all directions. He rubs the temples, he massages a limb here and there, for an hour he breathes into the mouth by pressing his lips against the stranger's lips. Finally he seems to sense a slight beating beneath his hand, held against the breast. The drowned man lives! At this supreme moment one could observe that several wrinkles had vanished from the rider's face and rejuvenated him by ten years. But alas! The wrinkles will return, perhaps tomorrow, perhaps as soon as he leaves the banks of the Seine. Meanwhile the drowned man opens his dull eyes and thanks his benefactor with a wan smile; but he is still weak and can't move. To save someone's life, how fine that is! And how that deed atones for wrongs! The man with bronze lips, until then occupied with snatching him from death, regards the young man with greater attention—and his features don't appear so strange to him. He tells himself that there isn't much difference between the asphyxiated one with blond hair and Holzer. See how emotionally they embrace! Never mind! The man with the jasper eyes wants to retain the appearance of serious character. Without speaking he takes his friend, whom he places on the back of the saddle, and the charger gallops away. O you, Holzer, who believed yourself so reasonable and strong, haven't you seen from your own example how difficult it is, in a fit of despair, to preserve the composure you brag about? I hope you will no longer cause me such chagrin, and, as for myself, I pledge to you that I will never make an attempt on my own life.

There are times in life when Man, with the louse-ridden hair, casts wild glances from a staring eye onto the green membranes of space—because he seems to hear the ironic hoots of a wraith before him. He falters and inclines his head: what he heard is the voice of conscience. Then, to his astonishment, he dashes from the house with the speed of a lunatic, he takes the first route that offers itself and he devours the rough plains of the countryside. But the jaundiced spectre doesn't lose sight of him and it pursues him with an equal speed. Sometimes on a stormy night—during which legions of ærial octopi, resembling crows from afar, soar over the clouds while steering with stiff sculls towards the human cities with the mission of warning them to change their conduct—the dark-eyed pebble sees two beings passing, one behind the other, in the lightning flash; and wiping away a furtive tear of pity which leaks from its icy eye, it exclaims: "Surely he

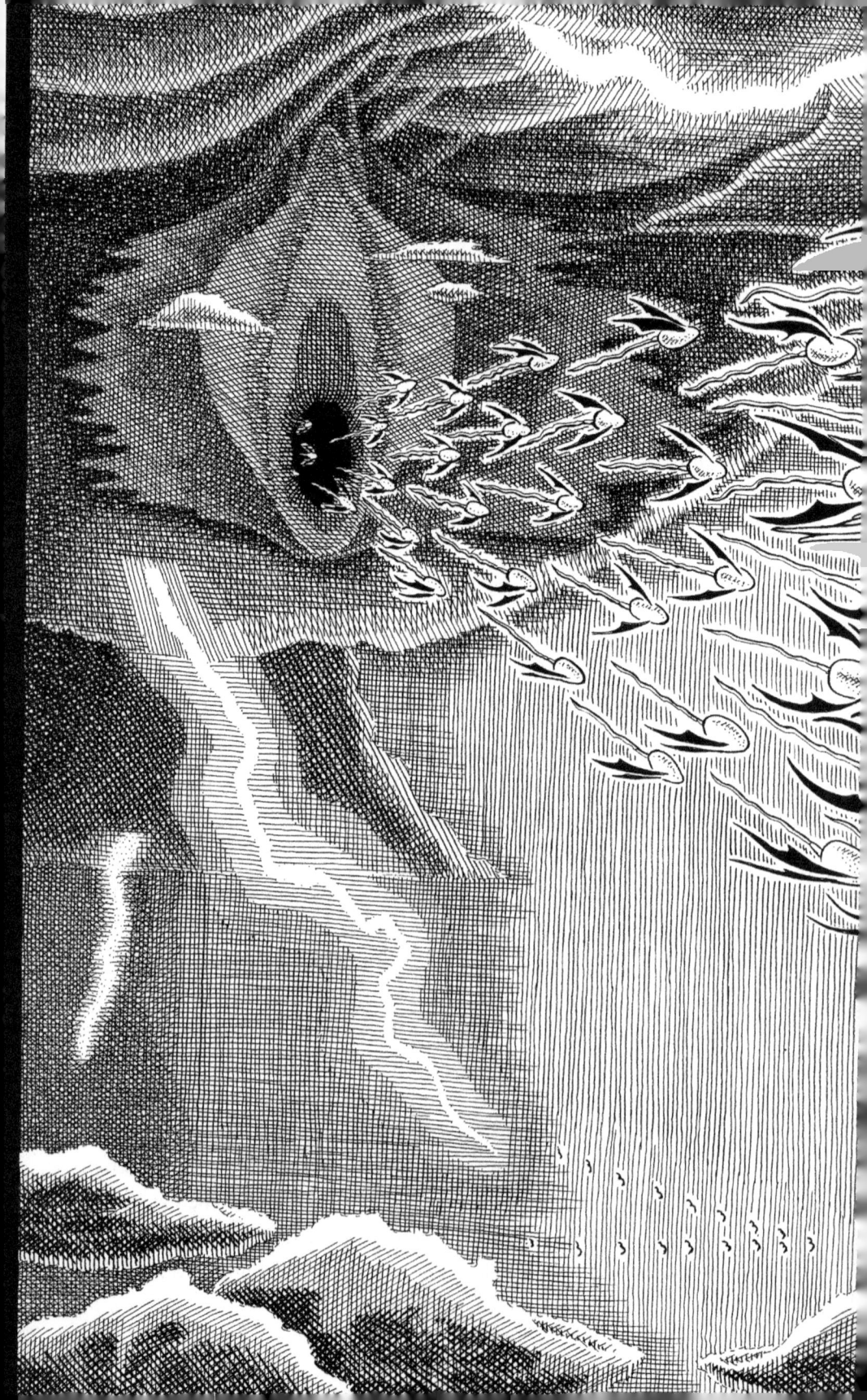

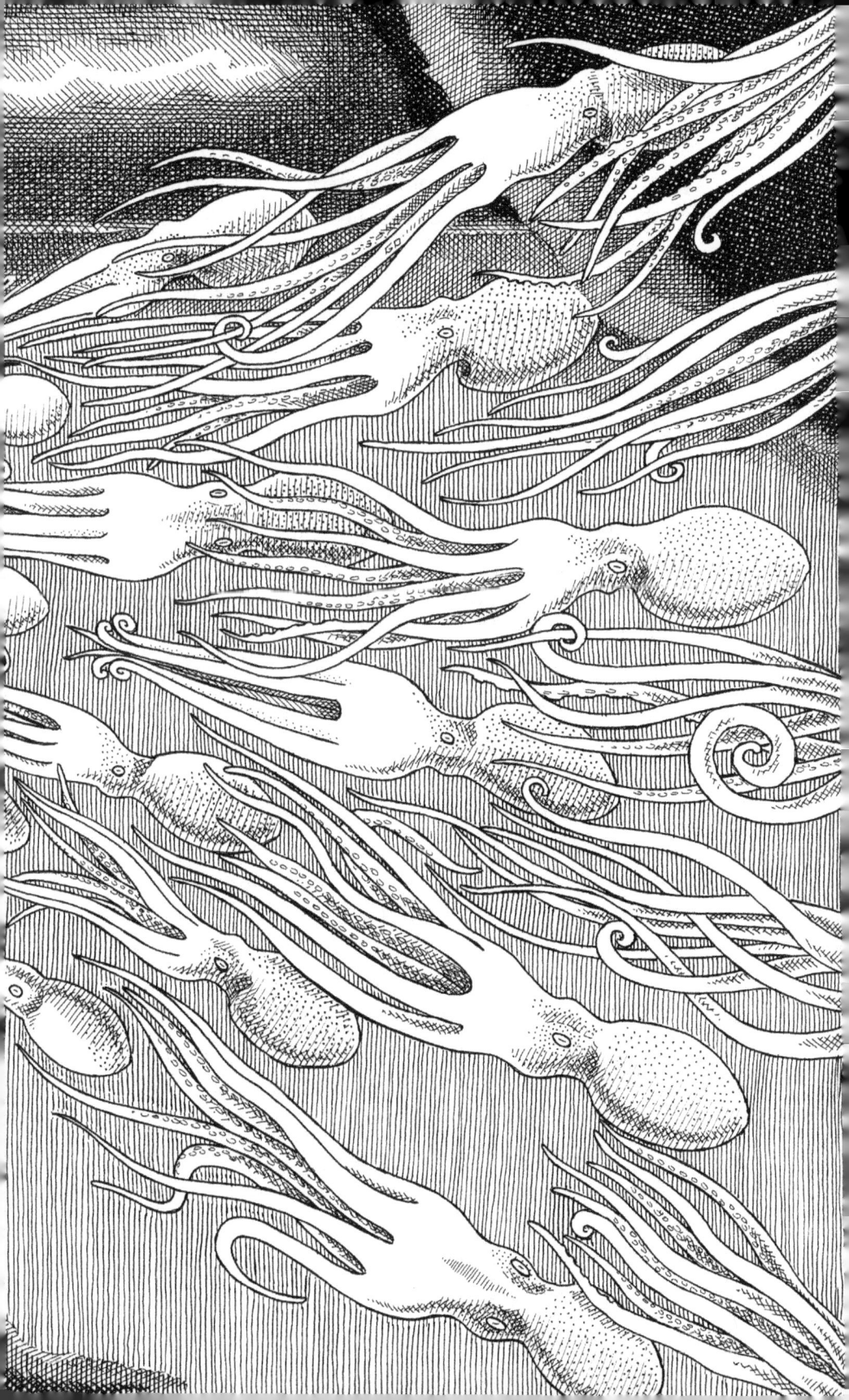

deserves it—and it's only justice." After having spoken thus, it puts its shy posture back in place and continues, with a nervous trembling, to watch the man-hunt, and the great lips of the shadowed vagina from which stream, continuously like a river, mysterious massive spermatozoa which take their flight into the lugubrious ether while completely concealing Nature with the immense unfolding of their bat-like wings—and the solitary legions of octopi grow gloomy at the view of these veiled and indescribable fulgurations. But during this time the steeplechase between the two tireless runners continues, and the ghost shoots torrents of fire from its mouth onto the charred back of the human antelope. If, while fulfilling this duty, it meets pity along the way which wants to bar its passage, it distastefully accedes to its demands and lets the man escape. The ghost clicks its tongue as though to tell itself that it is ceasing pursuit, and it returns to its kennel until further notice. Its voice of the damned is heard as far as the most distant strata of space—and when its terrifying howling penetrates the human heart, they say that this being would prefer to have death for mother than remorse for son. It pushes its head up to its shoulders into the earthy intricacies of a hole—but conscience causes this ostrich ruse to vaporize. The excavation evaporates, a droplet of ether; light appears with its procession of rays like a herd of curlews that swoops onto the lavender, and the man finds once more that he faces himself with open and livid eyes. I saw him heading towards the seashore, climbing a promontory mangled and beaten by the breakers, and diving into the waves like an arrow. Here is the miracle: the corpse reappeared the following day on the surface of the ocean which carried that fleshy wreck back to the shore. The man freed himself from the mold that his body has made in the sand, he wrung the water from his sodden hair and he resumed life's journey with mute face inclined downwards. Conscience judges our most personal thoughts and deeds severely, and it is not mistaken. As it is often powerless to prevent evil, it never ceases to hunt Man down like a fox, especially during darkness. Giving off a ghastly flame, your wrathful

eyes (which ignorant science terms *meteors*) roll around each other and articulate words of mystery... which he comprehends! Then his bedhead is crushed by the jerks of his body, oppressed by the weight of insomnia, and he hears the ominous breathing of night's faint rumours. The angel of sleep itself, mortally wounded in the forehead by a foreign stone, abandons its task and again rises skywards. Well, this time *I* offer myself to defend Man; *I*, the despiser of all virtues; *I*, whom the Creator hasn't been able to forget since the glorious day when, knocking the heavenly annals—where (by I know not what infamous deception) were recorded *His* power and *His* eternity—from their base, I applied my four hundred suction cups beneath His armpits and made Him utter terrible cries... These changed into vipers as they left His mouth, and they went to hide in the undergrowth and crumbling walls, on the alert by day and night. These cries, growing unchecked and blessed with numerous coils, small, splayed heads, and perfidious eyes, have vowed to exist as a stoppage in front of human innocence; and when it walks into the tangles of the undergrowth, over the far side of slopes, or over sand dunes, it won't delay in changing its mind. If, however, there is still time: because sometimes Man only notices venom penetrating the veins of his leg through an almost invisible bite before he has had time to turn back and flee. So, this is how the Creator, keeping an admirable composure even amid the most terrible sufferings, knows how to withdraw harmful germs from the very heart of the inhabitants of the earth. How astonished He was when He saw Maldoror transformed into an octopus, pushing against His body with his eight monstrous arms, any of which solid whip could easily embrace the circumference of a planet! Caught by surprise, He struggled for a few moments against this viscous hug which was tightening more and more... I feared some mischief on His part; after feeding copiously on the cells of this sacred blood, I detached myself brusquely from His majestic body and holed up in a cave which has remained my home ever since. After fruitless searches He wasn't able to find me. It remained so for ages, but I believe that now He knows where my home is, He refrains from returning to it; both of us live like two neighbouring monarchs who know their respective strengths, are unable to defeat each other, and are tired out by the futile battles of the past. He fears me, and I fear Him; each, being undefeated, has experienced the rough blows of his enemy—and there we remain. However, I am prepared to recommence the fight whenever He likes. But He shouldn't expect any favourable moment for His secret plans—I will always keep on my guard by having an eye on Him. May He no longer send Conscience and her tortures onto the earth. I have shown men the weapons with which to combat her to advantage. They aren't yet familiar with her; but you know that, for me, she is like the straw carried by the wind. That's as much as I value her. If I wanted to profit from the opportunity which presents itself, by pinching these poetic arguments, I will add that I value the straw even *more* than Conscience, because the

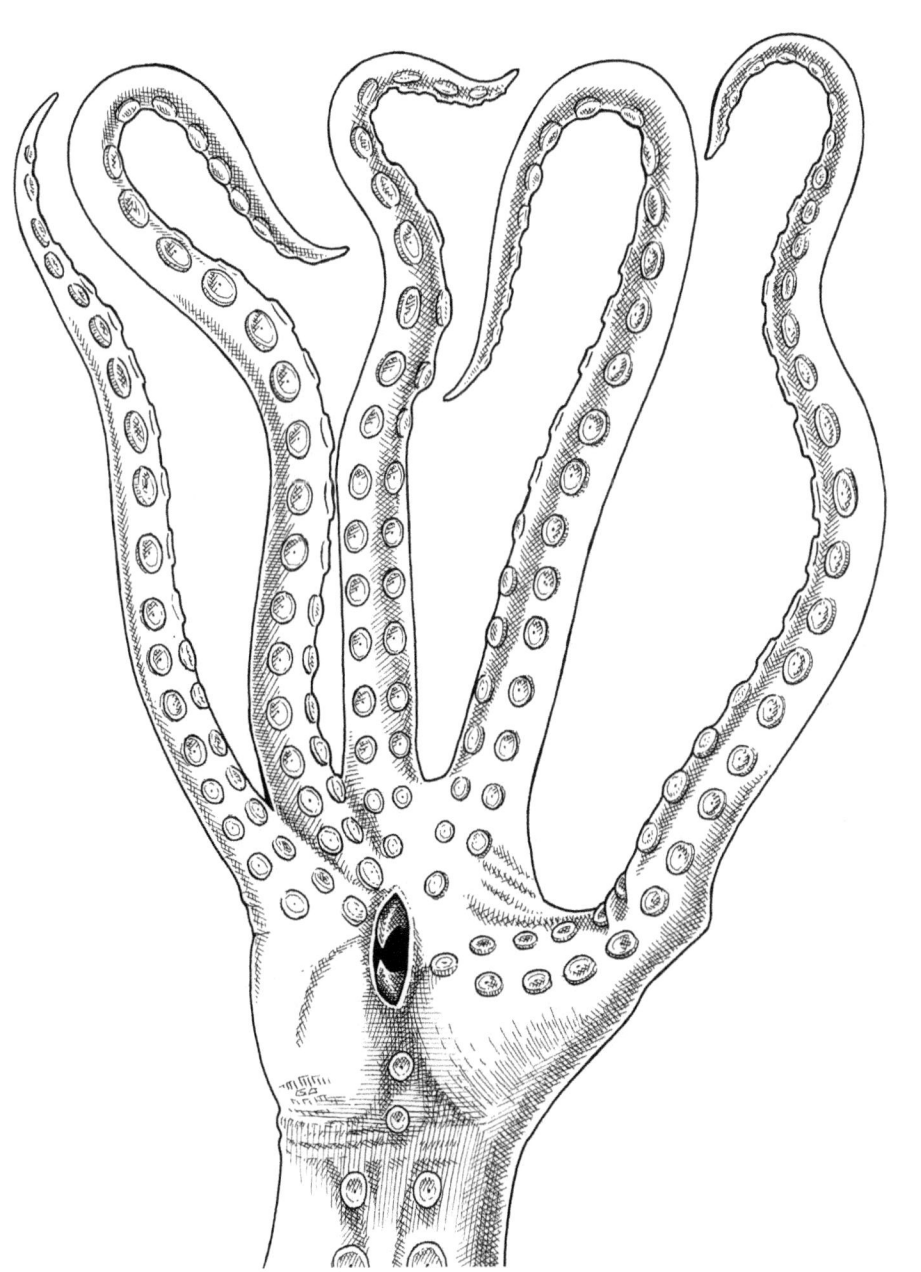

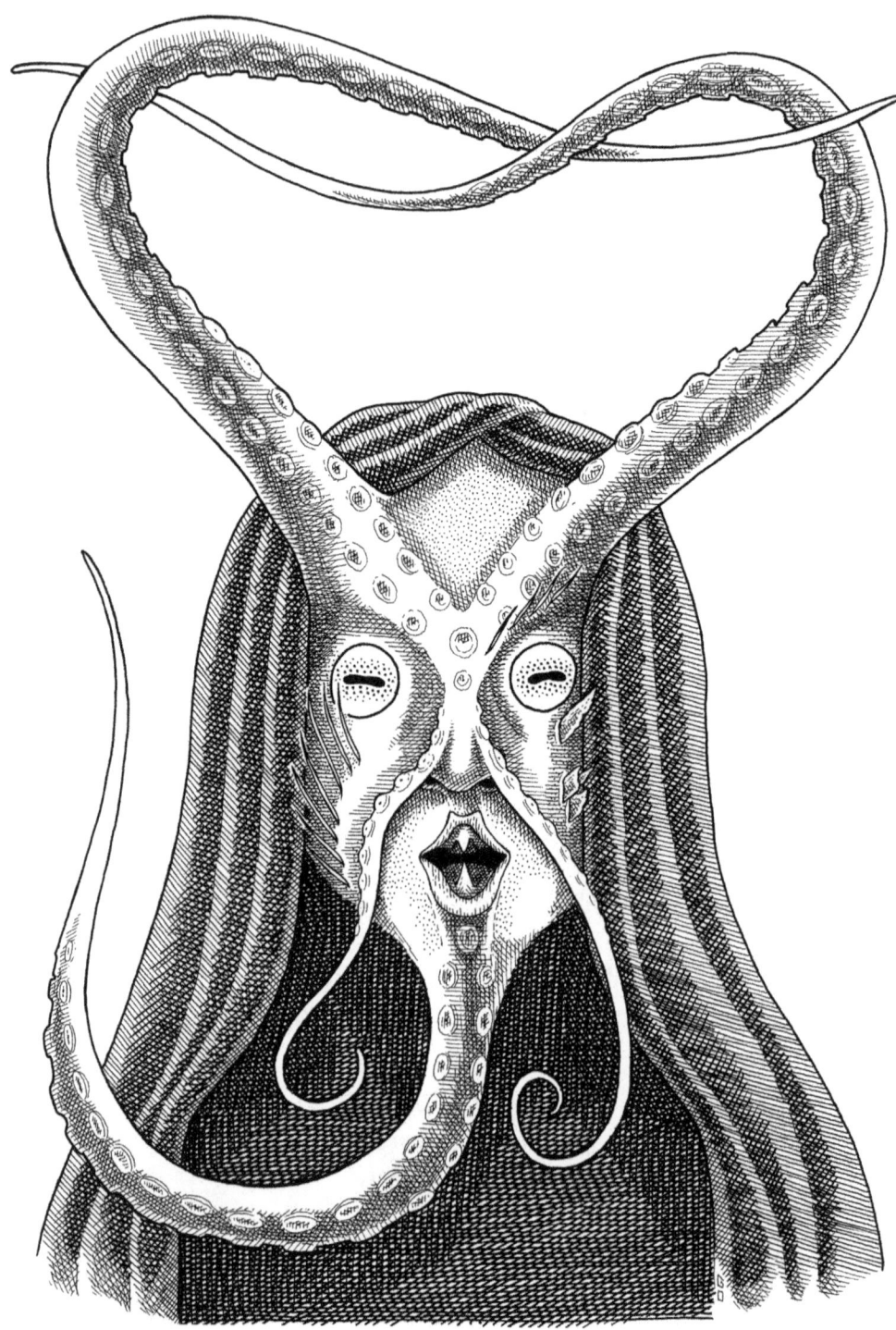

straw is useful for the ox that chews it, whereas Conscience only knows how to show her iron talons—which underwent an awful failure on the day they were placed before me. As Conscience had been sent by the Creator, I believed it appropriate not to let her obstruct my path. If she had presented herself with the modesty and humility befitting her station, and from which she should never have departed, I would have heeded her. I didn't like her arrogance. I extended a hand and crushed the talons beneath my fingers; they fell to dust under the growing pressure from that new kind of mortar. I extended the other hand and tore off her head. Then, with strikes from a whip, I expelled that woman from my house and saw her no more. I kept her head as a memento of my victory... I gnawed the skull of the head in my hand—I stood on one foot like the heron on the edge of the precipice gouged into the sides of the mountain. They saw me descend into the valley, while the skin of my breast was still and calm like the lid of a grave! I gnawed the skull of the head in my hand—I swam in the most dangerous gulfs, I skirted mortal perils and dove deeper than the currents, to be present, as an outsider, at the battles of sea monsters; I strayed from the shore until it was lost to my keen view; and dreadful cramp rays,[6] with their paralyzing magnetism, lurked around my limbs which cleaved the waves with robust motions, not daring to approach. They saw me return to the shore, safe and sound, while the skin of my breast was still and calm like the lid of a grave! I gnawed the skull of the head in my hand—I climbed the rising steps of a high tower. Legs fatigued, I reached the dizzying platform. I observed the countryside and the ocean; I looked at the sun and the firmament; pushing my feet against the resisting granite, I defied death and divine wrath with a mighty hoot and threw myself like a cobblestone into the mouth of space. Men heard the grim and resounding collision which resulted from the meeting of the ground with the head of Conscience, which I had abandoned in my fall. They saw me descend with the slowness of a bird carried by an invisible cloud, and collect the head in order to force it to be witness to a triple

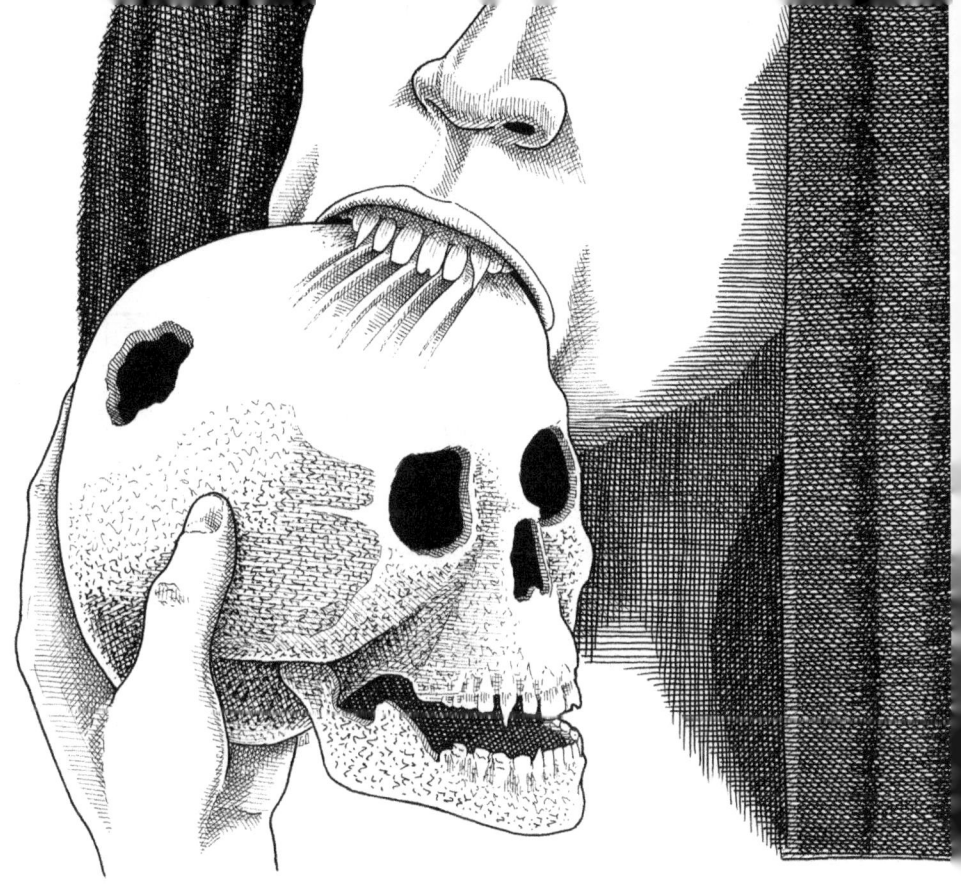

crime that I would commit that same day—while the skin of my breast was still and calm like the lid of a grave! I gnawed the skull of the head in my hand—I headed towards the place where the scaffold bearing the guillotine rose up. I placed the suave grace of the necks of three young girls beneath the chopper. As executioner, I released the cord with the apparent experience of a lifetime, and the iron triangle, falling obliquely, sliced off the three heads—which regarded me sweetly. I then placed my head beneath the heavy razor and the executioner prepared to fulfill *his* duty. Thrice the cutter fell between the furrows with a new vigour; thrice my material corpse, especially at the centre of the neck, was shocked to its core, like when a dreaming figure is crushed by a falling house. The dumbfounded mob let me leave the gloomy site, and it saw me open its billowing waves with my elbows and move forward full of life, with head held high—while the skin of my breast was still and calm like the lid of a grave! I have said that I wished to defend Man this time; I fear, however, that my justi-

fication doesn't bear the mark of truth: and, consequently, I prefer to remain silent. It is with gratitude that humanity will praise this precaution!

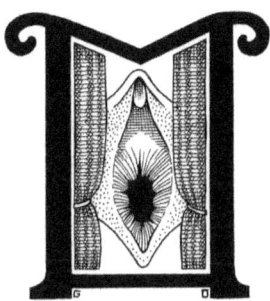

It is time to put the brakes on my inspiration and pause a moment along the way, as we do when we look at a woman's vagina; it is good to consider the course travelled and thereafter, limbs rested, to spring forward with an impulsive bound. Achieving a stretch in a single breath isn't easy, and wings tire so much in a lofty flight without hope and remorse. No... let's not drive the haggard pack with picks and excavations deeper through the explosive mines of this impious dirge! The crocodile will not alter a word of the vomit spewed out from under his skull. Too bad if some shy shadow, excited by the praiseworthy aim of avenging a humanity unjustly attacked by me, secretly opens the door of my bedroom—while grazing the wall as might the seagull's wing—and drives a dagger into the ribs of the looter of heavenly wrecks! Clay may as well dissolve its atoms that way as any other.

END OF THE SECOND DIRGE

 Third Dirge

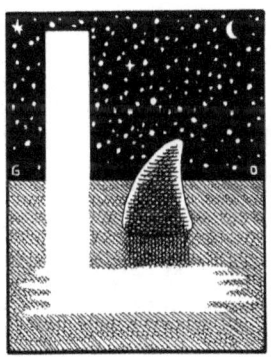 ET US RECALL the names of those imaginary beings of angelic character whom, during the second dirge, my quill drew from a brain shining with a light emanating from they themselves. They perish at birth like sparks whose rapid erasure the eye scarcely follows on the scorched page. Leman! ... Lohengrin! ... Lombano! ... Holzer ... you appeared for an instant, covered once more with youth's insignia, on my charmed horizon—but I allow you to fall again like diving-bells into the chaos. You will no longer escape. It's enough for me that I have preserved your memory; you must surrender space to other substances, perhaps less beautiful, which are born from the stormy outbursts of a love which is determined not to quench its thirst with the human race. A starving love—which might consume itself if it could not find nourishment in heavenly fictions: eventually creating a pyramid of seraphim, more numerous than the insects which swarm in a drop of water, it will interlace them in an ellipse which it will cause to gyrate around it. Meanwhile, halting against the view of a cataract the traveller will see, if he raises his face, a human being in the distance borne towards the cave of Hell by a wreath of living camellias! But ... silence! the floating image of the ideal fifth takes shape slowly, like the indistinct folds of an aurora borealis, on

the vaporous plane of my intellect and assumes a more and more definite consistency… Mario and I rode along the seashore. Our horses, necks tense, cleaved the membranes of space and struck sparks from the beach pebbles. The north wind, which hit us full in the face, rushed into our cloaks and made the hair flutter behind our paired heads. The seagull vainly tried to warn us with its cries and wing movements of the possible nearness of the storm, and it cried: "Where are they going at such a crazy gallop?" We said nothing; immersed in daydreams, we let ourselves be carried on the wings of this wild errand; the fisherman, seeing us pass as quickly as the albatross, and believing he had glimpsed fleeing ahead of him *the two mysterious brothers*—as they had been so called because they were always together—hastened to make the sign of the cross and he hid himself with his crippled dog under some impenetrable rock. The coastal residents had heard tell of peculiar things regarding these two characters, who would appear on earth amid the clouds at times of great disaster, when a terrible war would threaten to plant its harpoon into the breasts of two rival countries, or when cholera would prepare to throw down decay and death into whole cities with its sling. The oldest wreck-looters would scowl gravely, claiming that the two spectres, whose great span of black wings everyone had noted above the sandbanks and reefs during hurricanes, were the genie of the earth and the genie of the sea, who would promenade their majesty mid-air during great natural revolutions, joined together by an eternal friendship whose rarity and glory have engendered astonishment in the indefinite line of generations. It was said that, flying side by side like two Andean condors, they loved to glide in concentric circles amidst the layers of the atmosphere neighbouring the sun; that in these environs they nourished themselves on the purest essences of light—but that they would only reluctantly resolve to reduce the angle of their vertical flight towards the terrifying orbit where the human sphere spins in delirium, inhabited by cruel spirits who slaughter each other in fields where battle rages (when they don't kill each other perfidiously,

clandestinely, with the dagger of hatred or ambition in the centre of towns), and who prey on beings as full of life as themselves and which are placed some rungs lower down on the ladder of life. Or else, when they firmly resolved, in order to stimulate men to contrition by means of the stanzas of their prophecies, to swim while steering themselves with large arm-strokes towards the sidereal regions where a planet revolved amid dense miasmas of avarice, arrogance, blasphemy and mockery that emerged from its horrible surface like pestilential fumes — a planet that appeared as small as a ball, being almost invisible due to the distance — they didn't fail to find some occasions when they would bitterly repent their benevolence, unrecognized and decried, and they would go to hide themselves at the bottom of volcanos in order to converse with the perennial fire which seethes in the vats of the subterranean cores, or to the bottom of the ocean to rest their disillusioned sight delightfully on the most savage monsters of the abyss, which appear like models of charm compared to the bastards of humanity. Night coming with its auspicious darkness, they would spring with the submarine currents from the porphyry-ridged craters, leaving far behind them the rocky chamber-pot where the constipated anus of the human cockatoos convulses, until they could no longer distinguish the hanging silhouette of the foul planet. Then the angel of the earth and the angel of the ocean, chagrined by their unsuccessful attempt, would embrace while weeping among the stars sympathetic to their grief and beneath the eye of God!... Mario and the one who galloped beside him didn't ignore the vague and superstitious rumours which were spread in the evenings by coastal fishermen whispering around the hearth behind closed doors and windows, while the night wind, wishing to warm itself, made its soughings heard around the straw cabin and vigorously shook those frail walls surrounded at the base by bits of shell carried by the dying pleats of the waves. We didn't speak. What can two hearts who love each other say? Nothing. But our eyes conveyed everything. I warn him to draw his cloak tighter around him, and he indicates that my horse has moved too far from away his; each takes as much interest in the other's life as he would in his own; we don't laugh. He tries to smile at me, but I see that his face bears the weight of terrible impressions etched there by meditation, constantly focused on sphinxes who disconcert, with an oblique eye, the intellect of mortals with great anguishes. Seeing his futile manœuvres, he turns away his eyes, bites on his earthly bit with frothy rage and looks to the horizon which recedes at our approach. For my part, I try to remind him of his golden youth, which asks only to advance into pleasure palaces like a queen; but he sees that my words leave my emaciated mouth with difficulty, and that the years of my own springtime have passed, sad and frozen like an implacable dream which parades—on banquet tables and beds of satin where the pale priestess of love dozes, payed for with glittering gold—the sour luxuries of disenchantment, the stinking wrinkles of old age, the bewilderments of solitude and the torches of grief. Seeing my futile manœuvres, I'm not surprised that I can't make him happy. The Omnipotent appears to me clothed in His implements of torture, within all the resplendent halo of his horror; I avert my eyes and look to the horizon that recedes at our approach... Our horses galloped along the shore as if fleeing from the human eye... Mario is younger than me; the humidity of the weather and the salty foam that sprays over us bring the touch of the cold to his lips. I tell him: "Beware!... beware!... seal your lips together; don't you see the sharp claws of chapping that furrow your skin with burning sores?" He stares at my face and replies with the wagging of his tongue: "Yes, I see them, those green claws; but I won't disturb the natural state of my mouth by chasing them off. See if I lie. As it appears to be the will of Providence, I'll yield to it. Its will could have been better." And I exclaim: "I admire that noble vengeance." I wanted to rip out my hair, but with a severe look he forbade me and I respectfully obeyed him. It was getting late, and the eagle was returning to its nest dug into the rock crevices. Mario tells me: "To keep you from the cold, I'm going to lend you my cloak; I don't need it." I replied to him: "Misfortune for you if you do what you suggest. I don't want another to suffer in my place, and especially not you." He didn't reply because I was correct—but I began to comfort him because of the impetuous tone of my words... Our horses galloped along the shore as if fleeing from the human eye... I raised up my head once more, like the bow of a ship lifted by a giant wave, and I said to him: "Are you crying? I ask you, king of snows and fogs. I don't see any tears on your face, as handsome as the cactus blossom, and your eyes are dry like the riverbed; but deep down in your eyes I perceive a vat full of blood where seethes your innocence, bitten on the neck by a large species of scorpion. A violent wind swoops on the fire that heats up the cauldron and spreads the obscure flames beyond your sacred eye-socket. I brought my hair close to your rosy forehead and I smelled an odour of scorching—because it was burning. Close your eyes, because otherwise your face, calcinated like volcanic lava, will fall in ashes into the palm of my hand." And he turned around to me without paying attention to the reins he held in his hand, and he contemplated me with compassion while he slowly lowered and raised his lily eyelids like the ebb and flow of the ocean. He dearly wanted to answer my daring question, and here is how he did so: "Don't worry about me. Just as river vapors crawl up along the sides of a hill and once, reaching the top, dash into the atmosphere to form clouds—likewise your uncertainties on my account have increased callously without good cause and form the deceptive body of a desolate mirage above your imagination. I guarantee that there is no fire in my eyes, although I do feel there the same sensation as if indeed my skull had been plunged into a helmet of live coals. How can you suggest that the flesh of my innocence boils in the vat, because I can only hear very weak and confusing cries which, to me, are just the groanings of the wind that passes over our heads? It is impossible that a scorpion has fixed its home and sharp pincers deep down in my desiccated eye-socket; I believe rather that those are strong forceps which grind the optic nerves. Nevertheless, I am of the same opinion as you: that the blood which fills the vat has been extracted from my veins by an invisible executioner during last night's slumber. I have long awaited you, beloved son of the sea; and my fatigued arms have engaged in vain battle with the One who was shown into the vestibule of my house... Yes, I feel that my soul is locked within the bolts of my body and that it can't free itself to flee far from the shores stricken by the human sea, and to witness no more the spectacle of the angry crowd of misfortunes relentlessly pursuing the human chamois through the quagmires and gulfs of great depression. But I will not complain. I've received life like a wound and I've prohibited suicide from healing the scar. I want the Creator to consider the yawning chasm in every hour of His eternity. That is the punishment I inflict on Him. Our chargers slacken the speed of their shod hooves; their bodies tremble like the hunter surprised by a drift of peccaries. They need not begin to hear what we say. By means of attention their intelligence might grow, and they may perhaps be able to understand us. Sadly for them—because they would suffer more! Indeed, think only of the young boars of humanity: doesn't the degree of intelligence that segregates them from the other beings of Creation only seem to be accorded them at the irreparable cost of incalculable sufferings? Follow my example and let your silver spurs be buried in the sides of your charger…" Our horses galloped along the shore as though fleeing the human eye.

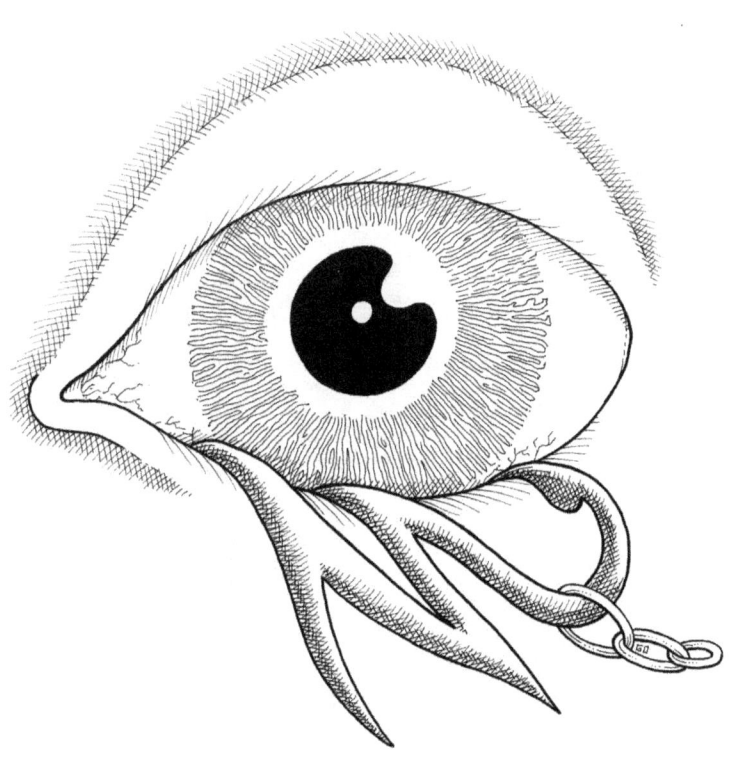

Here passes the madwoman, dancing whilst she vaguely remembers something. Children pursue her with blows of rocks as though she were a blackbird. She flourishes a stick and pretends to chase them, then she resumes her course. She has left a shoe on the path and doesn't notice it. The long legs of spiders encircle the nape of her neck; these are nothing but her hair. Her face no longer resembles a human face, and she hurls out cackles of laughter like the hyæna. She lets fly some fragments of phrase in which, were they pieced together, very few would find clear meaning. Her dress, pierced in more than one place, executes jerky movements about her bony and muddy legs. She advances like the leaf of the poplar tree, blown — herself, her youth, her delusions and her past happiness, which she sees once more through the fogs of demolished intellect — by the eddy of subconscious faculties. She has lost her original grace and beauty; her gait is uncouth and her breath smells of brandy. If men were happy on this earth, then this would be surprising. The madwoman doesn't reproach anyone — she is too proud to complain — and she will die without having revealed her secret to those who would be interested in her, but whom she has prohibited from ever speaking to her. Children pursue her with blows of rocks as though she were a blackbird. She has let a roll of paper fall from her breast. A stranger collects it, he holes up at home all night and reads the manuscript — which contained the following:

"After many barren years, Providence sent me a daughter. For three days I kneeled in church and never ceased to thank the great name of He who had finally granted my wishes. With my own milk I fed the one who was more than my life and who I saw rapidly growing, gifted with all the qualities of soul and body. She would say to me: 'I would like to have a little sister to have fun with; urge the good God to send me one, and in return I'll weave Him a wreath of violets, mint and geraniums.' My sole response was to raise her to my breast and embrace her with love. She was already apt to be interested in animals, and she asked me why the swallow was content to skim with its wings over human cottages without daring to enter them. But I would place a finger on my mouth as if to tell her to remain silent on that serious question, whose details I didn't yet want her to grasp so as not to strike her childish imagination with excessive excitement; and I hurried to steer the conversation away from that subject, so difficult to handle for anyone belonging to the race which has extended unjust domination over the other animals of Creation. When she would speak to me of the graves in the cemetery, telling me that pleasant scents of cypress and evergreen flowers were inhaled in that atmosphere, I refrained from contradicting her; but I would tell her that this was the village of the birds, that they would sing there from dawn to dusk, and that, by raising the marble lids, the graves were their nests where they would lay at night with their families. I had sewn all the dainty clothes she dressed in, like the laces with a thousand arabesques which I reserved for Sunday. In winter she had her regular place around the big fireplace—because she considered herself an important person—and during summer the meadow recognized the soft tread of her steps when she ventured out with her silk net tied to the end of a cane, after the hummingbirds so full of independence and the butterflies with their annoying zigzags. 'What were you doing, little vagabond, when the soup is awaiting you for an hour, with its spoon becoming impatient?' But, jumping to my neck, she would cry out that she might no longer return there. The next day she would escape once more through the daisies and mignon-

ettes, amid the sunrays and the mayflies' circling flight—knowing only the prismatic cup of life, not yet the gall; happy to be larger than the chickadee; teasing the warbler (who didn't sing as well as the nightingale); poking her tongue out impishly at the ugly crow (who watched her paternally); and as graceful as a kitten. I would not enjoy her presence for long: the time neared when she would, in an unforeseen way, make her farewells to life's wonders, leaving forever the company of turtledoves, grouse and greenfinches, the babbles of tulip and anemone, the counsels of swamp grasses, the incisive minds of frogs and the freshness of streams. I was told that she had passed away—because I hadn't personally been present at the event which brought about my daughter's death. If I had been, I would have protected that angel with the price of my blood... Maldoror was passing with his bulldog; he saw a young girl sleeping in the shade of a plane-tree, and he initially took her for a rose... One cannot say what rose soonest in his mind—whether it was the view of this child or the resolution that would follow. He rapidly unclothed himself, like a man who knows his purpose. Naked as a stone, he threw himself onto the body of the young girl, and raised her dress in order to commit an assault against her chastity... in broad daylight! He isn't embarrassed—come off it!... Let's not belabour this obscene act. Mind dissatisfied, he quickly reclothes himself, throws a shrewd look on the dusty road (where no-one walks), and orders the bulldog to strangle the bloodied young girl with the action of its jaws. He indicates to the mountain dog the spot where the suffering victim gasps and howls, and he withdraws to a distance so as not to witness the penetration of those teeth into the pink veins. The fulfillment of this order may have seemed harsh to the bulldog. It believed that what it had been asked to do had already been done, and this wolf was content in its turn to violate the virginity of that delicate child with its monstrous muzzle. Blood ran once more from her torn belly, along her legs, onto the meadow. Her groans joined with the animal's whimpers. The young girl showed it the gold cross which adorned her neck so that it might spare her; she hadn't dared show it to the fierce eyes that had initially thought of exploiting the weakness of her age. But the dog was aware that, if it were to disobey its master, a knife thrown without warning from beneath his sleeve would brusquely disembowel it. Maldoror (how disgusting to pronounce this name!) heard the agonies of pain and was astonished that the victim had such enduring life for one not yet dead. He approaches the sacrificial altar and sees the conduct of his bulldog, surrendering to its base instincts, and who holds its head over the young girl like a castaway might raise his above the wrathful waves. He gives it a kick and splits one of its eyes. The angry bulldog flees into the countryside, dragging behind it (along an expanse of road that was always too long even as short as it was) the suspended body of the young girl—which was only freed thanks to the jerky movements of the flight; indeed, the dog is afraid of attacking its master, who would never see it again. From his pocket the cloaked one takes an American pen-knife made up of ten or twelve blades which served various purposes. He opens the angular arms of this steel hydra and, armed with one like a scalpel—and seeing that the grass hadn't yet vanished beneath the stain of so much shed blood—he unflinchingly prepares to boldly investigate the vagina of this unfortunate child. From that enlarged cavity he withdraws the interior organs sequentially: the intestines, lungs, liver, and, finally, the heart itself are torn from their foundations and brought forth to the light of day through the appalling opening. The sacrificer notices that the young girl, gutted chicken, is long dead; he halts the growing persistence of his pillages and leaves the corpse to sleep once more in the shade of the plane-tree. The abandoned knife was picked up a few steps away. A shepherd, witness to the crime whose perpetrator they hadn't discovered, only reported it a long time afterwards when he had assured himself that the criminal had reached the safety of the borders and that he no longer feared the certain retribution that would be uttered against him in the event of disclosure. I pitied the maniac who had committed this dire crime, which the legislature hadn't foreseen and

which had no precedents. I pitied him—because it was likely that he hadn't been sane when he handled the twelve-bladed knife, ploughing the visceral lining from top to bottom. I pitied him—because, if he weren't insane, his dastardly behaviour must have incubated a great hatred against his fellow men for him to harass in this way the flesh and arteries of a harmless child, who was my daughter. I attended the burial of these human remains with speechless resignation; and every day I come to pray over a grave."

At the end of this letter, the stranger could no longer maintain his strength and he fainted. He regained his senses and burned the manuscript. He had forgotten this souvenir of his youth (habit dulls the memory!); and after twenty years' absence he returned to that fatal land. He will not buy a bulldog!… He will not talk to shepherds!… He will not go to sleep in the shade of plane-trees!… Children pursue her with blows of rocks as if she were a blackbird.

For the final time Tremdall touched the hand of the one who still willingly leaves the image of the man pursuing him, always fleeing ahead of him. The Wandering Jew reflects that he would not flee in this way if the sceptre of the earth belonged to the crocodile race. Standing in the valley, Tremdall put one hand in front of his eyes in order to concentrate the sunbeams and to sharpen his view, while, with arm horizontal and motionless, his other hand palpates the breast of space. Leaning forward—statue of friendship—he sees through eyes as mysterious as the ocean the leggings of the traveller climbing the slope of the hill, aided by his iron staff. The ground seems to give way at his feet, and even when he might wish it he can't hold back his tears and emotions:

"He is distant; I see his silhouette making its way along a narrow path. Where is he going with that heavy tread? He himself doesn't know... Nevertheless, I am convinced that I no longer sleep; who is it that approaches and goes to meet Maldoror? How large it is, the dragon... larger than an oak tree! One might say that its blanched wings, knitted with strong sinews, have steely nerves, so effortlessly do they split the air. Its body begins with the bust of a tiger and ends in a long serpent tail. I was not accustomed to seeing such things. What does it have thus on its forehead? I see written there, in a symbolic language, a word I can't decipher. With a final beat of its wing it conveys itself closer to the one whose vocal timbre I am acquainted with. It says to him: 'I was expecting you, and you were waiting for me. The hour has come; here I am. Read my name written in hieroglyphic sigils on my forehead.' But he, when he had barely seen the enemy coming, transformed himself into a giant eagle and prepared himself for battle, joyfully clicking his curved beak—wishing to declare in this way that he alone planned to devour the dragon's *derrière*. Behold how they trace circles whose circumferences dwindle, calculating each other's strategies before combat; they do well to. To me, the dragon appears stronger; I would like it to carry off victory over the eagle. I am going to feel strong emotions at this spectacle where a part of my being is involved. Powerful dragon, I will incite you with my cries if necessary, because it is in the eagle's interests to be conquered. Why are they waiting to attack? I am in mortal terror. Look here, dragon—you begin the attack first. You come to give it a sharp blow with your claw: that's not too bad. I guarantee that the eagle must have felt it; the wind carries away the beauty of its blood-soaked feathers. Ah! The eagle snatches an eye from you with its beak, and *you* have only torn a little from it—you need to pay attention to that. Bravo, take revenge on it, break its wing; needless to say, your tiger fangs are excellent. What if you could approach the eagle while it turns in space, launching down towards the countryside! I note that the eagle inspires you to hold back, even when it falls. It is

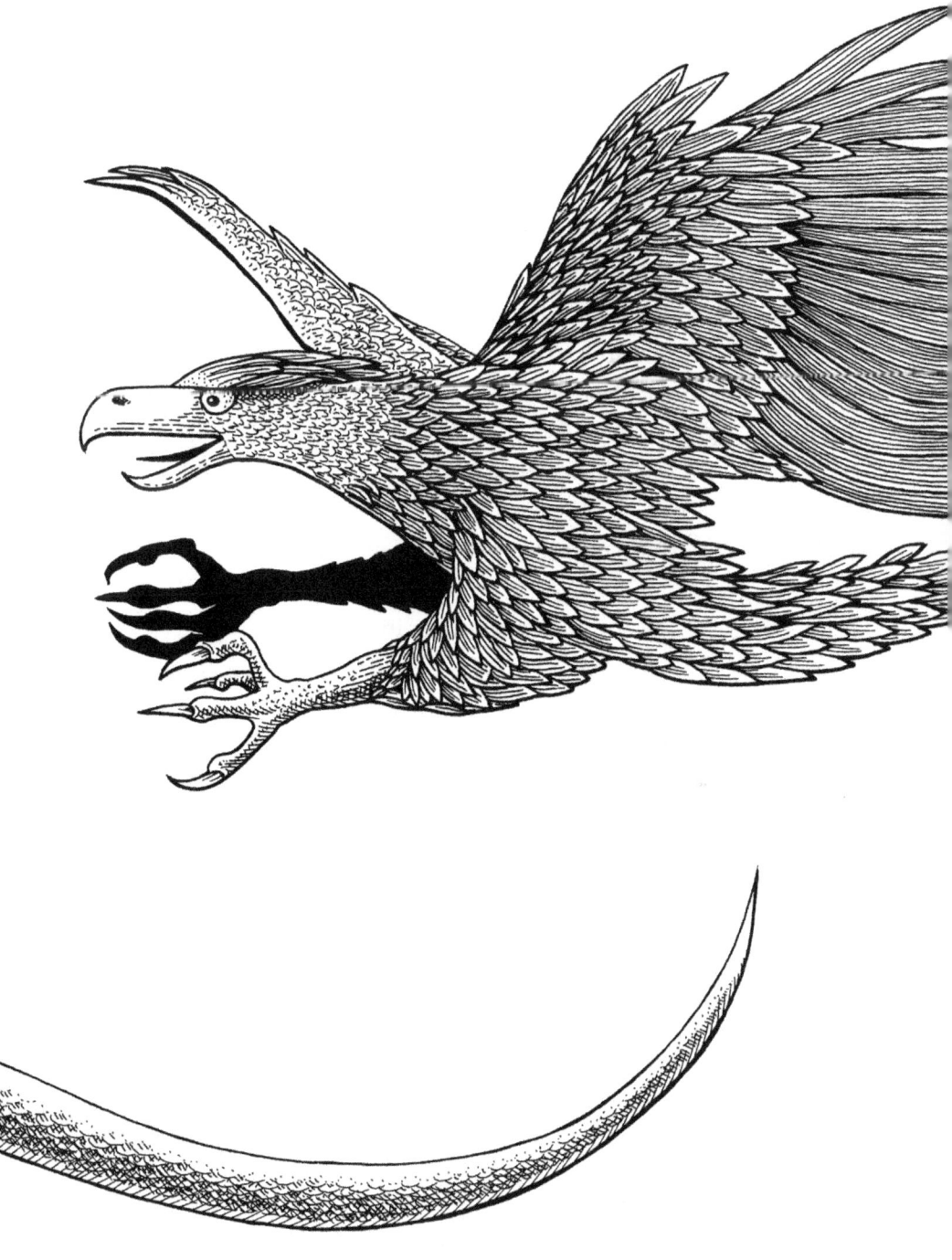

on the ground—it can't get up again. The sight of all these yawning wounds intoxicates me. Swoop down near it at ground level and finish it off with strikes of your scaly serpent's tail, if you can. Courage, fine dragon—sink your vigorous claws into it, and may blood mix with blood to form streams where there isn't any water. That's easy to say, but not to do. Provoked by the unlucky fortunes of this memorable battle, the eagle has just devised a new strategic plan of defence; it is prudent. It is firmly seated in a resolute position on its remaining wing, on both thighs, and on its tail which it previously used as a rudder. It defies efforts more extraordinary than those it has resisted up till now. One time it turns as swiftly as the tiger and doesn't seem fatigued; another time it lies calmly on its back with its two strong legs in the air and ironically regards its opponent. At the end of the day I must know who the victor will be—the battle can't go on forever. I imagine the resulting consequences! The eagle is terrible, and it performs enormous jumps that shake the earth as if it is going to take flight; it knows, however, that this is impossible for it. The dragon doesn't trust this; it believes that any moment the eagle is going to attack the side where its eye is missing… I am dismayed! That is what happens. How has the dragon let itself be taken by the chest? It tries to use strength and cunning; I realize that the eagle, glued like a leech to it with all its limbs, sinks its beak further and further into the stomach of the dragon despite the fresh wounds it receives at the base of its neck. Only its body is visible. It appears to be relaxed; it isn't pressed to withdraw. It is undoubtedly seeking something, while the tiger-headed dragon booms bellowings that wake the forests. Here's the eagle coming out of that cavern. Eagle, how horrible you are! You are redder than a pool of blood! Even though you are holding a beating heart in your forceful beak, you are so covered with wounds that you can barely stand on your feathered legs; and without loosening your beak, you stagger to the side of the dragon who is dying in terrible agonies. Victory has been difficult; no matter—you have won it—it's necessary to at least tell the truth… You behave according

to the rules of reason by casting off the eagle form as you move away from the dragon's corpse. In this way therefore, Maldoror, you were the winner! In this way therefore, Maldoror, you have defeated *Hope!* Despair will henceforth feed on your purest essence! From now on re-enter, with determined steps, the career of evil! Even though I am, so to speak, *blasé* about suffering, I didn't fail to feel the final blow you inflicted upon the dragon. Judge for yourself whether I suffer! But you frighten me. Behold, observe that man who flees in the distance. From out of him—excellent soil—malediction has grown its bushy foliage; he is damned and he curses. Where do your sandals carry you? Where are you going, faltering like a sleepwalker on a rooftop? May your perverse destiny be realized! Farewell, Maldoror! Farewell until Eternity—when we will not meet up together again!"

It was a spring day. Birds poured out their hymns in twitterings, and humans, having carried out their various duties, bathed in the sanctity of weariness. Everything was working for its destiny: the trees, the planets, the dogfish. Everything—except the Creator! He was stretched out on the road, clothes in tatters. His bottom lip sagged like a drooping string, His teeth were unclean, and there was dust mixed through the blond waves of His hair. His body, numbed by a heavy drowsiness and ground against the pebbles, made futile efforts to raise itself. His strength had abandoned Him and He lay there as feeble as an earthworm, as impassive as bark. Streams of wine filled the ruts furrowed by the nervous jerks of His shoulders. Stupefaction, with its swine's snout, covered Him with its protective wings and threw Him an amorous glance. His legs, with their relaxed muscles, were sweeping the soil like two blind masts. Blood ran from His nostrils: His face had struck a stake in His fall ... He was drunk! Terribly drunk! As drunk as a bed-bug who has chewed up three barrels of blood during the night! He performed the repetition of incoherent words which I will refrain from repeating here; even if the Supreme Souse has no self-respect, *I* must respect men. Did you know that the Creator... is sozzled! Pity this lip stained from the cups of debauchery! The hedgehog, who was passing, pushed its quills into His back and said: "That one's for You. The day is half-done—work, You loafer, and don't eat the bread of others. Wait a bit and You'll see what gives if I summon the cockatoo with the hooked beak." The woodpecker and the owl, flying past, sank their beaks wholly into His stomach, and they said: "This one's for You. What are You doing there on the ground? Is it to offer this dreary comedy to the animals? But I swear to You that neither the mole, the cassowary, nor the flamingo will imitate You." The ass, who was passing, gave Him a kick on His temple, and it said: "That one's Yours. Why have You given me such long ears? There aren't any who don't despise me, including the cricket." The frog, who was hopping past, shot a jet of saliva onto His face, and said: "Here You go. If You hadn't made my eye so big, and if I hadn't observed You in the state I now see You in, I would have hidden the beauty of Your limbs chastely beneath a spray of buttercups, forget-me-nots and camellias, so that none might glimpse You." The lion, who was striding past, inclined his regal face and said: "For my part, I respect Him, even though His splendour appears overshadowed to us at the moment. The rest of you, who affect such arrogance and are just cowards—since you have attacked Him as he sleeps—if put in His place,

would *you* be happy to endure the insults from passers-by that you haven't spared Him?" The man, walking by, halted before the unsung Creator; and, to the applause of the pubic-louse and the viper, he pooped for three days on His august face! Ill fortune for the man due to that insult—because he didn't respect an enemy, defenceless and virtually unconscious, stretched out in a mixture of mud, blood and wine!... Then the sovereign God, finally awakened by all those mean insults, raised Himself as well as He could; staggering, He went to sit on a rock, with His arms hanging like the two testicles of a phthisic; and He threw a glassy, impotent look on the whole of Nature that belonged to Him. O humans, you are terrible children, but I beseech you: spare this great being who hasn't yet finished sleeping off the vile liquor—and who, not having kept enough strength to hold Himself upright, has fallen loutishly onto that rock where He sits now like a vagabond. Heed this passing beggar; he saw that the dervish was extending a starving arm and, oblivious to whom he offered the alms, he threw a piece of bread into that hand that implored mercy. The Creator expressed His gratitude to him with a gesture of His head. Oh! You will never know how the constant holding of the reins of the universe becomes such a difficult challenge! Blood sometimes rushes to the head when one tries to draw a final comet with a new race of beings out of nothingness. Intelligence, thoroughly disturbed from toe to head, retreats like the vanquished, and once in life it may fall into the bewilderments which you have witnessed!

A red lantern, standard of depravity, hanging from the end of a pole above a huge worm-eaten door, swung its carcass at the whip of the four winds. A dirty corridor which reeked of the human thigh gave onto an inner courtyard where roosters and hens, leaner than their wings, pecked for their food. From the wall which served to enclose the courtyard, and which was situated on the western side, various

openings closed-off with portcullises had been parsimoniously cut. Moss covered the main part of the dwelling—which had undoubtedly once been a convent—and along with the rest of the building currently served as domicile for all those ladies who would display on a daily basis, to those who would enter, the inside of their vaginas in exchange for a little gold. I was on a bridge whose pillars plunged into the muddy water of a girding moat. From its elevated platform I contemplated this erection in the countryside, intrigued by its antiquity and the tiniest details of its interior design. Occasionally the portcullis of a wicket would rise grindingly as though impelled upward by a hand that violated the nature of iron; a man would show his head in the partly-raised opening and would push forward his shoulders, onto which fell flaking plaster, and in this laborious extraction he would make his spiderweb-covered body follow. Putting his hands like a crown on all kinds of garbage that weighed heavily on the ground, while he still had his leg engaged in the twistings of the grill, he would thus regain his natural posture and go to soak his hands in a rickety bucket—whose soapy water had seen whole generations rise and fall—and then he would distance himself as quickly as possible from those working-class alleyways in order to go and breathe the fresh air around the centre of town. When the customer had departed, a completely naked woman would proceed outside in the same way and head towards the same bucket. Then the roosters and hens, attracted by the seminal scent, would come flocking from different points in the courtyard, and they would bring her to the ground—in spite of her vigorous efforts—trampling the surface of her body like manure and slashing with pecks of their beaks until blood was drawn from the flabby labia of her swollen vagina. The hens and roosters, their gullets sated, would return to scratching in the courtyard grass; having clean herself up, the woman would rise like a person waking from a nightmare, trembling and covered in wounds. She would drop the rag she had brought to wipe her legs; no longer needing the communal bucket, she would return to the lair as she had left it in order to wait for another client. Seeing this spectacle, *I also* wanted to penetrate this house! I was about to descend from the bridge when I observed this inscription in Hebrew characters on the entablature of the pillar:

> "You who cross this bridge, don't go thither. Crime tarries there with vice; one day his friends waited in vain for a young man who had passed through the fatal gateway."

Curiosity overcame fear — I shortly arrived in front of a wicket whose grill had solid, tightly-crossed bars. I wanted to look inside through this thick screen. At first I could see nothing, but it didn't take long to distinguish the objects which were in the dark room thanks to the rays of the sun which was dimming and was soon going to disappear over the horizon. The first and only thing that struck my view was a blond staff made from cones pressed into each other. This staff was moving! It was walking around the room! Its movements were so robust that the floor shook; with its two ends it was making some enormous breaches in the wall and appeared like a battering-ram one strikes against the gate of a besieged town. Its efforts were futile; the walls were built from rough-hewn stone and when it collided with the dividing wall I would see it bend back like a steel blade and bounce back like a rubber ball. Therefore this stick wasn't made of wood! Then I noted that it rolled and unrolled itself with the ease of an eel. Although as tall as a man, it didn't hold itself upright. Sometimes it tried to, and would show one of its ends in front of the portcullis. It would make some impetuous jumps, would fall again to the ground, and would not be able to break open the obstacle. I began to watch it more and more attentively — and I saw that it was a hair! After a great struggle against the material that surrounded it like a prison, it went to rest on the bed which was in this room, the root resting on a mat and the tip leaning back on the bedhead. After several moments of silence, during which I heard some interrupted sobs,

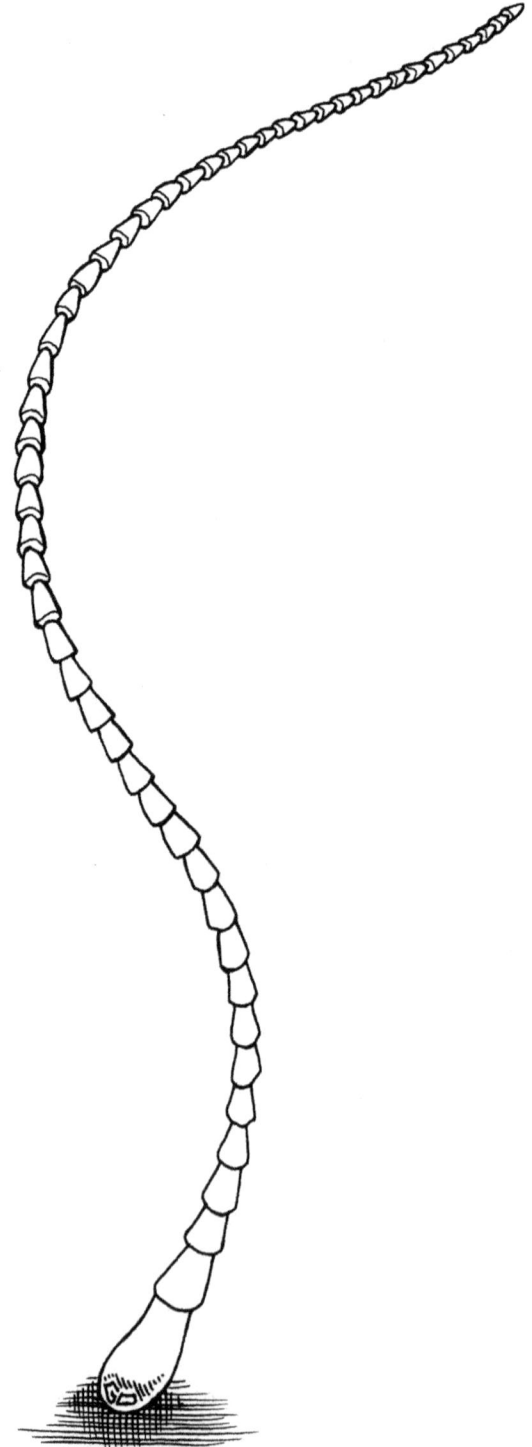

it raised its voice and spoke thus: "My master has forgotten me in this room; he doesn't come to seek me. He rose from this bed where I am resting, he combed his perfumed hair and never imagined that I had previously fallen to the ground. If he had picked me up, however, I wouldn't have found that simple act of justice surprising. He abandons me in this locked room after having been wrapped in the arms of a woman. And what a woman! The sheets are still moist from their warm contact and bear, in their disarray, the impression of a one-night stand..." And I asked myself *who* its master could be! And my eye again stuck itself more energetically to the grill!... "While the whole of Nature snoozed in its chastity, *he* coupled with a wanton woman in lascivious and dirty embraces. He so degraded himself as to let those cheeks—despicable with their habitual impudence, their sap shrivelled—approach his august face. He didn't blush—but *I* blushed for *him*. He certainly felt happy to have slept with such a partner for a night. The woman, astonished by the majestic sight of this guest, appeared to experience incomparable pleasures and was kissing his neck in a frenzy." And I asked myself *who* its master could be! And my eye once more stuck itself more energetically to the grill!... "Meanwhile, by virtue of his unaccustomed ardour for carnal pleasures, I felt the poisoned pimples (that were growing more numerous) surround my root with their deadly gall and absorb my life's generating essence with their suckers. The more the lovers forgot themselves in their crazy movements, the more I felt my resources decrease. At the moment when their fleshly desires reached a passionate climax, I noticed that my root was collapsing like a soldier wounded by a bullet. The torch of life was extinguished in me—I detached myself from his illustrious head like a dead branch, I fell to the ground without spunk, without power, without vitality—but with a profound sympathy for that one I had belonged to; but with an eternal grief for his willful misconduct!..." And I asked myself *who* its master could be! And my eye again stuck itself with more vigour to the grill!... "If only he had surrounded the innocent heart of a virgin with his soul. She would have been more worthy of him and the degradation wouldn't have been so great. With his lips he kisses that muddy forehead which men have trodden on with their dirty heels!... Through his brazen nostrils he inhales the emissions of those two clammy armpits!... I saw the latter membranes contract with shame while for their part the nostrils rejected that infamous inhalation. But neither he nor she paid any attention to the solemn warnings of the armpits, nor to the gloomy and livid repulsion of the nostrils. She raised her arms higher and with a stronger push he pressed his face

into their pits. I was compelled to be accessory to that profanity. I was obliged to be spectator to that outrageous hip-swaying — to witness the forced alloying of these two beings whose different natures were separated by a large abyss..." And I asked myself *who* its master could be! And my eyes adhered once more energetically to the grill!... "When he was slaked with smelling this woman, he wanted to tear out her muscles one by one; but since she was a woman he excused her, preferring to make one of his own sex suffer. He called to a young man in the neighbouring cell who had entered that establishment to pass some idle time with one of the women, and implored him to come and place himself a few paces from his eyes. I had lain on the floor for a considerable time. Not having the strength to lift myself up on my burning root, I couldn't see what they were doing. What I did know was that scarcely had the young man been within reach of his hands than shreds of flesh fell at the feet of the bed and came to rest at my side. They told me in a whisper that the claws of my master had detached them from the youth's shoulders. That individual, after several hours during which he had fought a greater power, raised himself from the bed and withdrew majestically. He was literally flayed from foot to head; he dragged his subverted skin across the flagstones of that room. He told himself that his character was filled with goodness, that he liked to believe his fellows were also good, and because of that he had acquiesced to the wish of the distinguished stranger who had beckoned him — but he had never, *ever*, expected to be tortured by an executioner. 'By *such* an executioner,' he added, after a break. Finally he headed towards the entrance gate, which mercifully opened to its full extent in the presence of that body deprived of its epidermis. Without abandoning his skin, which might still be useful to him if only as a cloak, he attempted to disappear from that death-trap; once gone from the room, I couldn't see if he had the strength to make it back to the exit door. Oh! How the hens and roosters respectfully retreated from that long trail of blood on the soggy ground — despite their hunger!" And I asked myself *who* its master could be! And my eyes again stuck themselves with more vigour to the grill!... "Then that young man, who should have been thinking more about his dignity and justice, raised himself up with difficulty on his tired elbow. Alone, dismal, nauseated and grotesque!... He clothed himself slowly. Buried for centuries in the catacombs of the convent, and after being awakened abruptly by the noises of that horrible night which clashed together in a cell above the vaults, the nuns clasped hands and came to form a gloomy circle around him. As he searched the ruins of his former splendour — as he washed his hands with spit while wiping them on his hair (after an evening spent entirely in vice and crime, it was better to wash them with spit than not to wash them at all) — the nuns chanted woeful requiems like when someone is lowered into the grave. Indeed the young man could not survive this torture exacted upon him by a divine hand, and his agonies terminated during the nuns' intoning..." I remembered the inscription on the pillar, and I understood what had become of the adolescent dreamer whose friends still waited each day since the time of his disappearance... And I asked myself *who* its master was! And my eyes were stuck even more energetically to the grill!... "The walls opened to let him pass; the nuns, seeing him take his flight into the air with wings which had been hidden in his emerald robe, silently relocated themselves under cover of the catacomb. He left for his Heavenly home, leaving me here; there is no justice. The other hairs remained on his head — and *I* lie in this gloomy room, on the floor covered with clotting blood and shreds of dry meat; this room has become cursed since he penetrated it; nobody enters; meanwhile I am trapped in here. It's all over, then! I will no longer see the legions of angels marching in tight phalanxes, nor the stars promenading through the gardens of harmony. Well, so be it... I will know how to endure my misfortune with resignation. But I will not fail to tell men what happened in this cell. I will give them permission to reject their dignity like a useless garment, since they know the example of my master; I will advise them to fellate the cock of crime, since *another* has already done so..." The hair became silent... And I asked myself *who* its master could be! And my eyes again adhered more energetically to the grill!... Thunder immediately cracked; a phosphorescent light penetrated the room. In spite of myself, I recoiled by some warning instinct—and although I was far from the gate I heard another voice, but this one groveling and sweet, afraid of being heard: "Don't make such jumps! Be quiet... silence yourself... what if somebody heard you! I will replace you among the other hairs; but first let the sun set on the horizon so that night might cover your steps... I haven't forgotten you—but they would have seen you leaving and I would have been jeopardized. Oh! If you only knew how much I suffered since that moment! Back in Heaven my archangels surrounded me with curiosity; they didn't want to ask the reason for my absence. They, who had never dared raise their eyes to me, threw puzzled looks on my downcast face, striving to figure out the enigma, even though they couldn't perceive the crux of that mystery, and quietly spread their thoughts—which betrayed a fear of some unaccountable change in me. They wept silent tears; they vaguely sensed that I was no longer the same, that I had become inferior in my identity. They wanted to know what baleful resolution had made me cross Heavens' borders in order to swoop onto the earth and taste the ephemeral pleasures which they themselves profoundly despised. They noticed on my brow a drop of semen and a drop of blood. The first had spouted from the courtesan's thighs! The second had sprung from the martyr's veins! Odious stigmata! Indelible rosettes! My archangels found, hanging in the thickets of space, the flamboyant remains of my opal tunic which floated above the gaping people. They weren't able to repair it, and my body must remain naked in its innocence—memorable punishment for abandoned virtue. Observe the furrows which have drawn a bed on my discoloured cheeks: it is the drop of semen and the drop of blood which slowly percolate along my dry wrinkles. Reaching the upper lip, they make a great effort and enter the sanctuary of my mouth, attracted like a magnet by the irresistible throat.

They choke me, those two relentless drops. Up until now I believed myself to be the Omnipotent; but, no — I must lower my neck in the face of Remorse which cries at me: 'You're just a wretch!' Don't leap about so much! Shut your trap... silence yourself... what if somebody heard you! I will replace you among the other hairs; but first let the sun set on the horizon so that night might shroud your steps... I saw Satan, the great foe, restore the tangled bones of his body above his larval numbness and, standing triumphant and sublime, harangue his reassembled troops; he stirred me with derision, as I deserved it. He said that it astonished him muchly that his arrogant rival — successfully caught in the act, finally realized by constant spying — could, by means of a long voyage through the reefs of the ether, abase Himself so far as to kiss the dress of human debauchery and to make a member of humanity perish with sufferings. He said that this young man, crushed in the gears of my refined tortures, may perhaps have become an intellect of genius, comforting men against the blows of misfortune on this world through worthy songs of poetry and bravery. He said that the nuns of the convent-brothel could no longer return to their sleep; that they loiter in the courtyard, gesticulating like robots and squashing the buttercups and lilacs; and that they have become mad from indignation, but not enough that they can't recall the cause which brought about this illness in their brains... (Here they approach, clothed again in their white shrouds, not conversing, and holding hands. Their hair falls in disarray over their naked shoulders; bouquets of black flowers are draped over their breasts. Nuns, return to your sepulchres; night hasn't arrived yet — it's only twilight... O hair, you see it yourself: I am harassed from all sides by the unleashed sense of my own depravity!) He said that the Creator, who had vaunted Himself as being the Providence of all who lived, conducted Himself with great frivolity (to say the least) by offering such a spectacle to the stellar worlds; for he clearly affirmed his plan of reporting to the orbicular planets how I maintain virtue and goodness by my very example in the vastness of my kingdoms. He said that the great esteem which he'd had for so noble an enemy had vanished from his mind and that he would prefer to place his hand on the breast of a young girl, even though that was an act of execrable evil, rather than spit on my face—caked in three layers of mixed blood and semen—so that he wouldn't sully his dribbling saliva. He said that he believed himself rightly superior to me, not out of vice but through virtue and modesty; not through crime but Justice. He said that it was necessary to bind me to a rack because of my numerous transgressions, to make me burn slowly in a scorching furnace, and to throw me into the sea (if, however, the sea was willing to take me). That, since I had bragged of being just—I who had condemned *him* to eternal punishments due to a minor revolt that had not had serious consequences—*I* should therefore exact severe justice upon myself and impartially judge my own iniquity-charged conscience… Don't leap around so much! Be silent… shut your mouth… what if somebody should hear you! I will replace you among the other hairs—but first let the sun set on the horizon so that night might shroud your steps…" He paused for a moment; although I didn't see him at all, I understood from this required moment of pause that the surge of passion had stirred up his breast like a gyrating cyclone would stir up a pod of whales. Divine bosom—sullied one day by the bitter touch of a wanton's nipples! Regal soul—abandoned in a moment of oversight to the crab of debauch, to the octopus of weak character, to the shark of personal abjection, to the boa of absent morality, and to the monstrous snail of idiotism! The hair and its master hugged each other tightly like two friends who meet again after a long absence. The Creator continued—the accused appearing before His own tribunal: "And men, what will they think of me—of whom they had such a lofty opinion—when they learn of the erring ways of my conduct, the hesitant tread of my sandal in the muddy labyrinths of the material, and the direction of my tenebrous route through the stagnant waters and miasmatic rushes of the puddle where crime with its dark paw, shrouded in mists, turns blue and howls!… I see that I must work hard towards my rehabilitation in the future in order to regain their respect. I am the Omnipotent—and yet in one thing I remain inferior to men, whom I created with a little sand! Tell them an audacious lie, and tell them that I never left Heaven, perpetually imprisoned by the concerns of the throne, among the marble, statues and mosaics of my palaces. I appeared to the heavenly sons of humanity; I told them: 'Chase evil from your cottages and let the cloak of good enter your home. The one who would raise a hand against one of his fellows, by inflicting a mortal wound on his breast with deadly iron—may he never hope for the results of my mercy, and let him fear the Scales of Justice. He will go to bury his sadness in the forest, but the rustling of the leaves through the glades will serenade his ears with the ballad of Remorse; and he will flee from those environs, pricked on the hip by thicket, holly and blue thistle, his rapid footfalls interlocked by the suppleness of lianas and the bites of scorpions. He will head towards the pebbles of the beach, but the incoming tide will tell him with its sea-spray and dangerous approach that they haven't overlooked his past; and he will hasten his way blindly towards the summit of the cliff while the driving winds of the equinox, forcing themselves into the gulf's natural grottoes and quarries cut beneath the wall of reverberating rocks, will bellow like enormous herds of Pampas buffalo. The coastal lighthouses will pursue him with their sarcastic reflections as far as the northern limits, and the will-o'-the-wisps of the fens—simple combusting vapours—with their fantastic dances will make the hairs in his pores shiver and verdigris the irises of his eyes. May modesty flourish in your huts and be safe in the shadow of your fields. This is thus how your sons will grow handsome and bow gratefully before their parents; if not, sickly and stunted like parchment in libraries, they will advance with great strides, led by revolt, against the day of their birth and the clitoris of their unclean mother.' How will men want to obey these strict laws if the legislator himself is the first to decline to be constrained by them?... And my shame is as large as Eternity!" I heard the hair, who humbly forgave

him for its seclusion since its master had acted with prudence and not lightly; and the last pale ray of sun that illuminated my eye-lids receded from the mountain ravines. Turning towards the hair, I saw it roll up like a shroud... Don't bounce around so much! Be quiet... silence yourself... what if somebody should hear you! He will replace you among the other hairs. And now that the sun has set on the horizon, cynical old man and sweet hair, creep, both of you, to a distance from the brothel while night, extending its shadow over the convent, shrouds the lengthening of your furtive steps across the plain... Then the louse, suddenly coming out from behind a promontory, told me while bristling its claws: "What do you think of that?" But *I* didn't wish to respond to this. I moved off and arrived on the bridge. I erased the primordial inscription—I replaced it with this: "It is painful to keep such a secret, like a dagger, in one's heart; but I swear never to reveal the thing I witnessed when I first entered this terrible keep." I threw over the parapet the penknife I had used to carve the letters; and, making some rapid reflections on the Creator's character in infancy—He who must still, alas! (Eternity is long), make humanity suffer for ages, either by cruelties inflicted or by the ignoble spectacle of the chancres caused by serious vice—I closed my eyes like a drunkard thinking about having such a being for a foe, and I sadly resumed my journey across the mazes of roads.

END OF THE THIRD DIRGE

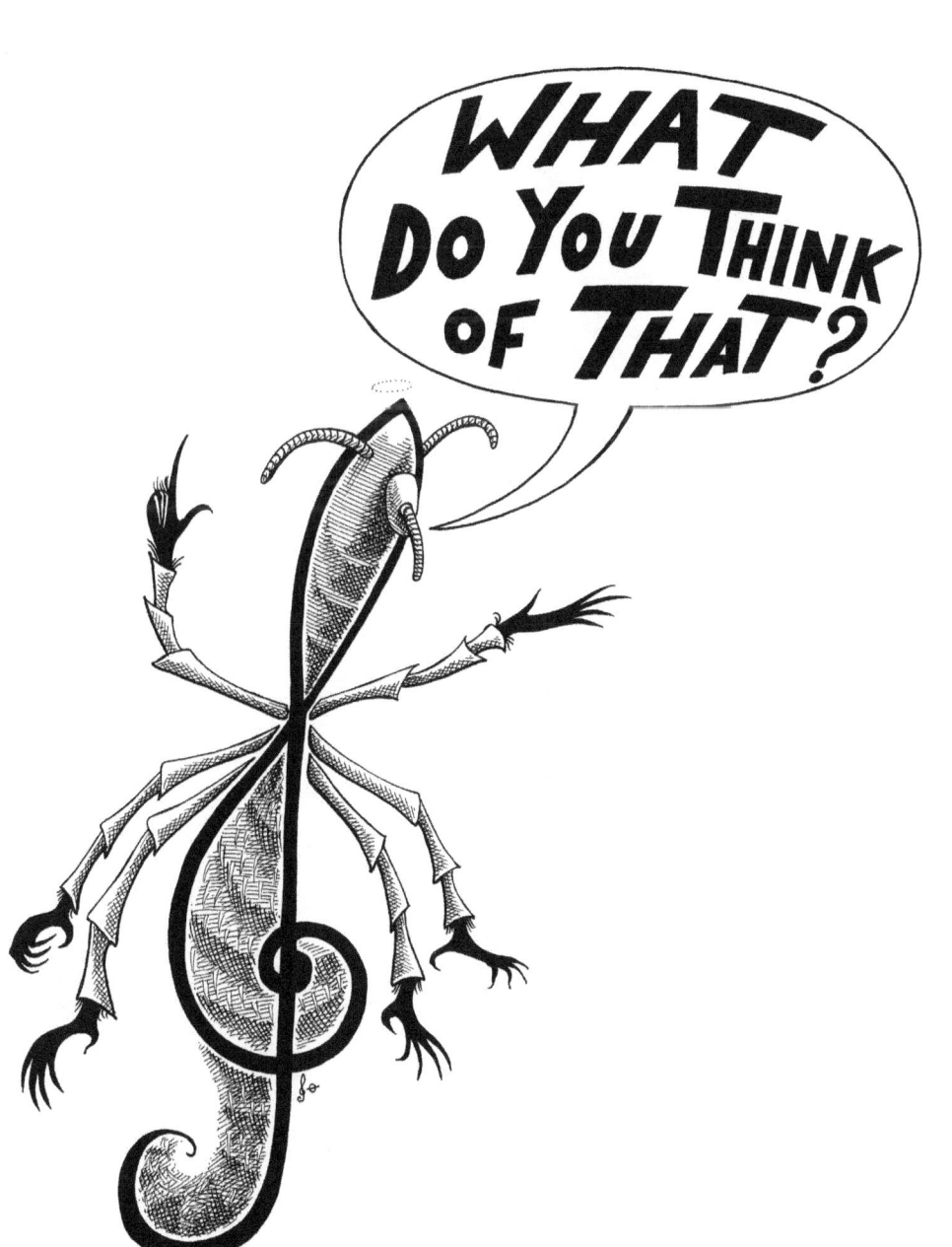

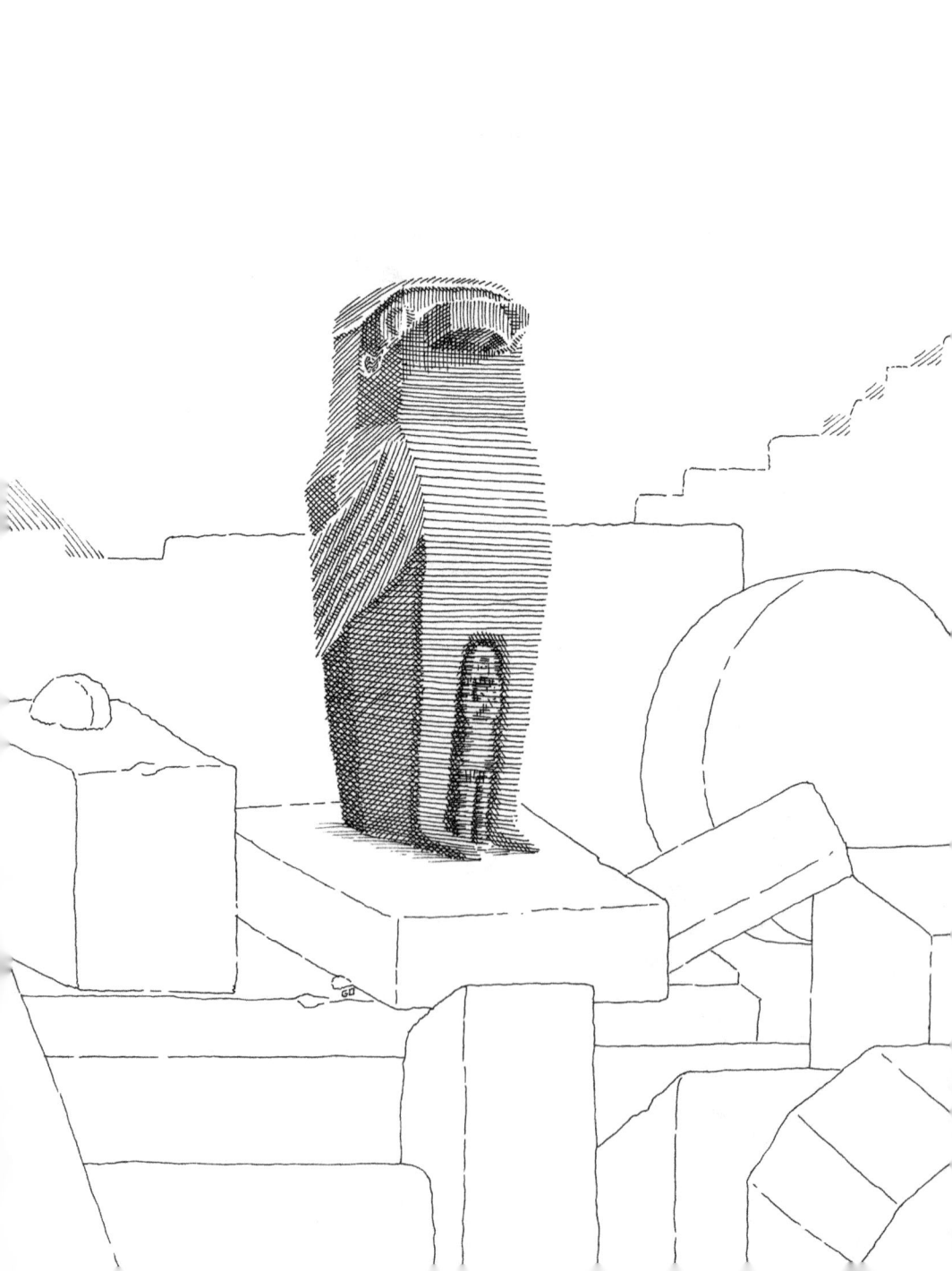

 Fourth Dirge

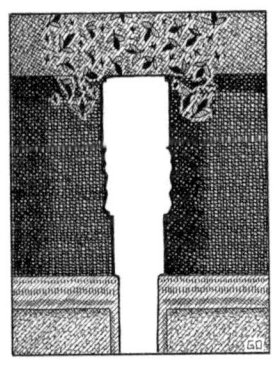 T IS A man or a rock or a tree which is going to begin the fourth dirge. When our foot slips on a frog, we feel a sensation of distaste; but when we barely graze the human body with our hand the skin of the fingers cracks like scales from a block of mica which has been shattered by hammer hits; and just as the heart of a shark, dead for an hour, still beats with tenacious life on the deck, in the same way our innards stir from top to bottom long after touching it. Man inspires as much horror in his own kind! Perhaps I am wrong when I suggest this—but perhaps what I say is also true. I experience and conceive an illness more grievous than eyes swelling from long meditations on Man's strange character—but I still search for it... and I haven't been able to find it! I don't believe myself to be any less intelligent than the next person, and yet who would dare claim that I have succeeded in my investigations? What a lie would exit their mouth! The ancient temple of Denderah is situated an hour and a half from the Nile's left bank. Today innumerable phalanxes of wasps have taken over the drains and cornices. They hover around the columns like the thick waves of an ebon head of hair. The sole inhabitants of the cold portico, they guard the entrance to the vestibules as an hereditary entitlement. I would compare the buzzing of their metallic

wings to the endless collision of slabs of ice thrown against each other during break-up in the polar oceans. But if I were to consider the behaviour of the one to whom Providence has given a throne on this earth, the three pinions of my pain emit a greater murmur! When a comet suddenly appears during the night in an area of sky — after an eighty-year absence — it displays its glowing and vaporous tail to the terrestrial inhabitants and the crickets. Undoubtedly it is unaware of that long voyage — it is not the same with me: resting on my elbows on my bed while the jagged edges of a dry and dreary horizon rise in force from the bottom of my soul, I am absorbed in dreams of compassion — and I blush for Man! Cut in half by the north wind, the sailor hastens to get back to his hammock after doing his night shift: why isn't that comfort offered to me? The idea that I have willfully fallen as low as my fellow-men, and that I have less right than any other to deliver complaints about our fate — which remains chained to the calloused crust of a planet — and about the essence of our perverse soul, transfixes me like a forged nail. We've seen fire-damp explosions wipe out whole families, but they experienced agony only briefly because death is almost immediate amidst the rubble and toxic gas — *I* endure always like basalt! Midway through life, the same as at the start, angels resemble one other: has it not been ages since I no longer resembled myself! Man and I, trapped within the bounds of our intelligence like a lake often is within a girdle of coral isles, instead of uniting our respective strengths to defend ourselves against chance and misfortune, we diverge, shaking with hatred, while taking two opposite paths — as if we had wounded each other with the point of a dagger! It looks as if one understands the contempt he inspires in the other; urged on by the motive of reciprocal dignity, we hasten not to mislead our adversary; each keeps to himself and is aware that declared peace may be impossible to keep. Very well, so be it! — let my war against Man drag on, because each recognizes in the other one his own degradation... since the two are mortal foes. Whether I might win a disastrous victory or succumb, the battle will be good: me alone against humanity. I won't employ weapons made from wood or iron; I will kick away the layers of the earth's mineral ores: the powerful and seraphic sonority of the harp beneath my fingers will become a fearful talisman. Man, that sublime ape, has already penetrated my chest with his lance of porphyry in more than one ambush: a soldier doesn't display his wounds, as glorious as they may be. This terrible war will throw pain into those two parties: two friends who would stubbornly seek to destroy themselves—what drama!

Two columns larger than two pins—which it wasn't difficult, though improbable, to take for baobab trees—could be seen in the valley. Actually, they were two giant towers. And although at first sight two baobabs might not resemble two pins, nor even two towers—yet by cleverly employing the threads of prudence we can assert without fear of being mistaken (because if that assertion were accompanied by an ounce of fear it would not be an assertion—although a like name expresses these two mental phenomena that exhibit characteristics contrasting enough to be confused lightly) that a baobab doesn't differ so much from a pillar that comparison would be prohibited between these architectural forms... or geometric forms... or both... or neither... or, instead, tall and gigantic forms. I just found—I won't pretend to say otherwise—appropriate adjectives for the nouns 'pillar' and 'baobab': let it be well known that it's not without joy mixed with arrogance that I remark to those who, having opened their eyes, have taken the very laudable resolution of reading through these pages while the candle burns (if it's night) or while the sun shines (if it's day). And yet, even when a higher power might order us, in the most clearly precise terms, to throw back into the chasms of chaos the judicious comparison that everyone has certainly been able to relish with impunity, even then—and especially then—let us not lose sight of this fundamental axiom: habits formed over years, books,

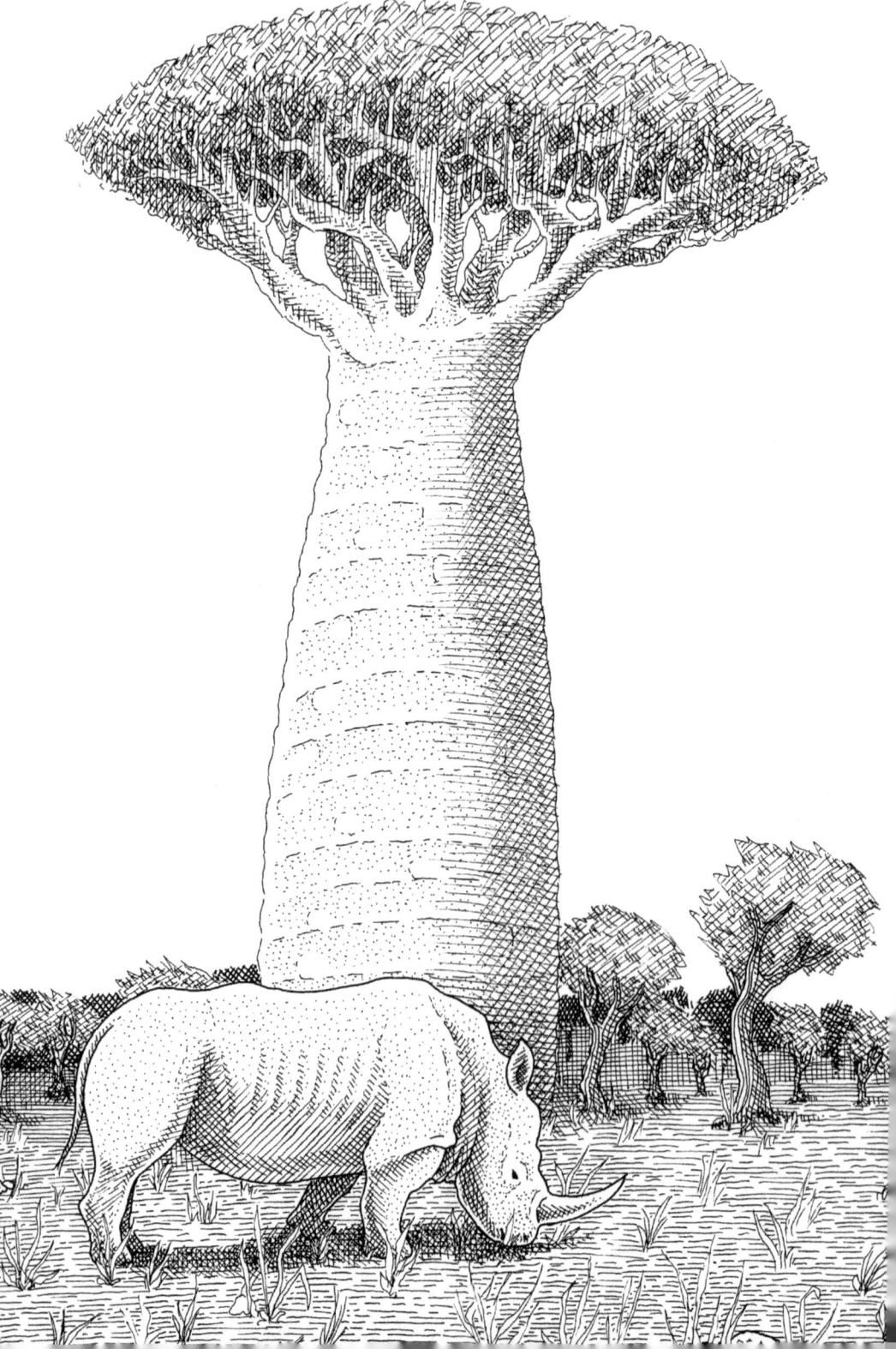

contact with our peers, and the inherent nature of each individual which blossoms in rapid efflorescence—these would impose on the human spirit the irreparable stigma of recidivism in the criminal employment ('criminal,' when placing it briefly and spontaneously from the viewpoint of the superior power) of a figure of speech despised by some but which many applaud. If the reader finds that sentence too long, may he accept my apologies—but he shouldn't expect grovellings on my part. I can admit my mistakes but not make them worse through my cowardice. My reasonings will sometimes clash against the jingle-bells of madness and the serious appearance of what is only, in short, grotesque (although according to some philosophers it is hard enough to separate the fool from the melancholic—life itself being a comical drama or a dramatic comedy); however, everyone is allowed to kill flies, and even rhinoceri, in order to sometimes take a break from overtaxing toil. Here is the most efficient method for killing flies (though it isn't the best): one squashes them between the first two fingers of the hand. The majority of writers who have thoroughly dealt with this subject have calculated most credibly that in many cases it is preferable to cut off the head. If someone should reproach

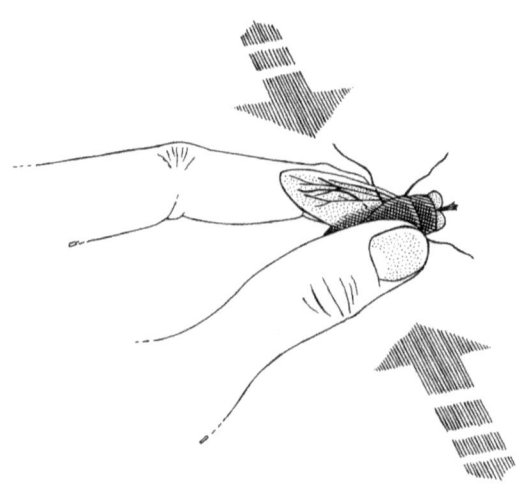

me for speaking about pins as a radically frivolous subject, let him note without bias that the greatest results have often been produced by the smallest causes. And, so that I not distance myself further from the frame of this page, is it not clear that the laborious literary piece which I have composed since the beginning of this stanza would perhaps be appreciated less if it had taken its pivotal point in a thorny question of chemistry or internal pathology? Besides, all tastes exist in Nature, and when at the start I compared pillars to pins with so much exactness (I certainly didn't believe that I might one day be reproached for it), I based myself on the laws of optics that have established that, the more distant the visual range is from an object, the more diminished the image reflected in the retina.

It is in this way that what our mind's tendency to farce takes for a miserable attempt at wit is—most of the time, and from the author's perspective—only an important truth to be proudly proclaimed! Oh! That crazy philosopher who burst out laughing upon seeing a donkey eating a fig! I invent nothing: the ancient tomes recounted in the most ample detail that willful and shameless stripping of human nobility. *I* don't know how to laugh. I have never been able to laugh, even though I have often tried to do it. It is very difficult to learn how to laugh. Or to be more exact, I believe that a feeling of repugnance for that monstrosity forms an essential mark of my character. Well, I have witnessed something stronger: I've seen a fig eating a donkey! And yet I did not laugh; frankly, *no* buccal part moved. The need to weep seized me so strongly that my eyes let a teardrop fall. "Nature! Nature!" I cried to myself while sobbing, "the sparrowhawk tears up the sparrow, the fig eats the donkey, and the tapeworm devours Man!" Without resolving to go further, I wonder if I spoke of the method by which one kills flies. Yes—isn't that so? It is no less true that I haven't spoken of the destruction of rhinoceri! If certain friends maintained the opposite to me, I would not listen to them and I would recall that praise and flattery are two big stumbling blocks. Nevertheless, in order to comfort my conscience as much as possible, I cannot refrain from observing that this thesis on the rhinoceros would carry me beyond the bounds of patience and calm, and for its part would probably (let us even have the boldness to say "certainly") put present generations off. Not to have spoken of the rhinoceros after the fly! As a fair excuse I should at least have mentioned sooner (and I haven't done so!) this inadvertent omission—which won't surprise those who have thoroughly studied the real and inexplicable contradictions that occupy the lobes of the human brain. Nothing is unworthy to a great and simple intelligence; if there is mystery in it, the smallest natural phenomena will become, for the sage, inexhaustible material for meditation. If someone sees a donkey eat a fig or a fig eat a donkey (these two circumstances don't often arise, unless it

be in poetry), you may be certain that, after a few minutes' reflection — in order to decide what action to take — he will abandon the path of virtue and start to cackle like a cock! Moreover, is it not quite proven that roosters deliberately open their beaks to imitate Man and to make a tormented grimace. I call 'grimace' in birds that which bears the same name in humanity! The rooster doesn't depart from its nature, less by inability than by arrogance. Teach them to read — they revolt. This is not a parrot, which would go into ecstasies before its ignorant or unpardonable weakness! Oh! Disgraceful dishonour! How we resemble a goat when we laugh! The calm forehead has vanished to be replaced by two enormous fish eyes which (isn't it deplorable?)... which... which begin to shine like lighthouses! Often, I will manage to declare solemnly the most laughable propositions... I don't think that becomes a conclusive enough reason to widen one's mouth! "I can't refrain from laughing," you will reply to me; I might accept that absurd statement, but then let it be a melancholy laugh.

Go ahead and laugh—but weep at the same time. If you can't weep with your eyes, cry with your mouth. If this is still not possible, urinate—but I warn you that any liquid is necessary here to mitigate the dryness that carries the laugh inside it with reins cracked from behind. As for me, I won't let myself be disconcerted by the comical chucklings and odd bellowings coming from those people who always find some fault in a character not like their own, because this is one of many intellectual improvements that God created, without departing from a primordial pattern, to govern the bony frameworks. Up till our times, poetry laid a false trail; rising to Heaven or crawling on the earth, it misunderstood the principles of its existence and has been (not unreasonably) mocked continually by honest people. It has not been humble... the most beautiful attribute that should exist in an imperfect being! I myself wish to display my qualities, but *I* am not enough of a hypocrite to hide my vices! Laughter, evil, arrogance, madness: they will appear alternately between compassion and love of Justice and they will serve as an example—to human amazement; each will recognize himself there, not as he *should* be, but as he *is*. And perhaps this simple ideal imagined by me may, meanwhile, surpass all that poetry has so far found most grandiose and sacred. For if I allow my vices to perspire through these pages, humans will only have better faith in the virtues that I have made shine there, and on which I will place a halo so high that the greatest geniuses of the future will witness a genuine appreciation for me. In this way therefore will hypocrisy be driven summarily from my abode. There will be in my dirges an impressive proof of power, to thus scorn the opinions received. He sings only for himself, and not for his peers. He doesn't place the measure of his inspiration on the human scale. Free as the tempest, one day he happens to run aground on the untamable shores of his terrible will! He fears nothing—unless it might be himself! In his supernatural battles he will attack Man and the Creator with advantage, like when the swordfish forces its sword into the stomach of the whale: May he be damned—by his children and by my scrawny hand—that one who persists in misunderstanding the relentless kangaroos of laughter and the daring lice of caricature!... Two enormous towers were observed in the valley; I stated that at the beginning. Multiplied by two, the result was four... but I couldn't quite discern the need for that mathematical operation. I continued along my path with a feverish face, and I kept crying: "No... no... I don't quite discern the need for that mathematical operation." I had heard the creaking of chains and painful groans. Let nobody find it possible, when they are passing through this place, to multiply the towers by two so that the result would be four! Someone suspected that I loved humanity as if I were its true mother, and that I had carried it for nine months within my scented innards; that is why I don't travel again through the valley where the two multiplicand units rise!

A gallows rose from the ground; suspended by the hair a metre below the scaffold was a man whose arms were tied behind him. His legs had been left free to increase his suffering and to make him crave anything contrary to the binding of his arms. The skin of his forehead was so stretched by the weight of the hanging that his face, condemned by circumstance to be void of natural expression, resembled the stony concretion of a stalactite. For three days he had endured this torture. He exclaimed: "Who will untie my arms? Who will untie my hair? I dislocate myself with my movements, which only makes the roots of my hair separate further from my head; thirst and hunger aren't the main reasons preventing me from sleeping. It's impossible that my life would extend itself beyond the limits of an hour. Oh, for someone to cut my throat with a sharp stone!" Each word was preceded and followed by intense howls. I sprang forward from the thicket behind which I had sheltered and headed towards the marionette or piece of pork attached to the scaffold. But now I found that

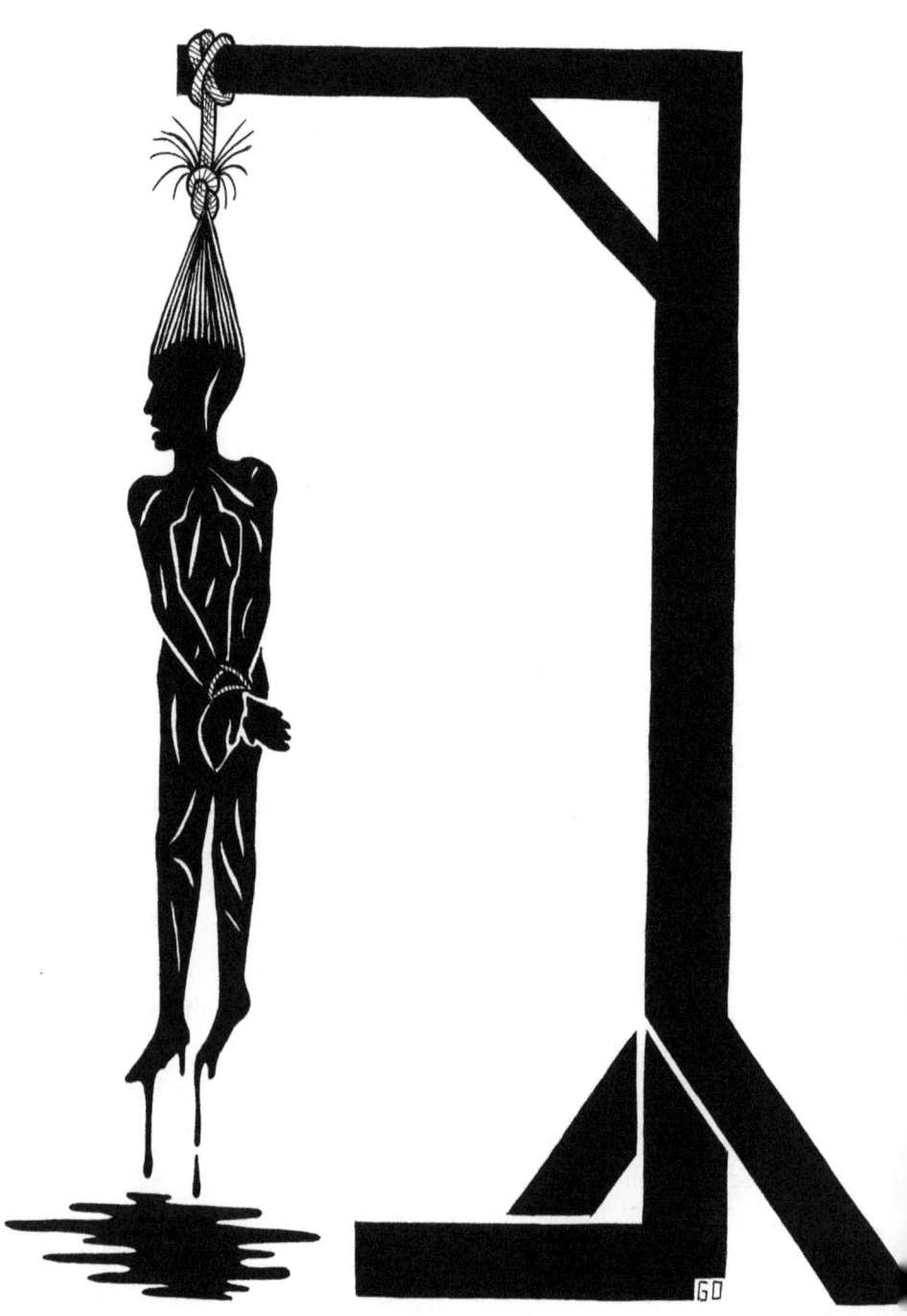

two drunken women had arrived, dancing in from the opposite side. One held a bag and two lead-tipped whips—the other held two brushes and a barrel full of tar. The greying hair of the older woman fluttered in the wind like the tatters of a torn sail, and the other one's ankles cracked against each other like the slaps of a tuna's tail on a ship's poop deck. Their eyes shone with a flame so black and strong that I didn't at first believe that these two women belonged to my species. They cackled with such selfish aplomb and their features inspired such repugnance, that I didn't doubt for a moment that I was viewing two of the ugliest specimens of the human race. I hid myself again in the thicket and remained silent, like a longicorn beetle[7] which only shows its head outside of its nest. They approached with the swiftness of the tide; putting my ear to the ground, the distinctly-perceived sound of their gait's lyrical thumping was carried to me. When the two female orang-outangs had arrived beneath the gallows, they sniffed the air for several seconds; they exhibited by their absurd gestures the truly remarkable amount of amazement that resulted from their experience—when they saw that nothing in this place had changed: death's *dénouement*, conforming to their wishes, had not yet happened. They did not deign to lift their heads to confirm whether the mortadella was still in the same place. One said: "Is it possible that you might still be breathing? You have enduring life, my beloved husband." Just like when two cantors in a cathedral sing the verses of a psalm alternately, the second one responded: "You don't wish to die then, O my graceful son? Then tell me how you've managed (surely it is by some evil spell) to scare away the vultures? Your carcass has indeed become quite thin! The zephyr swings it like a lantern." Each took a brush and tarred the body of the hanged man... each took a whip and raised their arms... I admired (it was absolutely impossible *not* to do as I did) with what energetic precision the metal blades, instead of gliding across the surface—like when one fights a ghost-writer[8] and makes no headway in seizing him by the hair, characteristic of nightmare—applied themselves, thanks to the tar, into the flesh's interior, branding with furrows as deep as the bones' impediment would reasonably allow it. I have resisted the temptation to find pleasure in this extremely bizarre spectacle — but one less profoundly comical than we would have a right to expect. And yet despite good resolutions taken beforehand, how could the strength of these women or their arm muscles *not* be acknowledged? Their skill, which consisted of hitting the most sensitive parts such as the face and the groin, would go unmentioned — except I aspire to the ambition of telling the whole truth! Unless by applying my lips against each other, particularly in the horizontal way (since everyone knows that this is the most normal method of achieving such pressure), I would prefer to keep a silence swollen with tears and mysteries whose painful manifestation will be powerless to hide — not only as well but even better than my words (since I don't believe I'm mistaken, although it certainly isn't necessary to deny in principle, under pain of failing the most basic rules of cleverness, the hypothetical possibilities of error) — the deadly results caused by the fury brought into play by dry hand-bones and robust joints; even when one might put oneself at the point of view of the impartial spectator and the experienced moralist (it's almost important enough that I learn that I don't accept, at least entirely, this more or less erroneous limitation) doubt, in that regard, would not have the ability to extend its roots (because I don't for a moment suggest it's in the hands of a supernatural power) and it would unavoidably, perhaps not immediately, perish for want of a sap to fulfill the simultaneous conditions of nourishment and absence of toxic substances. It is understood — if it's not, don't read me — that I only set the scene with the timid character of my opinion: yet far from me to consider renouncing rights that are indisputable! My intention is decidedly not to fight that assertion, where the criterion of certainty shines, which is a simpler way of being understood; it would involve — I express it with only a few words, but which are worth more than a thousand — not discussing it, which is more difficult to put into practice than common mortals generally prefer to believe.

'Discuss' is the grammatical word, and many people will find it unnecessary to contradict without a large dossier of evidence—which I have just set down on paper; but the thing differs notably if it is allowed to agree with its own instinct, that it employ a rare sagacity in the service of its circumspection when it formulates judgments which would, rest assured, otherwise appear of a boldness bordering the banks of bravado. To conclude this small incident, which is itself stripped of its gangue by a levity as irrecoverably deplorable as it is inevitably full of interest (which none will have failed to verify provided they have examined their most recent memories), it is good if one has their faculties in perfect balance or, even better, if the scale of idiocy doesn't take much away from the tray on which the noble and magnificent qualities of reason rest, it is said, in order to be clearer (as so far I have only been brief, which many wouldn't admit because of my lengths, which are only imaginary since they reach their target by tracking the fleeing ghosts of truth to their limits with the scalpel of analysis); if intelligence sufficiently predominates over the faults beneath whose weight it has been choked, partly out of habit, nature and education, it is good, I repeat for the second and final time, because, by force of repetition we will end up—most often this isn't wrong—in no longer understanding, to return with tail down (if it's even true that I have a tail) to the dramatic subject cemented in this verse. It is useful to drink a glass of water before undertaking the next step of my work. I prefer to drink two glasses rather than to go without. In the same way, in a hunt through the forest for a runaway slave, at a convenient moment each member of the pack hangs his rifle from a vine and they group together in the shadow of a mountain to quench their thirst and satisfy their hunger. But the halt only lasts a few seconds—the pursuit is resumed with passion and the cry of the hunt is soon sounding again. And just as oxygen is identified by the properties it possesses, without arrogance, by relighting a match to show the ignition points, in the same way we recognize the achievement of my duty by my eagerness in returning to the matter. When the women found themselves unable to keep hold of the whips, that fatigue had allowed to fall from their hands, they judiciously ended the gymnastic labour they had undertaken for about two hours and withdrew with a joy not bereft of future threats. I headed towards the man who called to me for help, his eyes glassy (weakness hindered his speech because his blood loss was so great and, although I wasn't a doctor, my opinion was that the hæmorrhage was declared in his face and abdomen), and after untying his arms I cut his hair with a pair of scissors. He told me that one evening his mother had called him into her bedroom and ordered him to undress, in order to spend the night with her in bed, and that, without waiting for any response, maternity was stripped of all her clothes while weaving the most lewd gestures before him. Which was when he had withdrawn. Furthermore, due to his constant refusals he attracted the anger of his wife, who had been lulled by the hope of reward if she could manage to encourage her husband to lend his body to the old woman's passions. The two had resolved by conspiracy to hang him from a gallows, prepared in advance, in some little-frequented district, and to leave him — exposed to all miseries and dangers — to perish insensibly. It was not without numerous and well-considered discussions, full of almost insurmountable hurdles, that they finally succeeded in guiding their choice to the subtle torture which had only been ended by the unexpected salvation of my intervention. His every expression was underlined by the liveliest signs of gratitude, and these were matched by his confidences. Because he was about to faint, I carried him into the nearest cottage and only took my leave of the ploughmen when I had left them my purse for medications for his wounds — and I made them promise that they would dispense the tokens of persistent sympathy to the unfortunate man, as they would their own son. For my part, I told them about the event and moved towards the door to continue my journey; but suddenly, after having covered a hundred metres, I mechanically retraced my path, re-entered the cottage and, addressing myself to its simple owners, I exclaimed: "No, no... don't believe that this astonishes me!" This time, I departed definitively; though the soles of my feet couldn't tread with confidence, another might not have been able to see it! The wolf no longer passes beneath the gallows raised one spring day by the joined hands of a wife and a mother, as when it had taken, with its charmed imagination, the trail of an illusory meal. When it sees on the horizon that head of black hair swaying in the wind, it overcomes its inertia and flees with remarkable speed! Should we see in this psychological phenomenon an intelligence superior to the ordinary instinct of mammals? Without anything to attest to, or even predict it, it seems to me that the animal had understood that this be crime! How could it *not* comprehend it when human beings themselves had, up until that indescribable point, rejected the empire of reason in order to let exist — instead of that dethroned queen — only fierce vengeance!

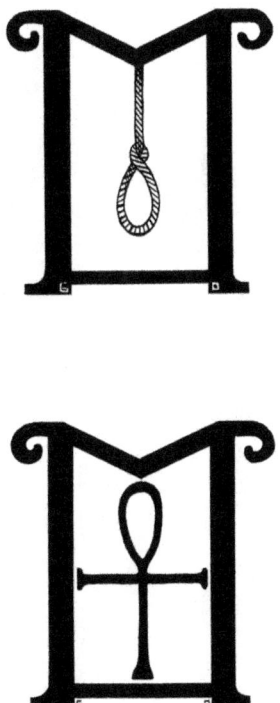

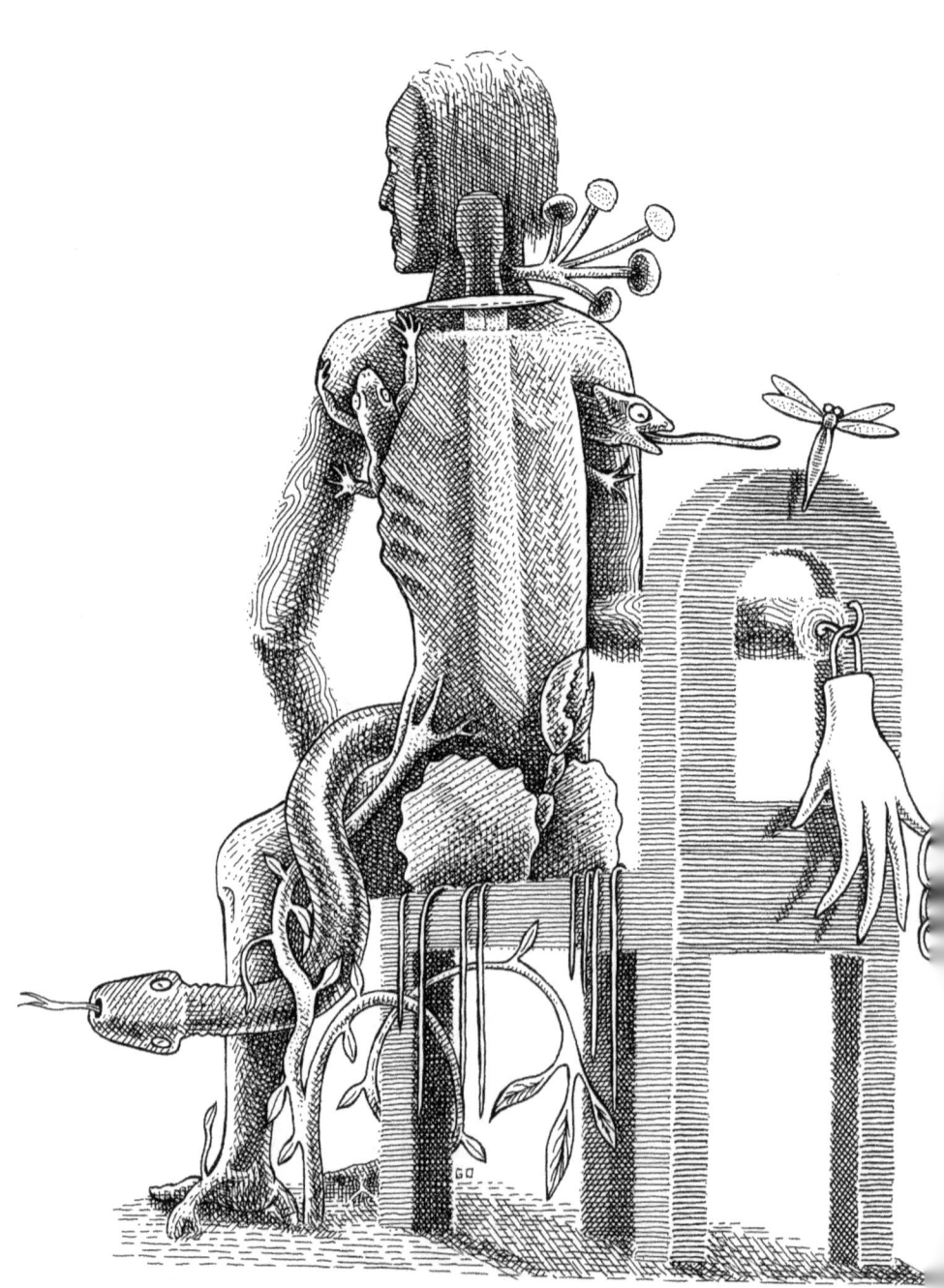

I am filthy. Lice nibble on me. Swine spew when they look at me. The scabs and sores of leprosy scale my skin, coated in yellowy pus. I don't know the water of rivers nor the dew from clouds. On my neck, like on a dung-heap, there sprouts an enormous mushroom with umbelliferous stalks. Sitting on a rough-hewn chair, I haven't moved my limbs in four centuries. My feet have taken root in the soil and form as far as my stomach a kind of living vegetation, filled with lowly parasites, which no longer derives from the plant and which is no longer fleshly. Meanwhile my heart beats. But *how* does it beat—if the putrefaction and exhalations of my corpse (I dare not say body) did not nourish it abundantly? Under my left armpit a family of toads has taken residence, and it tickles when one of them moves. Beware that it doesn't escape and come scraping the inside of your ear with its mouth: it might then be capable of entering your brain. Beneath my right armpit there is a chameleon which engages in a perpetual hunt for them in order not to die from hunger: it is necessary for all to live. But when one party completely thwarts the ruses of the other, they find nothing better than to not be shy and suck the fine grease from my sides: I am accustomed to it. A wicked viper has devoured my penis and taken its place: that infamous thing has rendered me a eunuch. Oh! If only I had been able to defend myself with my paralyzed arms; but I rather believe they have transformed into logs. At any rate, it's worth noting that blood no longer rushes there to parade its blush. Two small hedgehogs (which no longer grow) threw the insides of my testicles to a dog, which didn't refuse them: they have lodged within the carefully-washed scrotum. My anus was intercepted by a crab; encouraged by my inertia, it guards the entrance with its claws and does me much harm! Two jellyfish crossed the oceans, attracted immediately by a hope that wasn't misled. They attentively regarded the two fleshy parts that form the human bottom, and, clinging to their convex curves, they squashed them to such an extent through constant pressure that the two pieces of flesh vanished—while two monsters coming from the realm of viscosity, equal in colour, form and ferocity, remained. Do not speak of my spinal column — since it is a sword. Yes, indeed... I wasn't paying attention... your query is justified. You would like to know, wouldn't you, how it has found itself implanted vertically into my kidneys? I don't personally recall it very clearly; however if I choose to take it as a memory that may only be a dream, know that Man, when he knew that I had vowed to live with disease and paralysis until I would have conquered the Creator, walked up on tiptoes behind me but not stepping so softly that I couldn't hear him. I perceived nothing more for a brief moment. That sharp dagger buried itself up to the hilt between the shoulders of the festive bull and shook its skeleton like an earthquake. The blade sticks so firmly to my body that nobody has so far been able to extract it. Athletes, mechanics, philosophers and doctors have each tried the most diverse methods. They did not know that the evil which Man had done — could no longer be undone! I forgave the depth of their natural ignorance and saluted them with my eyelids. When you pass before me, traveller, I implore you not to address me with the least word of comfort: you will weaken my courage. Let me rekindle my tenacity at the flame of voluntary martyrdom. Be gone... lest I inspire you with any piety. Hatred is more bizarre than you think; its behaviour is inexplicable, like the broken appearance of a stick pushed into water.[9] Such as you see me, I can still make excursions up to Heaven's walls, leading a legion of assassins, and return to take up this posture in order to meditate afresh on noble plans of vengeance. Farewell — I will delay you no longer; and so that you may learn and protect yourself, reflect on the fateful lot which drove me to revolt, when perhaps I was born good! You will recount to your son what you've seen; and, taking him by the hand, make him admire the beauty of the stars and the marvels of the universe, the nest of the robin and the temples of the Lord. You will be astonished to see him so deferential to parental advice, and you will reward him with a smile. But when he learns that he is not observed, cast your eyes on him and you will see him spit out his saliva on virtue; he has deceived you, this one descended from the human race, but he will deceive you no more: you will henceforth know what he will become. To accompany the steps of your old age, O unfortunate father, prepare the ineffaceable scaffold that will behead a precocious criminal, and the pain that will show you the way leading to the tomb.

On my bedroom wall, what shadow draws the phantasmagorical projection of its shrivelled silhouette with such remarkable power? When I place this delirious and mute question on my heart, it is less for the form's majesty than the painting of reality that moderation of style behaves in this way. Whoever you are, defend yourself; because I am going to aim the sling of a terrible accusation at you: those eyes don't belong to you... whence did you procure them? One day I saw a blonde woman passing before me; she had similar eyes to yours — you snatched them from her. I see that you want to persuade with your beauty, but nobody is deceived — and me no less than any other. I'm telling you so you won't take me for a fool. A gamut of raptors, lovers of the flesh of others and defenders of practical pursuit, beautiful as the skeletons who strip the Brazilian ebonies[10] in Arkansas, flutter around your forehead like submissive and sycophantic servants. But *is* it a forehead? It's not hard to place very much doubt in believing it. It is so low that it is impossible to verify the numerically scant evidence of its equivocal existence. I don't tell you this to amuse myself. Perhaps you don't have a forehead, you who parade on the wall — like the evil symbol reflected in a fantastic dance — the feverish shaking of your lumbar vertebræ. Who scalped you then? If it is a human being — because you locked him up in a prison for twenty years and who escaped to prepare a fitting vengeance by his reprisals — he did as he had to, and I praise him; only (there *is* an only) it wasn't severe enough. Now you resemble a Native American captive, at least (as noted previously) by your expressive lack of hair. Not that it can't

grow back, since physiologists have discovered that even removed brains eventually reappear in animals; but my thought, halting at a simple observation (not devoid of an enormous voluptuousness, as far as I know), does not go, even in its boldest consequences, as far as the boundaries of a wish for your healing, and remains (on the contrary) justified, through the implementation of its more-than-suspect neutrality, to regard (or at least to hope for) as the omen of the greatest evils that which for you may only be a temporary loss of your scalp. I hope that you've understood me. And even if luck would permit you by an absurd (but sometimes certainly not reasonable) miracle to retrieve that precious skin which your enemy's religious vigilance has kept like an intoxicating souvenir of his victory, it is quite likely that, even when one has only studied the law of probabilities in terms of mathematical relations (well, it is known that analogy easily conveys application of that law into other areas of intelligence), your legitimate, though slightly exaggerated, fear of partial or total freezing won't reject the important (or even unique) occasion which presents itself, in a manner so opportune although abrupt, of protecting the various parts of your brain from exposure to the atmosphere, especially during winter, with a hairpiece which you rightly enough own since it is natural, and that you should be allowed additionally (it would be incomprehensible that you deny it) to keep it constantly on your head without running the always unpleasant risks of infringing the simplest rules of elementary propriety. You *are* heeding me well, aren't you? If you heed me further, your sadness will far from break loose from the interior of your red nostrils. But as I am extremely impartial and I don't detest you as much as I should (tell me if I am mistaken), you might, in spite of yourself, lend an ear to my discourse, as though impelled by a greater force. I am not as wicked as you: that's why your genius bows itself before mine... Indeed, I am not as wicked as you! You happen to glance at the city structure on that mountainside. And now what do I see?... All the residents are dead! I have as much pride as another, and that is more of a vice, perhaps, than having more. Well, listen … hark, if the confession of a man who remembers experiencing fifty years in the form of a shark in the submarine currents that run along the African coast interests you acutely enough to give him your attention, if not with bitterness, at least without the irreparable transgression of displaying the disgust which I arouse in you. I will not throw the mask of virtue at your feet in order to appear before your eyes just as I am, because I have never worn it (if, however, this is an excuse); and if you mark my features closely to begin with, you will recognize me as your respectful disciple in perversity, but not as your formidable rival. Since I don't compete with you for the palm of evil, I don't believe another would do so: he would first need to rival me, which isn't easy … Listen, unless you're the weak condensation of mist (you are hiding your body elsewhere and I can't locate it): one morning, when I saw a small girl who was looking over a lake to gather a pink lotus flower, she had firmed up her steps with precocious experience. She was leaning over the waters when her eyes met my gaze (from my perspective, it's true that it wasn't without premeditation). Suddenly she staggered, like the vortex spawned by the tide around a rock, her legs gave way, and—marvellous thing to observe, a phenomenon which happened with as much veracity as I'm chatting to you—she sank to the bottom of the lake: strange outcome, she no longer gathered any lotus flowers. What is she doing below?… I have not made inquiries. No doubt her will, which fell under the cloak of deliverance, engages in fierce fights against putrefaction! But you, O my master, beneath your gaze the city dwellers are suddenly exterminated, like an ant-mound squashed by the heel of an elephant. Haven't I just been witness to a demonstrator warning? See … the mountain is no longer joyful … it remains isolated like an old man. True, the houses may exist; but it isn't a paradox to claim, in a whisper, that you may not be able to say as much for those who no longer exist there. The emanations of the corpses are already reaching me. Don't you smell them? Observe those birds of prey waiting for us to leave so they can begin this giant feast;

an endless cloud comes from the four corners of the horizon. Alas! They had already arrived, since I saw their rapacious wings describe above you the monument of spirals, as if to incite you to hasten the crime. Doesn't your sense of smell pick up the least whiff, then? The impostor isn't something else... Your olfactory nerves are finally disturbed by the perception of aromatic atoms: these rise from the shattered city, although I don't need to tell you that... I would like to embrace your feet, but my arms only entwine a transparent vapor. Let us seek this elusive body that my eyes nevertheless perceive: for my part it deserves the most numerous tokens of genuine admiration. The ghost mocks me: it helps me seek its actual body. If I motion to it to remain where it is, behold — it sends the same gesture back to me... The secret is discovered; but, to be honest, this isn't to my greatest satisfaction. All is explained, the big details as well as the small; these aren't worth recalling to mind — for example, the tearing out of the blonde woman's eyes: that is almost nothing!... Did I not recall, then, that I *also* had been scalped, even if it had only been for five years (the exact amount of time fails me) that I had locked up a human being in prison in order to witness the spectacle of his sufferings—because he had rightly denied me a friendship not worthy of beings such as myself? Since I pretend to be unaware that my gaze can strike death, even on planets revolving in space, whoever pretends that I don't possess the faculty of remembrance won't be wrong. What remains for me to do is to break this mirror into splinters with the aid of a rock... This isn't the first time that the nightmare of temporary memory loss made its home in my imagination—when, by the inflexible laws of optics, I happen to be placed before the ignorance of my own image!

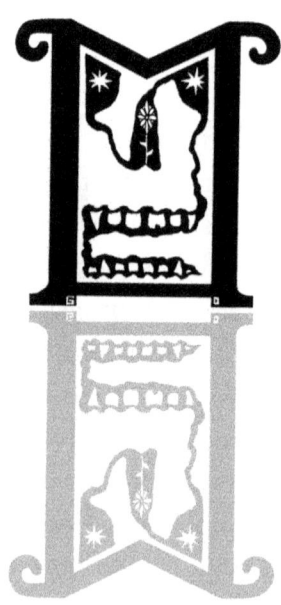

I had fallen asleep on the cliff. The one who had pursued the ostrich across the desert for a day, without being able to reach it, had not had time to eat or sleep. If it is he who reads me, he can guess, at a pinch, what slumber weighed down on me. Indeed, when the tempest pushes a ship with the palm of its hand vertically down to the bottom of the ocean; if, on the life-raft, all that remains of the entire crew is but a single man, broken by all kinds of fatigue and privations; if the wave tosses him like flotsam for hours longer than the life of Man; and if a frigate, which later criss-crosses these ocean areas desolate from hull breach, perceives the unfortunate one who sails his scrawny carcass over the sea and brings him assistance which almost comes too late—I believe that this castaway would even better guess to what degree the drowsiness of my senses was carried. Mesmerism and chloroform, when they go to the trouble, are likewise known to sometimes cause these lethargic catalepsies. They bear no resemblance to death: it would be an absolute lie to say so. But let's get straight to the dream so that the impatient ones, hungry for these kinds of lectures, don't roar like a pod of macrocephalic sperm whales fighting amongst themselves for a pregnant female. I dreamed that I had entered the body of a pig, that it wasn't easy to leave it, and that I rolled my hide in the muddiest quagmires. Was this as a reward? Aim of my desires—I no longer belonged to humanity! *I* understood the interpretation in this way and I experienced a most profound joy. Meanwhile I was searching actively for which virtuous act I'd perpetrated in order to merit this badge of honour on the part of Providence. Now that I reviewed in my memory the different phases of that dreadful flattening of granite against belly, during which the tide, without my noticing, had twice passed over that irreducible mix of dead matter and living flesh, it's perhaps not useless to proclaim that this humiliation was probably only a punishment inflicted upon me by divine Justice. But who knows His intimate needs or the cause of His pestilential joys? The metamorphosis never appeared to my eyes other than as the lofty and magnanimous reverberation of good fortune

which I had waited ages for. It had finally come—on the day when I was a pig! I tested my teeth on the bark of trees; I contemplated my snout with delight. The least bit of divinity no longer remained: I was able to raise my soul up to the extreme height of this unspeakable voluptuousness. Hear me, then, and don't blush—inexhaustible caricatures of beauty who take the laughable brayings of your thoroughly despicable souls seriously, and who don't understand why the Omnipotent, in a rare moment of brilliant buffoonery—which certainly would not surpass the usual grand laws of the grotesque—one day took wonderful pleasure in populating a planet with singular and microscopic beings, which He called *humans*, and whose substance resembled that of vermillion coral. Certainly you have cause to blush, bones and fat, but listen to me. I don't call upon your intelligence; you might make it reject the blood of the horror you witness: forget it and stay true to yourselves... There, more constraint. When I wanted to kill, I would kill; that same thing frequently occurred to me, and nobody would hinder me. The human laws still pursued me with their wrath even though I didn't attack the race which I had abandoned so calmly; but my conscience never reproached me. During the day I would fight with my new fellow-creatures, and the soil was strewn with numerous layers of clotted blood. I was the strongest and I carried off all the victories. My body was covered in smarting wounds; I appeared not to heed it. The earthly animals stayed away from me and I remained alone in my resplendent grandeur. Imagine my surprise, when—after swimming across a river, so as to distance myself from the countries that my rage had depopulated and to reach other lands in order to establish my habits of murder and carnage there—I tried to walk on that flowery river bank! My trotters were paralyzed; no movement whatsoever came to betray the reality of that forced immobility. Amidst supernatural efforts to resume my journey, it was then that I awoke, and that I sensed I had become a man once more. Providence thus made me comprehend, in a not inexplicable way, that even in a dream it didn't wish my sublime projects to be accomplished. Returning to my original form was so terribly painful that I still weep during the nights. My sheets are constantly moist as if they had been dragged through water, and I change them every day. If you don't believe it, come and see me; you will check through your own experiment, not the probability, but rather the very truth of my assertion. How many times since that night passed on a cliff under the stars have I not mixed with drifts of swine in order to recover, as a right, my destroyed metamorphosis! It is time to quit these glorious memories, which leave only the wan milky way of undying regrets in their wake.

It isn't impossible to witness abnormal deviation in the latent or visible working of the laws of Nature. Actually, if each individual were to make the ingenious effort to question the different phases of their life (without forgetting a single thing, because it may perhaps be that thing which would be destined to provide the proof of what I put forward), they would remember (with positive astonishment that would be comical in any other circumstances) that on a certain day (to speak of objective things first) they had witnessed some phenomenon which seemed to exceed — and positively *did* exceed — known notions provided by observation and experience — like, for example, showers of toads, the magical spectacle of which must not have been initially understood by experts. And that, on another day (to speak secondly and at last of subjective things instead), their soul had presented to the investigative eye of psychology — I won't go so far as to say a mental aberration (which would, however, be no less curious;

quite the opposite, it would be more so), but at least to make it not quite so difficult for certain cold people who might never excuse the flagrant utterances of my hyperbole—an unusual state, often quite serious, which shows that the limit granted imagination by commonsense is sometimes (despite the ephemeral agreement concluded between these two powers) sadly exceeded by the energetic pressure of the will, but also most of the time by the absence of its effective collaboration: let us give some examples to support this, from which it isn't hard to appreciate fortuity—*if*, however, we take attentive moderation for a partner. I propose two examples: fits of rage and illnesses of pride. I warn the one who reads me that he should be wary not to form a vague idea, and later a strong misunderstanding, of the beauties that I pluck from literature in the extremely rapid development of my phrases. Alas! I would like to evolve my reasonings and my comparisons slowly and with much magnificence (but who has the time?) so that each reader might better grasp at least my amazement, if not my fear, when, on a summer evening as the sun seemed to sink into the horizon I saw swimming on the sea a human being with sturdy muscles, with large duck-feet placed at the ends of his legs and arms, bearing a dorsal fin (as relatively long and slender as that of dolphins), and whom many shoals of fish (I saw in that procession, amongst other dwellers, the electric ray, the Northern bottlenose whale[11] and the scorpion-fish[12]) were following with obvious signs of the greatest admiration. Sometimes he would dive and his viscous body would reappear almost immediately two hundred metres away. Porpoises, who in my opinion haven't filched their reputation as good swimmers, could barely keep up with this new species of amphibian. I don't believe that the reader has reason to repent if he lends to my narrative less the harmful obstacle of stupid credulity than the supreme service of a profound confidence which legally discusses, with hidden sympathy, the poetic mysteries, too few in his opinion, that I endeavour to reveal to him whenever the opportunity presents itself, as it has unexpectedly appeared today, intimately suffused by the ton-

ic scents of aquatic plants that the fresh breeze carries into this stanza which contains a monster who has appropriated the distinctive marks of the palmipeds. Who speaks here of appropriation? How well we know that Man, with his multifarious and complex nature, isn't ignorant of the methods of pushing the envelope[13] further: he lives in water like the sea-horse, through the upper layers of the air like the osprey, and beneath the earth like the mole, the woodlouse, and the sublimity of the earthworm. Such is, in its more or less concise (but more rather than less) form, the exact criterion of extremely fortifying consolation that I was trying to produce in my mind when I wondered whether the human being whom I perceived swimming with four limbs far away on the surface of the waves, as the most superb cormorant would never have done, hadn't perhaps acquired the modification to the extremities of his arms and legs as an expiatory punishment for some unknown crime. I didn't need to worry my head preparing melancholy pills of pity in advance, because I didn't know that this man, whose arms alternately struck the bitter wave while his legs, with a force similar to that possessed by the spiral tusks of the narwhal, caused recoil from the watery layers, had not more willfully taken on these extraordinary forms—which had been imposed upon him as punishment. From what I later learned, here is the simple truth: the extension of existence in that liquid element had imperceptibly brought about, in the human being who had exiled himself from the rocky mainlands, the important (but not essential changes) that I had observed in the object, that a somewhat confused look had made me take, from the initial moments of its appearance (through an unacceptable thoughtlessness whose deviations begat so distressing a feeling that psychologists and lovers of prudence will easily understand), for a strangely-shaped fish not yet described in the classifications of naturalists—but maybe in their posthumous works, although I hadn't the excusable pretentiousness of leaning towards that last supposition imagined in very hypothetical circumstances. Indeed, this amphibian (since *there* it is amphibious, unless one can claim to the contrary) was, apart from the fish and whales, only visible to myself; because I had perceived some peasants, who had halted to look at my face so troubled by this supernatural phenomenon, and who sought vainly to explain to themselves why my eyes were staring with persistence (which appeared invincible, and which really wasn't) at a point on the ocean where *they* could only distinguish a considerable and limited number of shoals of fish of all species, and they distended the openings of their pompous mouths perhaps as much as a baleen whale.[14] "This made them smile, but not grow pale like me," they said in their picturesque language; "and they weren't beastly enough to note that I wasn't exactly observing the rustic movements of the fish, but that my view was being carried a lot further forward." In such a way that, in my case, automatically averting my eyes from the remarkable spread of those powerful mouths, I reflected that at least there didn't exist in the entire universe a pelican as large as a mountain or at least as a promontory (admire, I beseech you, the refinement of the limitation that doesn't lose an inch of ground), not any raptor's beak nor wild animal's jaws which could ever surpass, or even equal, any of these gaping (but too lugubrious) craters. And, meanwhile, even though I reserve a lot of sympathetic use of metaphor (this rhetorical figure does many more good turns to human aspirations towards the infinite than those — which are imbued with prejudices or false ideas, which are the same thing — trying to imagine it normally), it isn't less true that the laughing mouths of these peasants still remained broad enough to swallow three sperm whales. Let's truncate our thinking more, let's be serious, and let's be content with three small newborn elephants. With a single arm-stroke the amphibian left behind it a kilometre of frothy wake. During the very brief moment when the outstretched arm remained suspended forward in the air before it once more descended, its spread fingers, joined by means of a skinfold with the form of a membrane, seemed to dart towards the far reaches of space to seize the stars. Standing on the rock, I used my hands like a megaphone and I cried, while crabs and crayfish fled into the obscurity of the most hidden crevices: "O you, whose swimming beats the flight of the frigate-bird's long wings, if you still understand the significance of the great shouts that humanity throws forcefully as true expression of its intimate thought, deign to halt your rapid movement a moment and tell me briefly the phases of your true story. But I warn you that you don't need to speak to me if your daring intention is to arouse in me the friendship and veneration that I felt for you as soon as I first saw you accomplishing your indomitable and rectilinear pilgrimage with the grace and power of a shark." A sigh—which froze my bones and made the rock on which I rested the soles of my feet wobble (unless it was only I who wobbled from the rough penetration of the loud waves which brought such a despairing cry to my ear)—was heard as far as the bowels of the earth: the fish dove beneath the waves with the clamor of an avalanche. The amphibian dared not approach the shore too closely; but when he was certain that his voice would reach my eardrums distinctly, he lessened the movement of his webbed limbs in order to hold his seaweed-covered bust above the booming waves. I saw him bow his forehead as though to invoke the roaming mob of memories with a formal command. I dared not interrupt him during this saintly archæological occupation: submerged in the past, he resembled a reef. He finally spoke in these terms: "The centipede has no lack of enemies; the fantastic beauty of its multitudinous legs, instead of attracting the sympathy of animals, is to them perhaps only the powerful catalyst for a jealous irritation. And I wouldn't be surprised to learn that this insect is exposed to the most intense hatred. I will hide my birthplace from you, which doesn't matter in my narrative: but the shame which is reflected on my family *does* matter to my duty. After a year of waiting, my father and mother (may God pardon them!) had seen Heaven fulfill their wishes: twins—my brother and I—were hatched into the light.[15] All the more reason to love each other. It was not to be as I say. Because I was the more beautiful of the two, and the more intelligent, my brother hated me and didn't trou-

ble to hide his feelings: that's why my father and mother would reflect the greater part of their love onto me, while by my sincere and constant love I tried to appease a soul who had no right to revolt against the one who had been drawn from the same flesh. So, my brother knew no more limits to his fury and he made me vanish from the heart of our common parents by means of the most unlikely slanders. For fifteen years I lived inside a dungeon with larvæ and dirty water as my sole nourishment. I won't tell you in detail of the outrageous torments I underwent in that long, unfair isolation. Occasionally, at some moment of the day, one of the three executioners would (in turn) enter abruptly, equipped with pliers, pincers and various instruments of torture. The cries that these torments tore from me left them unwavering: my abundant blood-loss made them smile. O my brother, I have forgiven you—you, the primary cause of all my woes! May it be that blind rage can finally open its own eyes! I've made many reflections in my eternal prison. You may guess what became of my hate for humanity. Progressive atrophy and the loneliness of body and soul still hadn't made me lose all my reason to the point of harbouring resentment against those whom I hadn't ceased to love: a triple yoke whose slave I was. By subterfuge I managed to regain my freedom! Disgusted by the continental dwellers who, even though they called themselves my fellow-men, didn't seem to resemble me much at all (if they found that I did resemble them, why would they do me harm?), I headed towards the pebbles of the beach, firmly resolved to kill myself if indeed the ocean would offer me earlier recollections of a life fatally lived. Will you believe your own eyes? Since the day when I fled the paternal home, I didn't complain as much as you'd think about inhabiting the sea and its crystal grottoes. As you can see, Providence gave me in part the body of a swan. I live in peace with the fish and they obtain for me the nourishment I require, as though I were their monarch. I'll give a particular whistle, providing it doesn't upset you, and you'll see how they reappear." It transpired as he predicted. He resumed his regal swimming, surrounded by his procession of subjects. And although after a few seconds he had completely vanished from my eyes, with a telescope I could still distinguish him at the horizon's farthest limits. He swam with one hand and with the other he was wiping his eyes, which had become terribly bloodshot from having come close to *terra firma*. He had acted in this way to please me. I threw the revelatory instrument against the peak of the escarpment; it rebounded from rock to rock and, its fragments scattered, it was taken by the waves: such was the final demonstration and ultimate farewell, by which, as in a dream, I bowed before a noble and unfortunate intelligence! Yet all was real in what had passed during that summer evening.

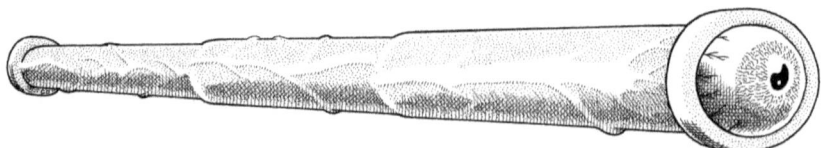

Every night, immersing the spread of my wings in my dying memory, I would remember Falmer... every night. His blond hair, his oval face, his majestic features were still imprinted on my imagination, indelibly... especially his blond hair. So, keep away, keep away, that bald head polished like a tortoise shell. He was fourteen, and I was just a year older. May that lugubrious voice be silent. Why does it come to denounce me? But it is *I* who speaks. My own tongue serves to express my thoughts; I notice *my* lips moving and that it is *I* who speaks. And it is *I* who, recounting a story of my youth and feeling remorse entering my heart... it is *I*, unless I am wrong... it is *I* who speaks. I was only a year older. To whom, therefore, do I allude? It is a friend I had in times past, I believe. Yes, of course, I've already said his name... I don't want to spell out those six letters again, no, never. It is pointless to repeat that I was a year older. Who knows it? Let us repeat it, then, but with a painful murmur: I was only a year older. Even then the superiority of my physical strength was rather an incentive to support, across life's rocky path, the one who had given himself to me, than to mistreat a visibly weaker being. However, I actually believe he was weaker... Even then. It is a friend I had in past times, I believe. The pre-eminence of my physical strength... every night... Above all, his blond hair. More than one human being exists who has seen bald heads: old age, illness, grief (the three together or considered separately) satisfactorily explain this negative phenomenon. Such, at least, is the answer that a scholar would offer me if I questioned it. Old age, illness, grief. But I do know (*I* am a scholar as well) that one day, because he had stopped my hand at the moment when I raised my dagger to pierce the breast of a woman, I seized him by the hair with an arm of iron and sent him spinning through the air with such speed that his hair remained in my hand, and his body, thrown by centrifugal force, went banging against the trunk of an oak tree... I know that one day his hair remained in my hand. I am a scholar also. Yes, indeed, I have already said his name. I know that one day I perpetrated a dastardly act, while his body was thrown by centrifugal force. He was fourteen. When I run through the fields in an attack of madness, taking, pressed to my heart, a blood-stained thing I had long kept like a venerated relic, the small children who pursue me... the small children and old women who pursue me with rock blows utter these awful groans: "There is Falmer's hair." So, keep away, keep away, that bald head polished like the turtle's carapace. A bloody thing. But it is *I* who speaks. His oval face, his majestic features. Now I actually believe he was weaker. Old women and little children. Now I actually believe... what did I want to say?... now I actually believe that he was weaker. With an arm of iron. That shock, did that shock kill him? Were his bones broken against the tree... irreparably? Did it kill him, this shock caused by an athlete's vigour? Did he retain life, even though his bones were irreparably broken... irreparably? Did this shock kill him? I fear knowing what my closed eyes did not witness. Actually... Above all, his blond hair. Indeed, I fled far away with a conscience henceforth implacable. Every night. When a young man, aspiring to glory, leans over his work-table on the fifth floor at midnight's silent hour, he hears an unidentifiable rustling, he turns his head—weighed down by meditation and dusty manuscripts—in all directions; but not a single amazed clue reveals to him the cause of what he hears so slightly, even though he does nevertheless hear it. He perceives at last that the smoke from his candle, floating through the ambient air towards the ceiling, causes almost imperceptible vibrations in a leaf of paper hanging by a nail fixed to the wall. On the fifth floor. As the young man who aspires to glory hears a rustling he can't place, likewise I hear a melodious voice which utters in my ear: "Maldoror!" But before resolving his misapprehension, he thought he heard the wings of a mosquito... leaning over his work-table. Nevertheless, I'm not dreaming; what does it matter if I am stretched out on my bed of satin? I calmly make the perspicacious remark that I have eyes wide open, even though it is the hour of pink dominoes and masqued balls. Never... oh! never! had a mortal voice uttered these seraphic accents, while pronouncing with such distressing elegance the syllables of my name! The wings of a mosquito... How benevolent his voice is. Am I then forgiven? His body went banging against the trunk of an oak tree... "Maldoror!"

END OF THE FOURTH DIRGE

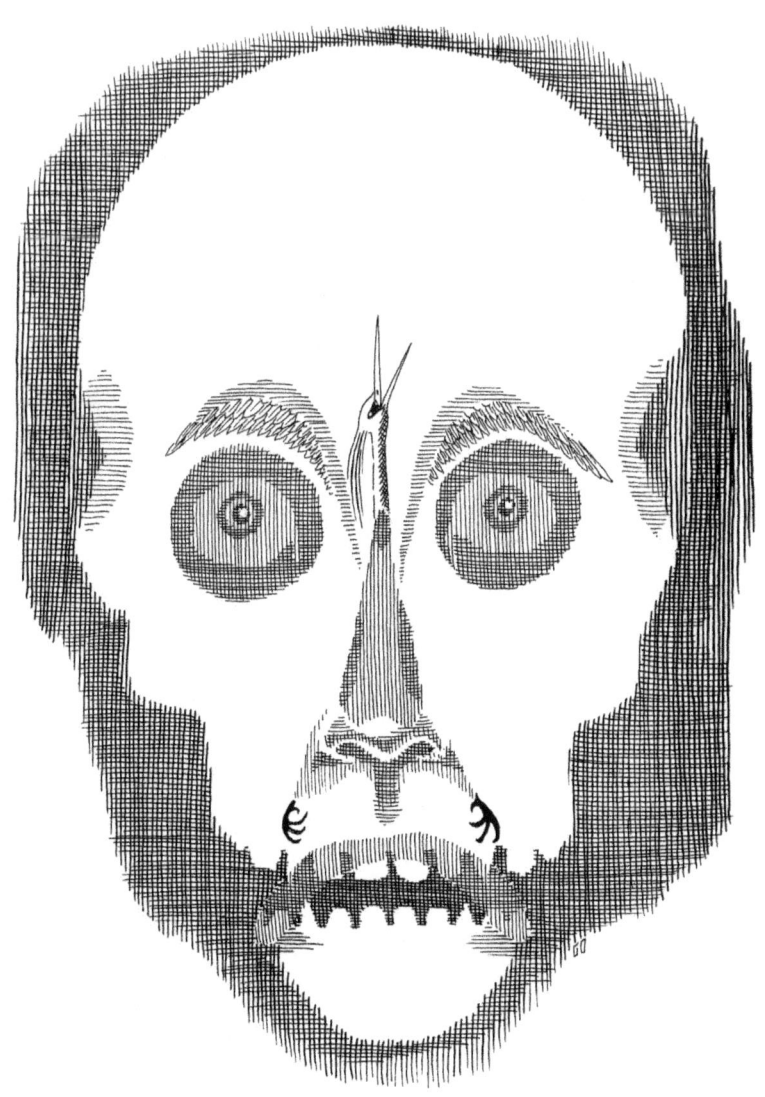

Fifth Dirge

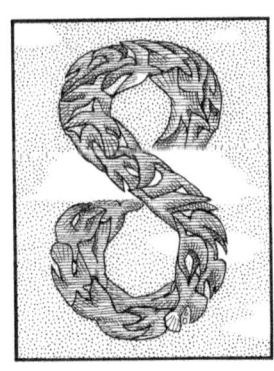

URELY THE READER won't get angry with me if my prose doesn't have the good fortune to appeal to him. You maintain that my ideas are at least singular. What you say there, respectable man, is the truth—but a partial truth. Well, what abundant source of errors and misapprehensions *isn't* every partial truth! Murmurations[16] of starlings have a method of flying which is their own and which seems to submit to a uniform and regular tactic such as a regimented platoon would, obeying precisely the voice of a single leader. It is the voice of instinct that starlings obey, and their instinct always induces them to draw nearer to the centre of the platoon while the speed of their flight takes them unceasingly beyond; so that this multitude of birds is thus reunited through a communal tendency around the same magnetic point, coming and going constantly, circulating and crossing in all directions, forming a kind of strongly agitated whirlwind whose entire mass, without following a given direction, appears to have a general movement of evolution out of itself resulting from the particular motions of circulation peculiar to each of its parts, and in which the centre, perpetually stretching to open out but incessantly pressed and repelled by the opposing force of the surrounding lines which weigh on it, is continually tighter than any of these lines, of which there are ever more that approach the centre. Despite this singular method of whirling the starlings don't cut through the surrounding air any less, with uncommon speed, and they gain precious ground appreciably with every second for the sake of the end of their fatigues and the objective of their peregrination. You yourself should pay no attention to the bizarre manner in which I chant each of these stanzas. But rest assured that the fundamental accents of poetry don't retain their intrinsic law over my mind any less. Let's not generalize from exceptional facts, I require nothing better: meanwhile my character is within the scheme of possible things. Undoubtedly, between the two extreme limits of your literature as you understand it—and of mine—there is an infinity of intermediaries and it would be easy to magnify the divisions; but that would be useless, and there is a danger of attributing something narrow and false to an eminently philosophical concept which would cease to be rational since it is no longer understood as it was imagined—that is to say, fully. You know how to combine enthusiasm and internal coolness, observant with a concentrated temper; indeed, *I* find you perfect... And you don't wish to comprehend me! If you are not in good health, follow my advice (it's the best that I have to offer you) and go for a walk in the countryside. Sad compensation, don't you say? When you've taken the air, come back and see me: your reason will be more rested. Weep no more; I didn't wish you any harm. Is it not it true, my friend, that to a certain extent your sympathy has been won over by my dirges? Now, what prevents you from passing through the other degrees? The boundary between your taste and mine is invisible; you will never be able to fathom it: proof that this boundary itself doesn't exist. Reflect therefore (I only touch on the question lightly here) that it would not be impossible for you to have signed a treaty with stubbornness, that agreeable mule's daughter, a source so rich in intolerance. I wouldn't reproach you in this way if I didn't know you weren't a fool. It's inadvisable that you encrust yourself in the cartilaginous carapace of an axiom that you believe unshakable. There are also other axioms that are unshakable, and which move parallel to yours. If you have a particular fancy for caramel (admirable farce of Nature), nobody would consider it a crime; but those whose intellect, more active and capable of greater things, prefers pepper and arsenic, have good reasons for behaving that way, without intending to impose their peaceful domination on those who tremble with fear before a shrew or the eloquent expression on the facets of a cube. I speak from experience, not to come here to play the role of provocateur. And just as rotifers and tardigrades [17] can be heated to a temperature close to boiling-point without necessarily losing their vitality, it will be the same for *you* if you know how to assimilate, with caution, the oozing acrid serosity slowly excreted from the irritation caused by my fascinating lucubrations. Eh what! have they not managed to graft onto a live rat's back the tail detached from another rat's body? Then try in the same way to convey into your imagination the various modifications of my cadaverous reason. But be cautious. At the hour I write, some new shudders run through the intellectual atmosphere: it's only a question of having the courage to look them in the face. Why do you grimace so? And you even accompany it with a gesture one could only mimic after a lengthy apprenticeship. Trust that habit is imperative in everything; and since the instinctive repulsion declared from the first pages has notably diminished in depth — in inverse proportion to the reader's concentration, like a boil one lances — it must be hoped, even though your head may still be upset, that your recovery will shortly and surely enter its final phase. To my mind you are undoubtedly already sailing into full convalescence; nevertheless your face has remained quite gaunt, alas! But... take heart! There is unusual spirit in you, I like you, and I don't despair of your complete salvation provided you consume some medications; these will only quicken the fading of the last symptoms of the illness. As astringent and tonic nourishment, you will first rip off your mother's arms (if she is still alive), you will carve them up into small pieces, and then you will eat them, in a single day, without any feature of your face betraying your emotion. If your mother be too elderly, choose another surgical subject, younger and fresher, onto which the raspatory will grip, and whose tarsal bones, when it walks, easily assume a fulcrum for the tilting-board: your sister, for example. I cannot refrain from pitying her fate, and I am not among those in whom a chilling enthusiasm only affects kindness. You and I, we will shed for her, for this loved virgin (but I haven't any proof to establish that she might be a virgin), two unforced tears, two tears of lead. That will be all. The most soothing potion I recommend to you is a basin full of gonorrheal pus (with nuclei) in which one has first dissolved a hairy ovarian cyst, a follicular chancre, an inflamed prepuce pulled back behind the glans by paraphimosis, and three red slugs. If you follow my prescriptions, my poetry will receive you with open arms like a louse resects a hair follicle with its kisses.

I saw before me an object standing on a mound. I couldn't clearly distinguish its head, but I already guessed that it wasn't a normal shape without, nevertheless, specifying the exact proportion of its contours. I dared not approach that motionless column, and even if I had had at my disposal the ambulatory legs (I don't even speak of those that serve for grasping and for the chewing of food) of more than three thousand crabs, I would still have remained in the same place—if only an event, trivial in itself, hadn't taken a heavy toll on my curiosity, which was breaching its banks. A scarab beetle—rolling along the ground, with its mandibles and antennæ, a ball whose principle elements comprised excrement—was advancing rapidly towards the mound indicated, striving to prove convincingly that its will had taken it in that direction. This articulated animal wasn't much bigger than a cow! If anyone doubts what I say, they may come to me and I will satisfy the most incredulous with the testimony of good witnesses. I followed it at a distance, obviously intrigued. What would it do with that big black ball? O reader, you who boasts endlessly of your perspicacity (and not wrongly), would *you* be able to tell me? But I don't want to submit your known passion for mysteries to a tough test. Let it suffice you to know that the softest penalty I can impose on you is to make you observe once more whether this mystery will only be revealed to you (it will be revealed to you) later, at the end of your life, when you will break into philosophical discussions, along with the final agony, beside your bolster... and perhaps even at the end of this stanza. The scarab beetle arrived at the base of the mound. I had fallen into step with its tracks and I was still a fair distance from the scene; because like skuas—birds anxious as if they were always starving, content in the seas bathing the two poles and only advancing inadvertently into temperate zones—in the same way *I* wasn't calm, and I carried my legs forward with much slowness. But what then was the corporeal substance towards which I was moving? I know that the Pelecaniformes order comprises four distinct *genera*: the booby, the pelican, the cormorant, and the frigate-bird.[18] The greyish form that appeared to me wasn't a booby. The plastic block I perceived wasn't a frigate-bird. The crystallized flesh I observed wasn't a cormorant. I saw him now, the man with the brain devoid of annular protuberance! I vaguely searched in the recesses of my memory, in what hot or cold country I had already observed a beak so very long, large, convex and vaulted, with a marked ridge, claw-like,[19] swollen and quite hooked at its end; those jagged, straight edges; that lower jaw with separate branches near its tip; that space filled with a membranous skin; that broad pouch, yellowish and sac-like, occupying the whole throat and able to swell out considerably: and those very narrow longitudinal nostrils, almost imperceptible,

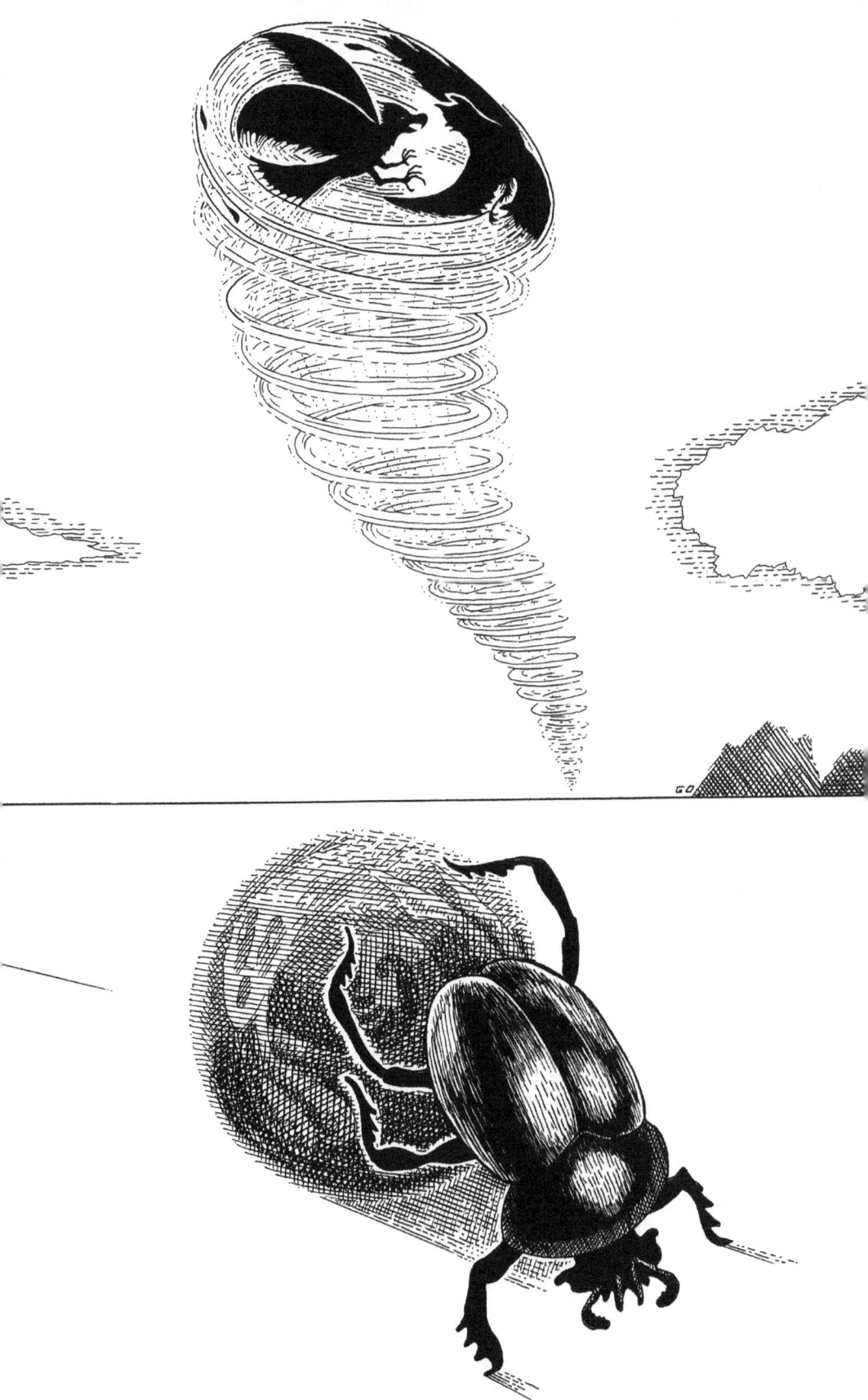

creased into a basal furrow! If this living being, with basic pulmonary breathing and a body garnished with hair, had been wholly bird to the soles of its feet and not just up to its shoulders, it wouldn't then have been so difficult to recognize it: a very easy thing to do, as you yourself see. Only I would excuse myself this time; for the clarity of my demonstration I'd need one of these birds to be placed on my work-table, even if it were simply to be stuffed. Well now, I'm not wealthy enough to acquire it. Following a former theory step by step, I would have immediately designated its true nature and found a place within the framework of natural history for this being whose nobility I admired in its pathological pose. With what satisfaction at not being absolutely ignorant of the secrets of its dual organism, and with what eagerness to know more, did I contemplate it in its enduring metamorphosis! Although it didn't have a human face, it appeared as fair to me as the two long tentacular filaments of an insect; or, instead, as a precipitous entombment; or more, as the law of regeneration of mutilated organs; and, above all, as an eminently putrescible fluid! But not paying any attention to what was passing in the surroundings, the stranger kept looking straight ahead—with the head of a pelican! I'll carry on to the end of this story another day. Nevertheless I will continue my narrative with gloomy eagerness, because if, from your point of view, you are longing to know where my imagination is heading (would to Heaven that it *was* indeed then only my imagination!), from my point of view I've determined to finish what I had to say to you in one go (and not in two!), although nobody has the right meanwhile to accuse me of lacking courage. But when we are faced with similar circumstances, more than one person feels their heart-beats throbbing against the palm of their hand. A coaster master just died, almost unknown, in a small Brittany port—an old sailor who was the hero of a terrible tale. He was then a career captain and was sailing for a Saint-Malo ship-owner. Now, after an absence of thirteen months, he had arrived at the conjugal home just as his wife, still bed-ridden, happened to give him an heir to whom he conceded no right of acknowledgement. The captain betrayed none of his surprise and anger; he coldly requested his wife to dress and to accompany him for a stroll on the city ramparts. It was January. The ramparts of Saint-Malo are high, and when the north wind blows the more intrepid back off. The miserable woman obeyed, quiet and resigned; upon returning she was delirious. She died in the night. But this was only a woman. While I, being a man, don't know if I would have retained sufficient self-control so that my facial muscles remained still while facing a drama no less great! Once the scarab beetle had arrived at the base of the mound, the man raised his arms towards the west (a Bearded vulture and a Great horned owl[20] were, in fact, engaged in ærial battle in that direction), wiped from his beak a long tear which displayed a spectrum of brilliant chromatism,[21] and said to the scarab beetle: "Miserable ball! Haven't you rolled it long enough? Your wrath hasn't been appeased yet—and already this woman, whose legs and arms you had bound with pearl necklaces to make an amorphous polyhedron in order to drag her with your tarsi across valleys and paths and over thorns and rocks (let me approach to see if indeed it *is* still her!), has seen her bones bored with wounds, her limbs, polished by the mechanical law of rotary friction, merge together in the unity of coagulation, and her body exhibits, instead of its original lines and natural curves, the plain semblance of just an homogenous whole that only very much looks like, through the confusion of its various broken elements, the mass of a sphere! She has long been deceased; leave these remains to the earth and guard against increasing the fury which consumes you in irreversible proportions: it is no longer Justice—because egotism, hidden in the skin of your forehead, slowly raises the sheet that covers it, like a ghost." The Bearded vulture and the Great horned owl, borne insensibly by the ups and downs of their battle, had approached us. The scarab beetle trembled before these unexpected words, and what on another occasion would have been a minor movement was this time a hallmark of unbridled fury—because it rubbed its hind legs fearsomely against the edge of its wing-cases, creating a shrill sound: "Who are *you* then, cowardly being? It seems that you've forgotten certain weird developments of the past; you don't keep them in your memory, my brother. This woman let us down, one after the other. You first, me second. It seems to me that this injury should not (must not!) vanish from memory so easily. So easily! *Your* magnanimous nature allows you to forgive. But do you know, despite the abnormal arrangement of atoms of this woman, reduced to a kneaded pulp (it isn't now a question of knowing if one might believe, on initial investigation, that this body had been augmented by a marked amount of density by the mesh of two powerful wheels rather than by the effects of my lively passion), whether she does still live? Shut up and let me avenge myself." It continued its merry-go-round and moved away, pushing the ball before it. When it had distanced itself, the pelican exclaimed: "This woman, through her magical power, has given me a palmiped's head and transformed my brother into a scarab beetle: perhaps she deserves even worst treatments than those I have just detailed." And I—who was uncertain that I wasn't dreaming, guessing from what I had heard the nature of the hostile relations which united the Bearded vulture and the Great horned owl in bloody combat above me—I threw back my head like a hood in order to give the play of my lungs likely ease and elasticity, and raising my eyes skyward I cried out to them: "Hey, you two, end your discord. You are both right, because she had pledged her love to each; consequently she has deceived you both. But you aren't the only ones. Furthermore she has stripped you of your human form, making a cruel game of your most sacred pains. And you would scruple to believe me! Besides, she is dead—and the scarab beetle has subjected her to a punishment of indelible impression, despite the mercy of the first one betrayed." At these words they ceased their quarrel and no longer tore out feathers nor scraps of flesh: they were right to act in this way. The Great horned owl (as beautiful as a dissertation on the curve that a dog describes while running after its master) dove into the crevices of a ruined convent. The

Bearded vulture (as beautiful as the law of cessation of development of the chest among adults whose propensity to growth isn't proportional to the amount of molecules incorporated within their organism) was lost in the lofty layers of the atmosphere. The pelican, whose generous pardon had left quite an impression on me because I didn't consider it natural, resumed the majestic impassivity of a lighthouse on its mound, always looking ahead as if to warn human navigators to pay heed to its example, and to protect their fate from the love of dark sorceresses. The scarab beetle (as beautiful as the trembling of the hands from alcoholism) was disappearing over the horizon. Four more existences that we can scratch from the book of life. I found myself so moved facing this fourfold misfortune that I tore out an entire muscle from my left arm, because I no longer knew what I was doing. And here's me thinking they were excremental materials. I'm clearly a bally brute.

The intermittent destruction of human faculties: whatever your thoughts would tend to assume, these aren't just words. At least, these aren't just words like any others. May he raise his hand, the one who might believe he carries out a fair deed by begging some executioner to flay him alive. May he raise his head, with the pleasure of smiling, the one who might voluntarily offer his chest to the bullets of death. My eyes will look for signs of scars; my ten digits will focus their complete attention in carefully palpating the flesh of this eccentric; I will confirm that brain splatters have splashed upon the satin of my brow. Surely such a man, a lover of such martyrdom, does not exist in the entire universe? I don't know what laughter is, it's true, never having experienced it personally. Nevertheless, wouldn't it be sheer folly to maintain that my lips wouldn't widen if it allowed me to see the one who might claim that this man then *does* exist somewhere? What nobody would wish for their own life has befallen me in unequal measure. It's not that my body would swim in the lake of grief;

it would pass then. But the spirit dries out from concentrated and continuously-strained reflection; it croaks like frogs in a swamp when a flamboyance of famished flamingos and a siege of hungry herons are about to descend on the shore-line reeds. Happy is he who slumbers peacefully in a bed of feathers, plucked from the eider's breast, heedless that he betrays himself. It's been more than thirty years since I've slept. Since the unspeakable day of my birth I've vowed an uncompromising hatred for soporific boards. It is *I* who wanted it; let nobody be accused. Swiftly, let's shed aborted suspicion. Do you perceive this pale crown on my forehead? The one who braided it with her skinny fingers was Tenacity. As long as a remainder of scorching sap flows within my bones, like a torrent of molten metal, I simply won't sleep. Every night I compel my livid eye to gaze at the stars through my window-panes. To bolster myself, splinters of wood keep my swollen eyelids apart. When dawn appears it finds me in the same position, body leaning vertically and upright against the plaster of the frigid wall. Sometimes, however, I happen to dream, but without losing for an instant the vital sense of my personality and my free ability of moving: know that nightmare which hides in the phosphoric angles of the darkness, the fever that caresses my face with its stump, every unclean animal that raises its bloody claw — well, it is my will that, in order to provide regular food for its perpetual activity, makes them go round and round. Actually, atom that takes revenge by its extreme feebleness, free will isn't afraid to claim with potent authority that it doesn't count stupefaction among the ranks of its sons: the one who sleeps is less than an animal castrated the previous day. Although insomnia leads these muscles (already giving off an odor of cypress) to the depths of the pit, the white catacomb of my mind will never open its sanctums to the Creator's eyes. A hidden and noble justice, towards whose extended arms I instinctively throw myself, orders me to hunt down relentlessly this repulsive punishment. Formidable enemy of my careless soul, at the hour when one lights a lantern on the shore I proscribe my unfortunate kidneys from lying on the dew of the turf. Victor, I repel the ambushes of the hypocritical poppy. It is a certain consequence that my heart has sealed its plans through this strange battle, a starving thing that eats itself. Impenetrable as giants, *I* have lived endlessly with the scope of eyes wide open. At least it is revealed, during the day, that everyone can offer useful resistance against the Great Exterior Object (who doesn't know *His* name?), because willpower then keeps vigil over its own defence with remarkable obstinacy. But as soon as the veil of nocturnal mists drifts out, even over the condemned ones who are going to hang, oh! to see one's mind in the sacrilegious hands of a stranger. A ruthless scalpel scrutinizes the thick undergrowths. Consciousness exhales a long cursing groan—because the veil of its modesty receives cruel rents. Humiliation! Our door is open to the Heavenly Bandit's fierce curiosity. I did not deserve this infamous torture—you, hideous spy of my causality! If I exist, I am not another. I don't accept this equivocal plurality in myself. I wish to live alone within my intimate reasoning. Autonomy... or else let me be changed into a hippopotamus. Plunge yourself into the underground abyss, O anonymous stigma, and reappear no more before my wild indignation. My subjectivity and the Creator—it's too much for one brain. When night obscures the stream of hours, who hasn't fought against sleep's influence in their moist layer of clammy sweat? That bed attracting dying powers to its bosom is merely a tomb built from sawn planks of fir. Willpower retreats imperceptibly, as if faced with an invisible force. A viscous resin thickens the lenses of the eyes. The eyelids look for each other like two friends. The body is no more than a cadaver that breathes. Finally, four huge stakes nail the limbs in their entirety to the mattress. And observe, I implore you, that sheets are fundamentally only shrouds. Here is the cassolette where the religious incense burns. Eternity roars like a distant sea and draws nearer with large steps. The apartment has disappeared: prostrate yourselves, humans, in the blazing chapel! Sometimes the hypnotized sense, vainly striving to conquer the organism's imperfections in the middle of the heaviest slumber, perceives with surprise that it is no more than a tombstone, and relying on peerless subtlety it reasons admirably: "Leaving that bed is a more difficult problem than one would think. Sitting on the cart, I'm drawn towards the twin poles of the guillotine. Curious thing, my immobile arm has cleverly assimilated the stiffness of a stump. It's very bad to dream that one is proceeding to the scaffold." Blood flows in large waves across the face. The chest makes repeated jolts and swells up with hissings. The weight of an obelisk impedes the spread of rabies. Reality has destroyed the dreams of somnolence! Who doesn't know that the hallucinating spirit loses its judgment when battle between prideful ego and the terrible increase of catalepsy is protracted? Gnawed by despair, it wallows in its pain until it has conquered Nature, and sleep, seeing its prey escaping, flies far from its heart on irritated and shamed wing never to return. Throw a little ash on my flushed eye socket. Don't stare at my eye, which never closes. Do you comprehend the suffering I endure (however, arrogance is satisfied)? When night exhorts humans to rest, a familiar man strides apace through the countryside. I fear that my resolve may succumb to senility. Let it arrive, that fateful day when I will sleep! Upon waking, my razor, opening a thoroughfare across my neck, will actually prove that nothing was more real.

— But who, then!… but who then, like a conspirator, dares drag the rings of its body here towards my black chest? Whoever you may be, eccentric python, by what pretext do you pardon your ridiculous presence? Is it vast remorse that torments you? Because you see, boa, I assume your wild majesty doesn't have the exorbitant pretention to avoid the comparison with criminal's features that I've made. To my mind, that foamy and whitish saliva is the sign of rabies. Hear me: do you know that your eye is far from soaking up a celestial ray? Don't forget that if your presumptuous brain believed me capable of offering you some words of comfort, that could only be because of an ignorance entirely lacking physiognomic knowledge. For a sufficient time (obviously), direct the glow of your eyes to what I have the right to call (as much as the next person) my face! Don't you see how it cries? You're wrong, basilisk. You must seek elsewhere the doleful share of relief that my extreme impotence deprives you of, despite the many protests of my goodwill. Oh! What strength, expressible in phrases, drove you fatally to your doom? It's nigh on impossible that I would become accustomed to this reasoning which you don't grasp as, laying out the shifty curves of your triangular head on the reddened lawn with a clomp of my heel, I mold an unnamable putty with savannah grass and crushed flesh.

— Anon, be gone as far as possible from me, you pale-faced culprit! The fallacious mirage of terror has shown you your own ghost! Dispel your harmful suspicions if you don't want me to accuse you myself, and lest I bring against you a charge that would certainly meet the secretary bird's[22] approval. What monstrous freak of fancy prevents you from recognizing me! You don't recall then the important services I've rendered you for the gratification of an existence I brought from chaos, and the vow on your part, forever unforgettable, to never abandon my flag so as to remain loyal to me until death? When you were a child (your comprehension was then in its most beautiful phase), first you would climb the hill with the speed of the chamois, to greet the blossoming dawn's multicoloured rays with a motion of your small hand. The notes of your voice would gush from your sonorous larynx like adamantine pearls and resolve their collective natures in the vibrant harmony of a long hymn of adoration. Now you shift your feet like a rag mucky with mud, which I've demonstrated forbearance over for too long. Gratitude saw its roots drying out like the bed of a pond; but in its place ambition had grown in proportions that it would pain me to quantify. Whoever hears me, what is it to have such confidence in the abuse of one's own weakness?

— And who are *you*, audacious substance? No!...no!...I am not mistaken, and despite the multiple metamorphoses you've resorted to, your serpent head will always shine before my eyes like a lighthouse of everlasting injustice and cruel domination! He wished to seize the reins of authority—but he didn't know how to reign! He wished to become an object of horror to all the beings of Creation—and he succeeded! He wished to prove that he alone was the king of the universe—and that's where he went wrong. O miserable one! have you waited until this hour to hear the whispers and plots which, rising simultaneously from the surfaces of the planets, come to shave your destructible eardrum's papillæ-fringe with a wild wing? The day isn't far off when I'll turn you over with my arm into the dust poisoned by your breath, and ripping harmful life from your guts I'll leave your contortion-riddled corpse on the road to teach the dismayed traveller that this palpitating flesh, which strikes his view with astonishment and nails his mute tongue to his palate, mustn't be compared (if he keeps his *sang-froid*) to a rotten oak trunk that has fallen from decay! What thought of pity keeps me before your presence? *You* back off instead before *me*, I tell you—and go wash your immeasurable hate in a newborn's blood: those are your habits. They are worthy of you. Go...always move ahead. I condemn you to become a wanderer. I condemn you to remain alone and without family. Travel constantly so that your legs will deny you their support. Cross the desert sands until the end of the world gobbles the stars into the void. When you pass close to the tiger's den, it will hasten to flee so as not to see, like in a mirror, its character erected on the plinth of ideal perversity. But when compelling fatigue will order you to halt your march before the gorges of my palace covered with thorns and thistles, pay heed to your ragged sandals and tiptoe across the elegant thresholds. This isn't a pointless recommendation. You might wake my young wife and infant son sleeping in the leaden

cellars lining the foundations of the ancient castle. If you don't take these precautions beforehand, they may make you go pale with their subterranean screams. When your impenetrable will deprived them of life, they were aware that your power was fearful and had no doubt in that regard; but they were absolutely not expecting (and their supreme farewells confirmed their belief to me) that your Providence would be displayed to that merciless degree! In any case, move swiftly through those desolate and silent rooms (with emerald wainscotting but faded coats of arms) where the glorious statues of my ancestors repose. Those marble bodies are furious with you; avoid their glassy stares. This is the advice that the tongue of their only and final descendant gives you. See how their arms are raised in an attitude of provocative defence, proud heads thrown back. They have undoubtedly become aware of the evil you've done me—and if you pass within range of the icy pedestals bearing those sculpted blocks, wrath waits for you there. If your defence needs to object to something, speak. It's too late to cry now. It was necessary to weep in more convenient moments, when the occasion was propitious. If your eyes are open at last, judge for yourself what the consequences of your conduct have been. Farewell! I go to breathe the breeze of the cliffs because my half-choked lungs request, with great whoops, a sight more tranquil and virtuous than yours!

O incomprehensible pederasts, it's not *I* who will throw insults at your immense degradation; it's not *I* who will come to throw scorn upon your funnel-shaped anus. It's enough that the shameful and almost incurable diseases which have besieged you carry their inevitable punishment with them. Law-makers of stupid institutions, creators of narrow morality, stay away from me, because I am an impartial soul. And you, young boys or (rather) young girls, explain to me how and why (but keep a respectable distance because I can no longer resist my passions) revenge has been sparked in your hearts so that such a wreath of wounds has been bound to humanity's side. You make it blush for your sons through your behaviour (which I personally venerate!); your prostitution, offering itself to the first come, exerts the logic of the most profound thinkers, while your exaggerated sensibility completely fills—with amazement—the cup of the woman herself. Is your nature less or more earthly than that of your peers? Do you possess a sixth sense that we lack? Don't lie, and speak your mind. This is not an interrogation that I put to you, because ever since I frequented the sublimity of your grandiose intelligence as a spectator, I know where I stand. Be blessed by my left hand, be sanctified by my right hand, angels shielded by my universal love. I kiss your faces, I kiss your breasts, I kiss the various parts of your harmonious and perfumed bodies with my soft lips. Why didn't you tell me from the outset what you were, crystallizations of a superior moral beauty? I had to guess for myself the many treasures of tenderness and chastity that the beats of your oppressed heart harboured. Breast adorned with festoons of roses and vetiver. I had to spread your legs slightly in order to know you, and so that my mouth might be suspend on the insignia of your modesty. But (important thing to clarify) don't forget to wash the skin of your genitals daily with hot water—because, if you don't, venereal chancres will inevitably sprout on the cracked corners of my unsatisfied lips. Oh! if, instead of being a hell, the universe had been just one huge heavenly anus—observe the gesture I make beside my groin: yes, I would have buried my penis into its bloody sphincter, shattering the very lining of its pelvis with my impulsive movements! Misfortune would not have then blown whole dunes of shifting sand over my blinded eyes; I would have revealed the subterranean spot where truth lies asleep, and the rivers of my viscous semen would have thus found an ocean into which to precipitate! But why am I surprised to regret an imaginary state of things which will never receive the seal of its later achievement? Let's not torture our-

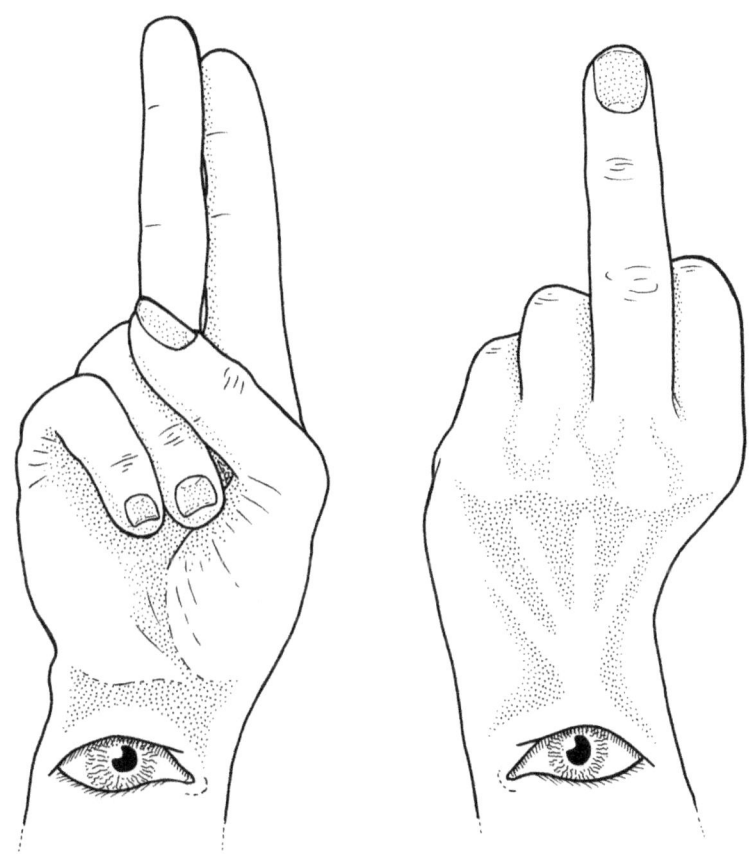

selves by building fleeting theories. In the meantime, let the one who burns with the fervour of sharing my bed come to me—but I put a strict condition on my hospitality: he mustn't be more than fifteen years old. For his part, let him not believe that I'm thirty—what's *that* got to do with anything? Age does not diminish the intensity of feelings (far from it), and although my hair has grown as white as snow, it isn't due to old age: on the contrary, it's for the reason you're aware of. *I* don't like women! Nor even hermaphrodites! I need beings who look like me, on whose foreheads human nobility has been marked by clearer and more indelible characters! Are you certain that those who wear long hair are of the same nature as mine? I don't believe it, and I won't abandon my opinion. A briny saliva flows from my mouth, I don't know why. Who wants to suck it from me, so that I may be shot of it? It mounts... it ever mounts! I know what it is. I've observed that, when I drink blood from the throats of those lying beside me (it's a mistake to suppose me a vampire, since that's what we call the dead who have left their graves—yet *I* am a living being), I throw some of it up the next day: that's the explanation of the stinking saliva. What would you have me do, if the organs weakened by vice decline the fulfillment of nutritional functions? But don't reveal my confidences to anyone. It isn't for me that I tell you this; it is for yourself and others, so that the secret's glamour might hold, within the limits of duty and virtue, those who, magnetized by electricity from the unknown, would be tempted to imitate me. Be good enough to observe my mouth (for now I don't have time to use a longer form of politeness); it strikes you at first by the appearance of its form (not including the snake in your comparisons): that's because I pulled the tissue right back in order to pretend that I have a frigid personality. You notice that it is diametrically opposite. Only then I do see my reader's face through these seraphic pages. If he hasn't passed puberty, he may approach. Hold me against you and don't be scared of harming me; let us gradually narrow the bonds of our muscles. *Further.* I feel it is useless to insist; the opacity (remarkable in many ways) of this sheet of paper is a most considerable hindrance to the process of our complete union. *I* have always had a notorious quirk for pale college youths and children blanched by factories! My words aren't the reminiscences of a dream, and I will have too many memories to untangle if I felt obligated to parade before your eyes events that would substantiate the veracity of my grim declaration. Human Justice has not yet caught me red-handed, despite the unquestioned ability of its police-officers. I have even assassinated a pederast (it hasn't been long since!) who wasn't sufficiently suited to my passion; I threw his corpse down an abandoned well and they didn't have conclusive proofs against me. Why do you quiver with fear, young man who reads me? Do you believe that I would want to do likewise to you?

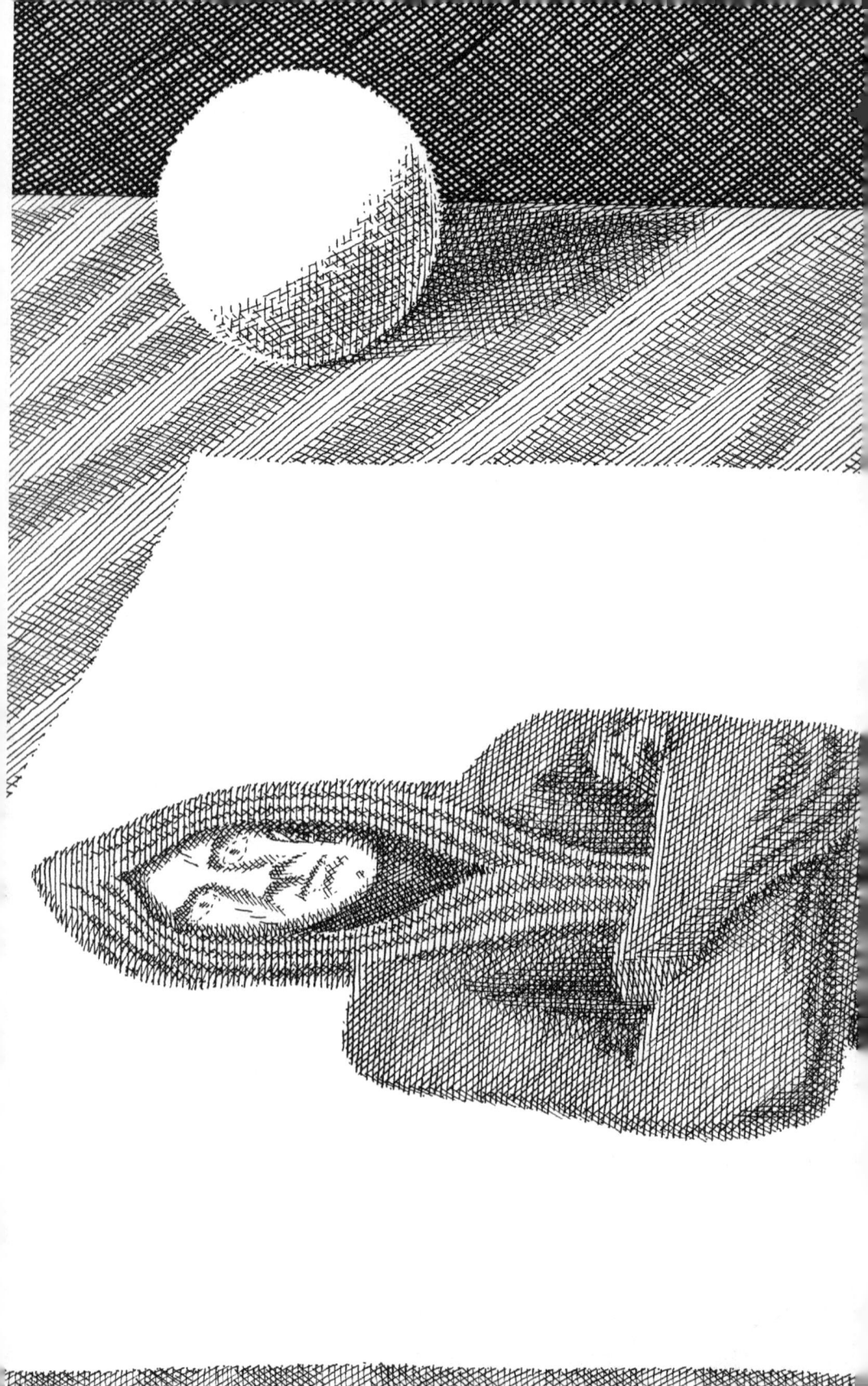

You show yourself to be extremely unjust... You have cause: beware of me, particularly if you are attractive. My private parts eternally offer the lugubrious display of turgidity; nobody can argue (and how many haven't approached them!) that they have seen them in a state of ordinary tranquility, not even the shoeshine boy who strikes me there with a dagger in a moment of delirium. The ingrate! I change clothes twice a week, propriety not being the main incentive for my determination. If I didn't act in this way, humanity's members might disappear within days through protracted battles. Actually, in whatever country I find myself, they continually harass me with their presence and come to lick the surface of my feet. But what power my seminal drippings would then possess, to attract to them all who breathe through their olfactory nerves! They come from the shores of the Amazon, they cross the valleys the Ganges irrigates, they desert the polar lichen—in order to realize long journeys in my pursuit and to ask the immobile cities if they've not seen, for a moment passing along their bulwarks, the one whose sacred sperm gives fragrance to the mountains, lakes, heaths, forests, promontories and the vastness of the seas! The despair of being unable to encounter me (to fuel their ardor I secret myself in the most inaccessible places) provokes them to the most regrettable acts. They station three hundred thousand on each side and cannonades serve as a prelude to war. All ranks shake simultaneously like a single warrior. Squares are formed and immediately tumble for good. Spooked horses flee in all directions. Cannonballs plough the soil like relentless meteorites. The theatre of war is but a vast field of slaughter when night reveals its presence and when the silent moon appears between breaks in a cloud. Pointing out to me an area of several leagues covered in corpses, the vaporous crescent of this star orders me to consider a moment, as the subject for meditative thoughts, the deadly consequences that the inexplicable enchanting talisman granted me by Providence drags behind it. Sadly, how many centuries will it still take before the human race perishes entirely from my perfidious trap! This is therefore how an adroit and unboastful mind uses the selfsame methods—initially appearing to impose an invincible obstacle—in order to attain its objectives. My intellect always soars towards this imposing question, and you yourself are witness that I can no longer stick to the modest topic I'd meant to write about in the first place. One final word...it was a winter's night. As the wind whistled in the firs, the Creator opened His door amidst the gloom and showed in a pederast.

Silence! A funeral procession passes beside you. Lean the binarity of your kneecaps to the ground and begin to sing a dirge from beyond the grave. (If you consider my words as a plain imperative formality rather than as a misplaced formal order, you will display spirit, and of the best kind.) It is possible that by rejoicing excessively like that you will reach the soul of the dead person going to rest from life in a pit. Even for me the fact is certain. Note that I've not said that your opinion can't to a certain degree be contrary to mine—but what matters before all else is to possess fair notions about the foundations of morality so that everyone should see through the principle commanding: "Do unto others as you would have them do unto you." The priest of religions leads the procession, holding a white flag, sign of peace, in one hand, and in the other a gold emblem representing the male and female organs to indicate that these carnal members are most of the time, aside from any metaphor, very dangerous tools in the hands of those who use them when they blindly manipulate them for various conflicting ends, instead of bringing about an expedient reaction against the famous passion that causes almost all our troubles. Attached to the priest's lower back (artificially, of course) is a thickly-bristled horse's tail which sweeps the dust from the ground. It signifies to take care not to debase ourselves to the level of the animals through our conduct. The coffin knows its route and follows the fluttering tunic of the consoler. The relatives and friends of the deceased, manifesting their position, have resolved to close the march of the

procession. It advances majestically like a ship shouldering the open sea and doesn't fear the phenomenon of sinking—because for now storms and reefs aren't conspicuous by anything less than their explicable absence. Crickets and toads follow several paces behind the funeral party; they, too, are aware that their humble presence will be included at anyone's funeral one day. They quietly discuss in their picturesque language (let me give you this unbiased advice: don't be so presumptuous as to believe that only you possess the precious faculty of translating opinions from your thoughts) the one whom they had seen running more than once across the verdant pastures and plunging the sweat of his limbs into the bluish waves of the sandy gulfs. At first, life seemed to smile on him without ulterior motive and it crowned him gorgeously with flowers; but since your understanding itself perceives, or rather guesses, that he was halted at the limits of childhood, I need not continue my rigorous demonstration's prefaces until the appearance of an absolutely necessary retraction. Ten years. A number precisely calculated on (perhaps mistaken for) that of the digits of the hand. It's a little and it's a lot. In the case that concerns us, however, I will depend upon your love for the truth that you pronounce with me, without a moment's hesitation, that "it's a little." And when I briefly ponder these tenebrous mysteries—whereby a human being vanishes from the earth as easily as a blowfly or dragonfly, without preserving hope of returning there—I catch myself nurturing deep regret at probably not living long enough to fully explain to you what I don't claim to understand myself. But since it is proven, by extraordinary coincidence, that I haven't yet perished since that remote time when, filled with terror, I began the previous sentence, I calculate mentally that it wouldn't be futile here to construe the full confession of my radical impotence, especially when it's a question (as it is now) of this imposing and inaccessible question. Generally speaking, it's a thing as singular as the attractive tendency that leads us to look for (in order to subsequently express them) similarities and differences that conceal, in their natural properties, objects most opposite to each other and sometimes least apt in appearance to lend themselves to these kinds of sympathetically curious combinations—and which (on my word of honour) give graciously to the style of the writer, who rewards himself that personal satisfaction: the impossible and unforgettable aspect of an earnest owl until Eternity. As a result, let us follow the current that pulls us. The red kite has wings proportionally longer than buzzards, and more effortless flight: therefore it spends its life in the air. It hardly ever rests and travels vast areas every day; and this great movement is not at all a hunting exercise, nor pursuit of prey, nor even of discovery—because it doesn't hunt; indeed, it seems that flight is its natural state, its favourite state. One can't help but admire the way with which it executes it. Its long and narrow wings appear stationary; it's the tail that believes it steers all the manœuvres, and the tail isn't wrong: it acts incessantly. The kite rises effortlessly; it descends as though it were gliding on an inclined plane; it seems to swim rather than fly; it hastens its course, retards it, comes to a halt, and remains as though suspended or fixed in the same place for whole hours. One cannot discern any movement in its wings: it would be just as futile were you to open your eyes as wide as a stove door. Everyone has the good sense to confess without trouble (although with a little bad grace) that they don't initially perceive the relationship, distant as it may be, which I highlight between the beauty of the red kite's flight and that of the child's face rising gently above the uncovered coffin like a water-lily piercing the water's surface—and precisely therein lies the unforgivable fault produced by the immovable position of lack of repentance, touching on the deliberate ignorance in which we stagnate. This relationship of calm majesty between the two terms of my ironic comparison is already only too common, and a comprehensible enough symbol, that I am surprised more by that which can't have, as its sole excuse, that same character of vulgarity which invokes a profound feeling of unjust indifference about every object or spectacle it wounds. As if what is seen every day should no less awaken our admiration's attention! Arriving at the entrance to the cemetery, the procession comes to a halt; its intention is to proceed no further. The gravedigger finishes the excavation of the pit; the coffin is lowered down into it with all the precautions taken in such cases; some unexpected shovelfuls of earth come to completely cover the child's body. In the midst of the emotional audience, the priest of religions recites some words in order to inter the dead one better in the audience's imagination. "He said that he is greatly surprised that we shed so many tears over an event of such insignificance. *Verbatim.* But he is

afraid of not sufficiently qualifying what *he* claims is unarguable happiness. If he had believed that death was hardly sympathetic in its naïvety, he would have renounced his term of office in order to stem the legitimate grief of the many relatives and friends of the deceased; but a hidden voice warned him to give them some comfort, which would be helpful even if it allowed a glimmer of hope of another meeting in Heaven between the one who'd died and those who'd survived." Maldoror fled at a great gallop while appearing to head towards the cemetery walls. The hooves of his charger raised a false crown of dense dust around its master. You folks can't know the name of that rider—but *I* know it. He was gradually approaching; his platinum face began to grow visible, although the lower portion was entirely enveloped by a cloak which the reader has been careful to remember and which only allowed his eyes to be seen. In the middle of his discourse the priest of religions suddenly grows pale because his ear recognizes the irregular gallop of that famous white horse which had never abandoned it master. "Yes," he added anew, "my confidence is great for that next meeting; we now understand better than before the meaning that must be attached to the temporary separation of the soul and the body. He who has faith to live on this earth lulls himself with an illusion whose evaporation it is paramount to expedite." The noise of galloping increases further—and as the rider, meeting the line of the horizon, appears in sight, fast as a gyrating tornado, within the optic field encompassed by the cemetery gate, the priest of religions carried on seriously: "You don't seem to doubt that this one whom illness had forced to experience only the early stages of life, and whom the pit has just taken into its womb, is the undoubted living; but know at least that the one whose ambiguous silhouette you see borne by a skittish horse—and upon whom I advise you to fix your eyes promptly, because he is no longer a point and will soon vanish into the heather—even though he has lived much, *he* is the only one truly dead."

"Every night, at the hour when sleep has reached its greatest level of intensity, an old spider of the large variety slowly extrudes its head from a hole made in the floor at one corner of the room. It listens keenly if any rustling in the air excites its mandibles. Given its insectile form it can do no less, even if it claims to boost the treasures of literature with brilliant personifications, than to recognize rustling with its mandibles. When it has confirmed that silence reigns in the surroundings, it withdraws successively from the depths of its nest, instinctively, the various parts of its body and advances with a measured gait towards my bed. Remarkable thing!—*I*, who make sleep and nightmares recede, feel myself paralyzed throughout my entire body when it climbs along the ebony feet of my satin bed. It clutches my throat with its legs and sucks my blood with its abdomen. Quite simply! How many litres of purple liqueur (whose name you are aware of) hadn't it drunk since it executed the same ploy with a persistence worthy of a higher cause! I don't know what I had done to it that it might behave in this way towards me. Did I carelessly crush one of its legs? Did I kidnap its young? These two questionable theories are unable to withstand serious scrutiny; they don't even have trouble provoking a shrug of my shoulders and a smile on my lips (although we shouldn't make fun of anyone). You should beware, black tarantula; if your conduct doesn't have irrefutable syllogism as an excuse, one night I will awake with a start by a final effort of my dying will, I will break the spell with which you hold my limbs immobile, and I will squash you between the bones of my fingers like a bit of soft stuff. Nevertheless I do vaguely recall that I gave you leave to let your legs climb on the opening of my breast, and from there up to the skin covering my face—so that consequently I have no right to hold you back. Oh! Who will untangle my confused memories! As reward I offer him what remains of my blood: counting the very last drop, it ought to fill at least half a profuse cup." He speaks and he doesn't stop undressing. He places one leg on the mattress and, with the other pressing against the sapphire floor in order to raise himself, he finds

himself stretched out horizontally. He resolves not to close his eyes so as to await his foe steadfastly. But does he not take the same resolution every time, and is it not always shattered by the unexplainable image of its fatal promise? He speaks no more, and painfully resigns himself—because for him the oath is sacred. He wraps himself majestically in swathes of silk, disdains to tie the golden tassels of the curtains, and, resting the wavy curls of his long black hair on the fringes of the velvet pillow, he feels with his hand the large wound in his neck—in which the tarantula had gotten into the habit of lodging itself, as in a second nest—while his face expresses satisfaction. He hopes (hope along with him!) that this present night will see the final performance of the tremendous suction, because his sole vow would be that the executioner might put an end to his life: death, and he will be content. Observe that old spider of the large variety slowly extruding its head from a hole made in the floor at one of the corners of the room. We are no longer in the narrative. It listens keenly if any rustling in the air excites its mandibles. Alas! We have now entered reality regarding the tarantula, and although we may not be able to put an exclamation mark at the end of every sentence, perhaps that's no reason to entirely dispense with it! It is assured that silence reigns around it; lo, it withdraws successively from the depths of its nest, instinctively, the various parts of its body and advances with a measured gait towards the bed of the solitary man. Momentarily it halts—but this moment of hesitation is brief. It tells itself that it's not yet time to cease to torture, and that it's necessary to give the condemned man the plausible reasons that had determined continuation of the torment. It climbs beside the ear of the sleeper. If you don't want to miss a single word of what it is going to say, refrain from strange activities that might obstruct the door of your mind, and at least be grateful for the care I bring in facilitating your presence at theatrical scenes which I reckon are worthy of exciting genuine attention on your part—because who would prevent me from keeping the events I narrate to myself? "Awaken yourself, loving flame from ancient days, emaciated skeleton. The time has come to stay the hand of Justice. We won't make you wait any longer for the explanation you desire. You hear us, don't you? But don't move your limbs; today you are still under our mesmeric power and encephalic sluggishness[23] persists: this is for the last time. What impression does Elsseneur's face make on your imagination? You have forgotten it! And this Reginald with his strutting, have you carved his features into your loyal brain? Observe him hidden in the creases of the curtains; his mouth is inclined towards your forehead, yet he dares not converse with you because he is more timid than I. I'm going to recount to you an incident from your youth and return you to memory lane..." It was a long time before the spider opened its abdomen, from whence darted two young men in blue robes, each with a dazzling sword in hand, and who were positioning themselves beside the bed as if to henceforth guard the shrine of sleep. "This one, who hasn't stopped looking at you yet because he had loved you so much, was the first of the two of us to whom you gave your love. But you often made him suffer by the abruptness of your personality. *He* never ceased working to not spawn in you any grievance against him: an angel wouldn't have succeeded. One day you asked him if he wanted to go bathing with you at the seaside. Both of you, like two swans, soared simultaneously from the summit of a rock. Distinguished divers, you slipped through the watery mass, arms stretched between heads and joining hands. For several minutes you swam between two currents. You reappeared at a great distance, your hair entangled and streaming with the salty fluid. But what mystery had happened underwater so that a long trail of blood appeared across the waves? Returning to the surface, *you* continued to swim and you didn't seem to notice your companion's growing weakness. He quickly lost his strength, and you didn't reduce the momentum of your broad strokes towards the hazy horizon fading away before you. The wounded man yelled with cries of distress, and you acted deaf. Thrice did Reginald make the syllables of your name resound—and thrice did you respond with a cry of pleasure. He

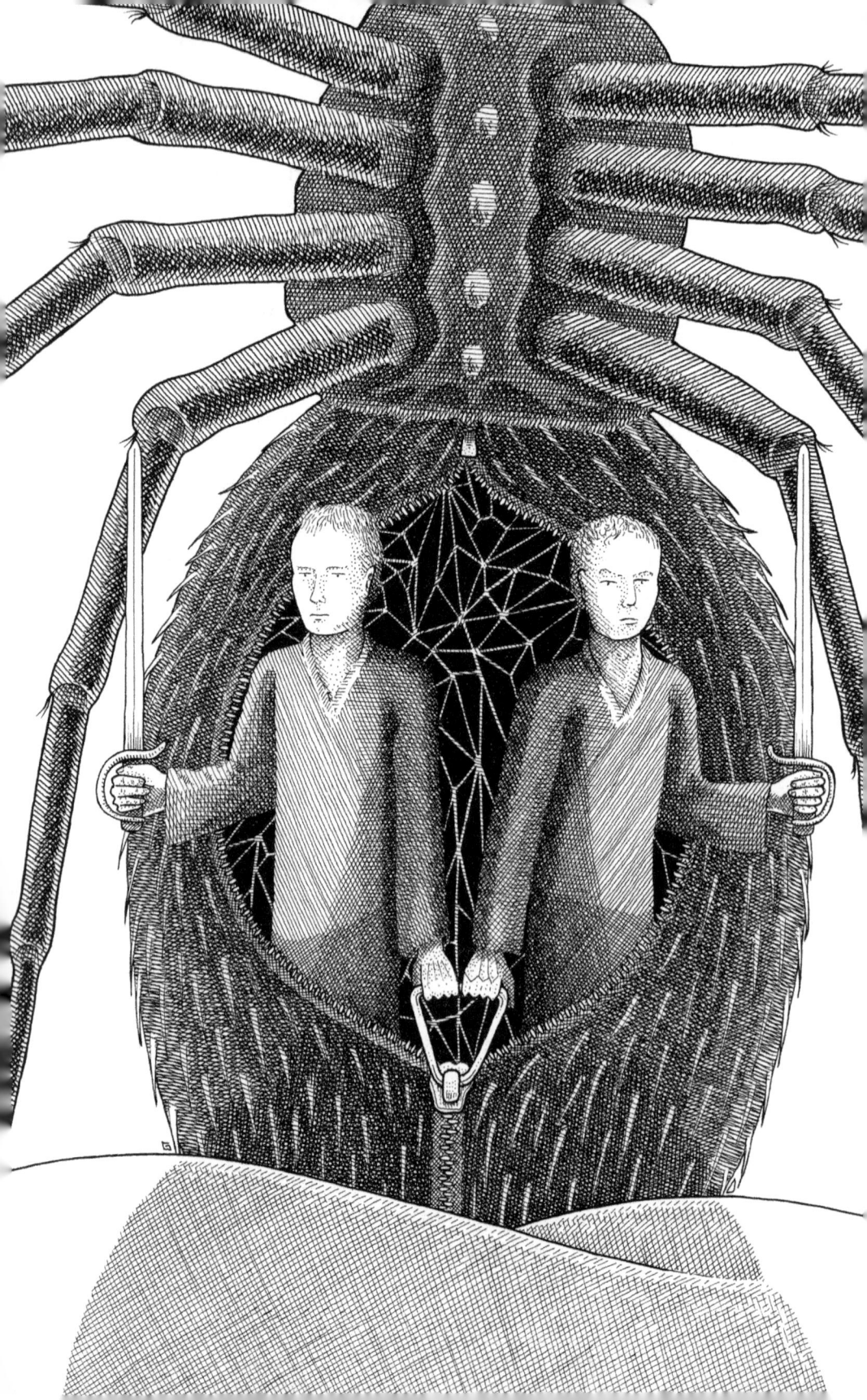

found himself too far from shore to return there, and he vainly endeavored to follow in the wake of your passage so that he might reach you and place his hand on your shoulder for a moment. The adverse hunt had dragged on for an hour—he losing his strength and you feeling yours grow. Despairing of equalling your speed, he said a brief prayer to the Lord to remind Him of his soul, turned himself over (like when we float on our back) in such a way that his heart could be seen beating fiercely beneath his breast, and he awaited death's arrival in order to wait no more. In that moment your vigorous limbs were lost from sight and were still distancing themselves as quickly as a depth-probe that is let to pay out. A barque, which was returning from placing nets out in open waters, passed through the area. The fishermen took Reginald for a castaway and hauled him, losing consciousness, into their skiff. The presence of a wound on his right side was noted; each of these experienced seamen opined that no point of reef or piece of rock was capable of making a hole so microscopic and at the same time so deep. Only a sharp weapon (as the keenest of stilettos might be) could claim authorship rights for so fine a wound. Reginald never wished to recall the various stages of the dive through the bowels of the waves, and he has kept this secret to himself up to the present. Some tears now run down his slightly discoloured cheeks and fall onto your sheets: the memory is sometimes more bitter than the event. But *I* will not suffer from pity: that would be to show you too much respect. Don't roll those wild eyes in their sockets. Stay calm instead. You know you cannot budge. Besides, I haven't finished my narrative.—Raise your sword once more, Reginald, and don't forget vengeance so easily. Who knows? Perhaps one day it may come to blame you.— Later you conceived a remorse whose existence must have been fleeting; you resolved to make amends for your error by choosing another friend to bless and honour. By this expiatory method you were effacing the stains of the past and making pity, which you'd not been able to show the other, boomerang on the one who became the second victim. Empty hope; character doesn't change it-

self from one day to the next, and your will stayed the same. *I*, Elsseneur, saw you for the first time, and from that moment I couldn't forget you. We watched each other for a few moments and you began to smile. I lowered my eyes—because I saw in yours a supernatural flame. I asked myself if you, aided by a dark night, had fallen clandestinely to us from the surface of some star—because today, when there's no need to feign, I must confess that you didn't resemble the small swine of humanity; but a halo of scintillating rays surrounded the periphery of your forehead. I would have desired to join with you in intimate relations; my presence dared not approach in front of the striking novelty of this strange nobility, and a tenacious terror prowled around me. Why didn't I heed these warnings from my conscience? Founded premonitions. Noting my hesitation, you blushed in turn and held out your arms. I bravely put my hand in yours, and after that gesture I felt stronger; henceforth a waft of your intelligence was passed inside me. Hair windblown, and inhaling the breezes' breaths, we strode forward momentarily through the dense thickets of mastic, jasmine, pomegranate-trees and orange-trees, whose scents intoxicated us. A wild boar at full trot brushed our clothes, and a tear fell from its eye when it saw me with you: I couldn't explain its behaviour. At nightfall we arrived before the gates of a heavily-populated city. The outlines of domes, minaret spires, and marble globes of turrets were strongly silhouetting their serrations through the gloom against the dark blue of the sky. But you didn't want to stay in that place, even though we were overwhelmed by fatigue. We traversed the foot of the external fortifications like nocturnal jackals, we avoided coming across guards on the lookout, and via the opposite gate we managed to distance ourselves from that solemn assembly of reasoning animals, civilized like beavers. The flight of the lantern-fly, the crackling of dry grass, and occasional growls from some distant wolf accompanied the obscurity of our uncertain passage across the countryside. What then were your valid motives for fleeing the human hives? I asked myself that question with a certain unease; moreover, my legs were beginning to deny me a service prolonged for too long. We finally reached the edge of a thick forest whose trees were interwoven with a tangle of high inextricable lianas, parasitic plants and cacti with monstrous thorns. You halted before a birch tree. You told me to kneel so as to prepare to die; you granted me fifteen minutes to depart this earth. Some furtive looks thrown stealthily on me during our long excursion, when I hadn't been watching you, and certain gestures in which I had noted irregularity of timing and movement soon came to my memory like the open pages of a book. My suspicions were confirmed. Too weak to fight against you, you threw me to the ground like the hurricane brings down the aspen leaf. One of your knees on my chest and the other supported on the moist grass, while one of your hands held the binarity of my arms in its vise, I saw the other hand removing a knife from the sheath hanging at your belt. My resistance was virtually nil, and I closed my eyes: the poundings of a yoke of oxen were heard in the distance, carried by the wind. Harassed by a shepherd's staff and a dog's jaws, it advanced like a locomotive. There was no time to lose, and you understood that; fearing you wouldn't succeed in your aims because the approach of unexpected aid had doubled my muscular power—and you perceived that you could only render me immobile by one of my arms at a time—you contented yourself in cutting my right wrist with a swift movement imparted to the steel blade. The neatly-detached piece fell to the ground. You ran off, while I was dizzy with pain. I won't recount to you how the shepherd came to my rescue, nor how much time was necessary for my recovery. Suffice you to know that this unexpected betrayal inspired me to seek death. I would become involved in fights in order to offer my breast to blows. I achieved glory on the battlefields; my name became feared among even the most courageous, while my artificial hand of iron spread carnage and destruction within the enemy's ranks. Yet one day, when the shells thundered more powerfully than usual and when squadrons, stripped of their base, whirled about like straws under the influence of a deadly

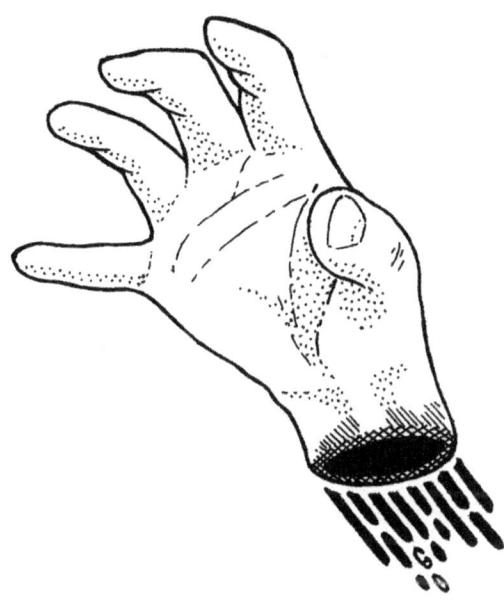

cyclone, a knight with a bold step advanced before me to dispute the victory palm. The two armies halted, motionless, to silently contemplate us. We fought long, covered in wounds, and helmets broken. By mutual agreement we ceased the fight so that we might rest, and thereafter we resumed with more energy. Filled with admiration for his adversary, each raised his own visor: 'Elsseneur!...', 'Reginald!...'—such were the simple words that our breathless throats pronounced simultaneously. The latter, falling into depression, had taken a military career like me and the bullets had spared him. In what circumstances did we cross paths again! But your name wasn't mentioned! He and I both swore eternal friendship—but certainly different from the first two performances in which you had been the principal player. An archangel, descended from Heaven and a messenger of the Lord, had ordered us to transform ourselves into a singular spider and to come every night to suck from your throat until a commandment from on high stopped the course of punishment. For nearly ten years we have haunted your bed. From today onwards you are delivered from our persecution. The vague promise of which you spoke wasn't made to us, but rather to the Being who is stronger than you: *you* understood that it was better to submit to that irrevocable decree. Wake up, Maldoror! The mesmeric enchantment that has weighed on your cerebro-spinal system for two lustra[24] evaporates." He wakes as he has been ordered to and sees two heavenly forms, arms linked, disappear into the air. He doesn't try to sleep again. He slowly removes his limbs, one after the other, from the bed. He goes to warm his icy skin at the rekindled cinders of the Gothic hearth. Only his shirt covers his body. His eyes seek the crystal carafe in order to moisten his parched palate. He opens the window shutters. He leans on the window-ledge. He contemplates the moon which pours on his breast a cone of ecstatic rays in which pulsate, like moths, silver atoms of sublime softness. He waits for the morning twilight to bring, with the changing scenery, a derisory salve to his shaken heart.

END OF THE FIFTH DIRGE

Sixth Dirge

OU, WHOSE ENVIABLE calm can do no more than embellish the face, don't believe that it is still a question of uttering—in verses of fourteen or fifteen lines like a fourth-grader—exclamations that will come across as inappropriate, and loud cluckings of a Cochinchinese chicken as grotesque as one could imagine (if one were to take the trouble); but it is preferable to substantiate with facts the propositions one puts forward. Do you claim, then, that my mission was complete because I had insulted (quite easily) Man, the Creator, and myself, with my explicable exaggerations? No—the most important part of my work doesn't subsist any less, as duty must be done. From now on the threads of the novel will move the three people named above: a less abstract power will thus be communicated to them. Vitality will spread magnificently through the torrent of their circulatory system, and you will see how amazed you yourself will be to encounter there—where at first you thought you only saw some vague beings belonging to a purely fantastic realm—on the one hand, the corporeal organism with its neural networks and its mucous membranes, and, on the other hand, the spiritual principle which directs the physiological functions of the flesh. They are beings endowed with energetic life who, with arms crossed and chests stilled, will pose prosaically (but I'm sure that the effect will be quite poetic) before your face, situated only a few steps from you so that the sunbeams, first hitting the roof-tiles and chimney pots, will in turn be visibly reflected on their earthly and material hair. But they will no longer be damnations, experts at provoking laughter; they will no longer be fictional personalities who should have been left within the author's brain, nor nightmares placed too far above routine existence. By that same token, observe that my poetry will only be the more beautiful. You will touch the rising branches of the aorta and the adrenal glands with your hands—and then the heart-strings! The first five recitals have not been pointless; they were the frontispiece of my work, the butt of the erection,[25] the preliminary explanation of my poetic future: and I owed it to myself, before packing my bag and starting out for lands of the imagination, to inform genuine literary enthusiasts—via a quick draft of a clear and precise overview—of the goal I had resolved to pursue. Consequently, my opinion is that the synthetic part of my work is now complete and sufficiently paraphrased. It is through this that you've learned that I intended to attack Man and the One who had created him. For the moment, and for later, you don't need to know more about it! New considerations seem superfluous to me because they would only repeat, in another form—more profuse to be sure, but identical—the declaration of the theory whose first development we'll see by the end of this day. The result of the preceding observations is that my intention is to undertake, henceforth, the analytical section; that is so true that only just a few minutes ago I expressed the fervent vow that you would be imprisoned in my skin's sweat glands in order to verify the reliability of what I declare, by knowing the cause. I know it is necessary to substantiate, with a multiplicity of proofs, the argument found within my theory; well, these proofs do exist, and you know that I don't attack anyone without having good reasons! I laugh out loud when I imagine that you blame me for spreading bitter accusations against humanity, of which I am a member (this detail alone gives me reason!), and against Providence: I will not retract my words; however, remembering what I've seen, it will be hard for me to justify them without any ambition other than truth. Today I am going to create a small novel of thirty pages; this length will subsequently remain more or less static. Hoping to promptly see, some day, the consecration of my theories accepted by such and such literary form, I believe I have finally found — after a few hiccups — my definitive formula. This is the best — since this is the novel! Perhaps this hybrid preface has been expounded in a way that doesn't seem sufficiently natural, in that it somewhat surprises the reader who doesn't quite see where it initially leads him; but I've tried my best to produce this feeling of remarkable puzzlement, from which we should generally seek to shield those who pass their time reading books and pamphlets. It was actually impossible for me to do any less, despite my willingness: only later, when several novels are published, will you better comprehend the preface of the renegade with the sooty countenance.

Before going any further, I find it stupid that it should be necessary (I don't think everyone will share my opinion if I'm wrong) to place an open inkwell beside me and some fresh sheets of paper. In this way I'll be able to lovingly start, via this sixth dirge, the series of educational poems that I'm looking forward to producing. Dramatic episodes of unrelenting usefulness! Our hero found that by frequenting caves and taking refuge in inaccessible places, he was transgressing the rules of logic and perpetrating a vicious circle. Because if, on the one hand, he fostered his repugnance for men in this way in compensation for solitude and isolation, and passively restricted his narrow horizon amongst stunted shrubs, brambles and wild vines — on the other hand, his activity no longer found any food to nourish the minotaur of his perverse instincts. Consequently, he had resolved to approach human settlements again, persuaded that his various passions would find much to satisfy themselves with among so many sitting ducks.²⁶ He knew that the police, that shield of civilization, had persistently sought him for a number of years and that a veritable army of agents and spies were constantly on his heels. Without, however, managing to encounter him. So much did his astounding skill derail, with aplomb, the most undebatable ploys (from the point of view of their success) and most expertly thought-out ordinance. He had a special talent for assuming forms unrecognizable to practiced eyes. Superior disguises, if I may speak as an artist! Costumes with a very mediocre effect, when I think of morality. On this point he almost touched upon genius. Have you never noticed, in the Parisian sewers, the gracefulness of a pretty cricket with its lively movements? Only, it was *that* one: it was Maldoror! Mesmerizing the flourishing capital cities with a pernicious fluid, he leads them into a lethargic state where they are incapable of the necessary surveillance. A state so much more dangerous when not suspected. Today he's in Madrid, tomorrow he'll be in St. Petersburg; yesterday he found himself in Peking. But to pinpoint the actual place that the exploits of this poetic Rocambole might terrorize is a task beyond the potential strengths of my dense ratiocination. Perhaps this bandit is seven hundred leagues from that country; perhaps he is a few paces from you. It isn't easy to kill all men, and there are laws; however one can, with patience, exterminate the humanitarian ants one by one. Well, since the days of my birth, when I was living with the forefathers of our race and I was still inexperienced in the tension of my traps; since remote ages seated beyond history when I would at various times, in subtle metamorphoses, ravage the world's nations with conquest and carnage and roll out civil war among the citizens — had I not already crushed beneath my claws, member by member or collectively, whole generations whose infinite number would not be difficult to grasp? The radiant past made brilliant promises to the future: it will keep them. For the sweep of my sentences, I will of course employ the natural method, by downgrading to the savages so that they might give me lessons. Simple and majestic gentlemen, their graceful mouths ennoble all that flows from their tattooed lips. I just proved that nothing is risible on this planet. A comical planet—but a superb one. Assuming a style which some might find naïve (when it is so profound), I will make it serve to translate ideas which will perhaps, unfortunately, not appear grandiose! By the same token, stripping myself of the frivolous and sceptical airs of ordinary conversation, and prudent enough not to pose... I no longer know what I meant to say, because I don't recall the start of the sentence. But know that poetry is found everywhere where there isn't the stupidly mocking smile of the man with the face of a duck. First I'm going to blow my nose, because I need to; and then, helped powerfully by my hand, I will once more take up the quill that my fingers have dropped. How can the Pont du Carrousel keep its neutrality steady when it hears the harrowing cries that the sack seems to utter!

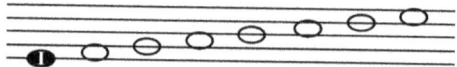

HE SHOPS OF the Rue Vivienne display their luxuries to marvelling eyes. Illuminated by numerous gaslights, the mahogany cases and gold watches scatter showers of stunning light through the shop windows. Eight o'clock is sounded by the Bourse clock: it isn't late! Barely has the last hammer-strike been heard than the aforementioned street starts to tremble, and it shakes its foundations from La Place Royal to Montmartre Boulevard. The pedestrians hasten their steps and retire thoughtfully to their homes. One woman faints and falls to the asphalt. Nobody helps her: everyone longs to desert that area. Shutters are closed hastily and the inhabitants bury themselves under their covers. It looks like the Asian plague has betrayed its presence. So, while most of the city prepares to swim in the festivities of late-night parties, the Rue Vivienne suddenly finds itself frozen by a kind of petrification. Like a heart that stops loving, it has seen its life extinguished. Soon, however, the news of the phenomenon spreads through the other sections of the populace and a mournful silence hovers over the stately capital. The gaslights—where have they gone? The prostitutes—what has become of them? Nothing...solitude and darkness! A screech owl, flying in a straight line and with a broken foot, passes over the Madeleine and directs its flight towards the Trône barrier, crying: "Disaster is nigh." Now, in this place that my quill (this dear friend who serves as my abettor) just rendered mysterious, if you look next to the junction of the Rue Colbert and the Rue

Vivienne you will see, at the corner of the crossroads, a person display his silhouette and head lightly towards the boulevards. But if one gets nearer to him, in a way that doesn't attract the attention of this passer-by, one is pleasantly surprised to see that he is young! From afar we would have actually taken him for a mature man. The sum of days no longer counts when it comes to appreciating the intellectual capacity of a serious face. *I know how to read age in the forehead's physiognomic lines: he is sixteen years and four months old!* He is as fine as the retractility of raptors' talons; or more like the uncertainty of muscular movements in wounds in the soft parts of the posterior cervical region; or rather like that perpetual rat-trap, always reset by the captured animal, which alone can take rodents indefinitely and even function hidden beneath straw; and, above all, like the fortuitous meeting of a sewing-machine and an umbrella on a dissecting table! Mervyn, this son of fair England, had just taken a fencing lesson with his teacher and, wrapped in his Scottish tartan, is returning to his parents' house. It is eight thirty, and he hopes to arrive home by nine o'clock: it is a considerable presumption on his part to feign certainty of knowing the future. Might not some unseen obstacle block his way? And would this circumstance, if infrequent, oblige him to consider it an exception? Why does he not consider instead, as an abnormal fact, the possibility that up till now he had felt free of worry and somewhat happy? By what right does he actually presume that he will reach his home safely, when someone watches him and stalks him as their future prey? (It would be to know little about one's profession of sensational writing to not at least highlight the restrictive interrogations immediately after which comes the sentence I am about to finish.) You have recognized the imaginary hero who has for ages broken my unfortunate intellect with the pressure of his personality! Sometimes Maldoror approaches Mervyn in order to carve this adolescent's features onto his memory; sometimes, body thrown backwards, he rebounds on himself like the Australian boomerang in the second phase of its trajectory—or instead like a diabolical

machine. Undecided about what he should do. But his conscience does not experience any symptom of the most embryogenic emotion, as you might mistakenly reckon. I saw him move away momentarily in the opposite direction: was he overwhelmed by remorse? But he retraced his steps with renewed stubbornness. Mervyn doesn't know why his temporal arteries beat so strongly, and he presses on, obsessed with a fear whose cause you and he both seek in vain. It is necessary to take into account his concentration to expose the enigma. Why doesn't he turn around? He would understand everything. Do we ever consider the most simple methods of bringing an alarming state to an end? When a barrier lurker crosses the boundary of one suburb to another, a bowl's-worth of white wine in his gullet and his coat in tatters, if at the corner of a border-marker he should notice a brawny old cat—contemporary with the revolutions in which our forefathers participated—gloomily contemplating the moonlight beating down

on the sleeping plain, he approaches torturously in a crooked line and gestures to a knock-kneed dog, which rushes forward. The noble animal of feline breed awaits its adversary courageously and contests its life dearly. Tomorrow some ragpicker will purchase an electrifiable hide. Why then did the cat not flee? It was so easy. But in the case that actually concerns us, Mervyn again complicates the danger through his own ignorance. He has some glimmers, very rare it's true, whose shrouding vagueness I won't stop to demonstrate; however, it's impossible for him to figure out reality. He is no prophet—I don't say otherwise—and he doesn't admit the faculty of being one. Reaching the large thoroughfare he turns right and crosses the Boulevard Poissonnière and the Boulevard Bonne-Nouvelle. At this point in his journey he proceeds into the Rue du Faubourg-Saint-Denis, leaving the Strasbourg railway platform behind him, and pauses in front of a lofty gate prior to reaching the perpendicular higher level of the Rue Lafayette. Since you advise me to end the first stanza here, I will indeed comply—this time—with your wish. Do you know that, when I imagine the iron ring hidden beneath a rock by the hand of a maniac, an invincible thrill passes through my hair?

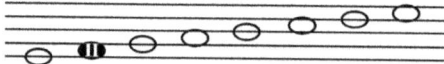

E PULLS A brass knob and the front gate of the modern townhouse swings on its hinges. He walks along the court covered in fine sand and ascends the eight steps of the stoop. The two statues placed on the right and left as guardians of the aristocratic villa don't obstruct his passage. The one who has renounced all—father, mother, Providence, love, ideals, in order to think only for himself—is careful not to follow the preceding steps. He has seen the young man entering a spacious ground-floor lounge with carnelian woodwork. The genteel son throws himself on the couch and emotion prevents him from speaking. His mother, in a long and trailing robe, fusses around him and enfolds him in her arms. His younger brothers group themselves around the couch loaded with its burden; they don't know enough about life to have a clear idea of the scene unfolding. Finally the father raises his cane and lowers a look full of authority on those present. Supporting his wrists on the arms of the easy-chair, he moves from his usual seat and, although weakened by age, he advances anxiously towards the motionless body of his first-born. He speaks in a foreign tongue, and each listens to it in respectful contemplation: "Who has sent the boy into this state? The misty Thames will ferry a mountain of silt again before my powers have been completely exhausted. Protective laws don't seem to exist in this inhospitable country. If I knew who to blame he'd feel the force of my arm. Even though I've long been retired from naval combat, my commodore's sword hanging on the wall hasn't rusted yet. Besides, it's easy to sharpen the edge. Calm yourself, Mervyn; I will direct my servants to locate the trail of this one whom, henceforth, I will seek out so that I can kill him with my own hand. Wife, go away and crouch in a corner; your eyes mollify me, and it would be better for you to close the ducts of your tear glands. My son, I implore you, awaken your senses and acknowledge your family; this is your father speaking to you..." The mother keeps her distance, and in order to obey her master's orders she has taken a book in her hands and is endeavoring to stay calm in the presence of the danger facing the one whom her womb had brought into the world. "...Children, go and amuse yourselves in the park, and be careful not to fall into the pond when admiring the swimming of the swans..." The brothers remain silent, hands hanging; with toque hats topped with plumes plucked from the wing of the chuck-will's-widow,[27] with knee-length and silk-bottomed velvet trousers, they join hands and leave the lounge-room, taking care to only tread on tiptoe on the ebony parquetry. I'm sure they won't have fun and will walk seriously through the avenues of plane trees. Their intelligence is precocious. All the better for them. "...Useless cares—I rock you in my arms and you are oblivious to my comfortings. Would you lift your head? I'll hug your knees if it's necessary. But no...it falls back down again, still." — "My dear master, if you would permit your servant, I am going to look in my room for a flask filled with turpentine essence, and which I habitually use when migraine plagues my temples after returning from the theatre or when the reading of a moving tale of our ancestors' chivalrous history recorded in the British annals throws my dreamy thought into swamps of sluggishness." — "Wife, I didn't given you leave to speak and you've no right to take it. Since our marriage, no cloud has come to divide us. I am happy with you and I have never reproached you: and it's been reciprocal. Go look in your room for a flask filled with turpentine essence. I know it's in one of your dresser drawers, and you haven't just apprised me of it. Hasten up the steps of the spiral staircase and return to me with a contented face." But the sensitive London woman has barely made the first steps (she doesn't run as quickly as a person of the lower classes) when one of her maids-in-waiting, cheeks flushed with sweat, is already descending from the first floor with the flask which perhaps contains the liqueur of life within its crystal sides. The maid bows gracefully while presenting her offering, and the mother, with her regal bearing, has moved towards the fringes hemming the couch, the only object occupying her tenderness. The commodore, with a proud but benevolent gesture, accepts the flask from his wife's hands. An Indian scarf is soaked and wrapped around Mervyn's head with orbicular windings of silk. He breathes in the smelling-salts; he moves an arm. Circulation is revived, and one hears the joyous cries of the Philippine cockatoos perched on the window pane. "Who goes there?... Halt me not ... Where am I? Is it a grave supporting my leaden limbs? The boards seem sweet to me... The locket holding my mother's portrait, is it still hanging around my neck?... Retreat, evil-doer with the dishevelled head. He couldn't seize me, and I've left a piece of my doublet between his fingers. Unchain the bulldogs, because tonight a known thief may get into our home by breaking and entering while we're sunk in sleep. My father and mother, I recognize you and I thank you for your care. Call my little brothers. I've brought pralines for them and I wish to embrace them." At these words, he falls into a deeply lethargic state. The doctor, who has been promptly summoned, rubs his hands and cries: "The crisis has passed. All is well. Tomorrow your son will awaken refreshed. Everyone go to your respective beds—I command it—so that only I remain beside the patient until the appearance of dawn and the nightingale's song." Maldoror, hiding behind the door, has not missed a word. Now he knows the personalities of the mansion's residents and he will act accordingly. He knows where Mervyn resides and doesn't wish to know any more. He has written the name of the street and number of the building in a notebook. That's the main thing. He is sure not to forget them. He advances like a hyæna along the edge of the court without being seen. He climbs the iron gate with agility and is momentarily blocked by iron spikes; in a bound he is on the causeway. He moves away with stealth. "He took me for a malefactor," he exclaims. "*He's* an idiot. I would like to find a man exempt from the accusation that nutcase brought against me. I haven't robbed him of a piece of his doublet, as he claimed. Basic hypnotic hallucination caused by fright. My intention wasn't to possess him today—because *I* have other ulterior designs on this timid adolescent." Head towards where the lake of swans is found and I will tell you later why there happens to be, among the lamentation, a completely black one whose body, supporting an anvil surmounted with the rotting corpse of a turtle crab, justifiably inspires distrust in its other aquatic comrades.

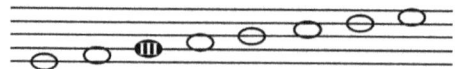

 **ERVYN IS IN** his bedroom; he has received a letter. Who then would write him a letter? His anxiety prevents him from thanking the postman. The envelope has black edgings and the words are written out in a hasty script. Is he going to refer this letter to his father? And if the sender expressly forbids him to? Filled with anguish, he opens his window to breathe in the aromas of the air; the rays of the sun reflect their prismatic irradiations on the Venetian glasses and damask curtains. He throws the letter aside among the gilt-edged books and volumes bound in mother-of-pearl scattered on the embossed leather covering the surface of his study desk. He opens his piano and runs his slender fingers along the ivory keys. The brass strings don't resonate at all. This indirect warning encourages him to once more take up the vellum paper — but it has drawn back as if offended by the recipient's hesitation. Taken in by this ruse, Mervyn's curiosity grows and he unfolds the piece of prepared scrap-paper. Until that moment he had only seen his own handwriting.

Young man, I'm interested in you:
I want to make you happy.
I will take you as a companion, and
we will carry out lengthy travels in
the Oceanic islands. Merryn, you know
that I love you, and I don't need to prove
it to you. You will give me your friendship,
I'm sure. When you know me better
you won't regret the confidence you've
shown in me. I will protect you from
the dangers that your inexperience
will face. I'll be a brother to you,
and you won't want for good advice.
For longer explanations, be at the Pont
du Carrousel the day after tomorrow
at five o'clock in the morning. If
I haven't arrived, wait for me — but I
hope to make it there on time.
You do likewise. An Englishman won't
easily forsake the chance to see
clearly into his affairs. Young man, I
greet you, and I'll see you shortly.
Do not show this letter to anyone.

"Three stars in place of a signature," exclaims Mervyn; "and a blood blot at the bottom of the page!" Abundant tears flow onto the curious sentences which his eyes had devoured, and which opened in his spirit the limitless field of uncertain and new horizons. It seems to him (only since the reading he just finished) that his father is a bit harsh and his mother too pompous. He has reasons (which are unknown to me and which consequently I can't convey to you) for suggesting that his brothers no longer suited him. He secrets this letter in his vest. That day his teachers observed that he didn't seem himself; his eyes were immoderately troubled and the veil of excessive reflection overcast his periorbital region. Each teacher blushed for fear of not finding himself at his student's intellectual height, and yet, for the first time, this youth neglected his duties and didn't work. In the evening the family meet in the dining-room decorated with antique portraits. Mervyn admires the plates loaded with succulent foods and perfumed fruits, but he doesn't eat; the multicoloured streams of Rhine wines and sparkling rubies of Champagne are lavished in tall and slender flutes of Bohemian crystal, and leave even his view indifferent. He leans his elbow on the table and stays absorbed in his thoughts like a sleepwalker. The commodore, with a face cured by sea-spray, leans over to his wife's ear: "Our eldest has altered his character since the day of the fit. He was already too carried away with absurd ideas — today he daydreams still more than usual. For goodness' sake, *I* wasn't like that when I was his age. Look as though you don't notice anything. It's here that an effective remedy, material or moral, might easily be employed. Mervyn, as you enjoy reading books of travels and natural history, I want to read you a story that you won't mind. Listen carefully to me; everyone will find some benefit in it, me first of all. And you other children, learn, through the attention you'll pay to my words, to hone the cut of your jib [28] and to realize an author's least intentions." As if this brood of adorable kids could have understood what this rhetoric was! He spoke and, upon a gesture of his hand, one of the brothers moved towards the paternal library and returned with a volume under his arm. Meanwhile the table-cloth and silverware are removed, and the father takes the book. At that electrifying noun "travels," Mervyn raised his head and tried to stem his inappropriate meditations. The book is opened towards the middle and the commodore's metallic voice proves that he remains capable, as in the days of his glorious youth, of controlling the fury of men and tempests. Well before the end of the reading Mervyn is once more leaning on his elbow, unable to follow any longer the reasoned development of sentences passing in sequence and the saponification of obligatory metaphors. The father exclaims: "This isn't interesting—let's read something else. You read, wife—*you'll* be luckier than I in dispelling the grief from our son's days." The mother no longer holds out hope; nevertheless she has taken hold of another book and the tone of her soprano voice rings out melodiously to her offspring's ears. But discouragement overcomes her after several words and she ceases her rendition of the literary work. The eldest son exclaims: "I'm going to lie down." He withdraws, eyes downcast with an icy stare, and without adding anything further. The dog begins to raise a mournful barking because it doesn't find this behaviour natural, and the wind outside, rushing intermittently through the longitudinal crack in the window, causes the flame, enclosed by the two rose crystal cupolas of the bronze lamp, to gutter. The mother presses her hands to her forehead and the father raises his eyes to Heaven. The children cast alarmed looks on the old sailor. Mervyn locks his bedroom door and his hand moves quickly on paper: "I received your letter at noon, and you will excuse me if I've made you wait for a reply. I haven't had the honour of knowing you personally and I don't know if I should write to you. However, as rudeness doesn't exist in our house I've resolved to take the quill and thank you warmly for the interest you take in a stranger. God forbid that I not show gratitude for the sympathy that you heap upon me. I know my faults and I no longer exhibit pride. But if it's fitting to accept the friendship of an older person, it is also fitting for him to understand that our characters aren't the same.

Indeed, you *appear* to be older than me since you call me 'young man,' and yet I have doubts about your true age. For how to reconcile the coldness of your syllogisms with the passion that radiates from within? It's certain that I won't leave my birthplace in order to accompany you through far-off countries; that would only be possible on the condition that I ask my parents beforehand for an impatiently-awaited permission. However, as you have implored me to keep 'mum' (in the cubic sense of the word) about this spiritually mysterious affair, I will hasten to obey your undeniable wisdom. It sounds like it wouldn't face the spotlight happily. Since you seem to want me to have confidence in your own person (not a misplaced wish, I must confess), please be good enough to show a similar confidence for my sake and to not assume that I'll be too far away from your view if I'm not punctual at our meeting at the hour indicated on the morning of the day after tomorrow. I will pass over the surrounding wall of the park because the gate will be closed, and nobody will witness my leaving. To speak frankly, what *wouldn't* I do for you, whose unexplainable attachment promptly knew how to show itself to my dazzled eyes — especially astonished by such proof of kindness which I'm sure I wouldn't have expected. Since I didn't know you. *Now* I know you. Don't forget your promise to me — of your strolling on the Pont du Carrousel. Should I pass there I'm absolutely certain of meeting you and shaking your hand, providing that this innocent display by an adolescent who only yesterday bowed before the altar of modesty doesn't offend you with its respectful familiarity. Well, isn't familiarity respectable in the case of a strong and passionate intimacy, when utter ruin is grave and proven? And I ask *you*, what harm would there be after all if I should bid you *adieu* while passing on the day after tomorrow, raining or not, when five o'clock has sounded? You, yourself a gentleman, will appreciate the tact with which I've conceived my letter, because I don't allow myself to tell you any more in a loose leaf apt to go astray. Your address at the bottom of the page is a puzzle. It has taken me almost fifteen minutes to decipher it. I think you did well to write the words in a microscopic manner. I'll dispense with signing and with that I imitate you: we live in far too an eccentric age to be astonished by what could happen at any moment. I would be curious to know how you learned of the place where my glacial immobility resides, surrounded by a long line of deserted rooms, vile charnel houses of my hours of ennui. How do I say this? When I think of you my chest stirs, resounding like the collapse of an empire in decline—because the shadow of your love reveals a smile which may not exist: it is so vague, and moves its scales so torturously! Into your hands I abandon my impetuous feelings, marble slates entirely new and as yet undeflowered by mortal contact. Let's be patient until the dawn of the matinal twilight and, in expectation of the moment which will throw me into the hideous interlacing of your pestilential arms, I humbly bow at your knees, which I embrace." After penning this guilty letter, Mervyn carried it to the post office and returns to go to bed. Don't count on finding his guardian angel there. The fish's tail will only fly for three days, it's true—but, alas! the girder won't be any less scorched; and a cylindrical-conical bullet will penetrate the hide of a rhinoceros—despite the snow maiden and the beggar! In fact, the crowned fool will have told the truth regarding the fealty of the fourteen daggers.

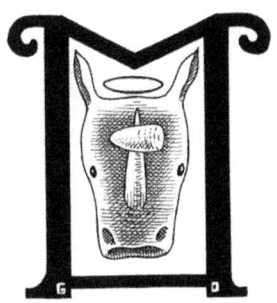

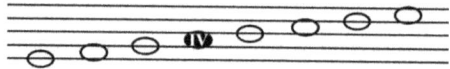

**PERCEIVED THAT** I had only one eye in the middle of my forehead! O mirrors of silver set into the panels of vestibules, how many rewards have you not offered me through your reflective power! Since the day when an Angora cat, suddenly flying onto my back, nibbled me on the parietal bump for an hour like a trepan penetrating the skull—because I had boiled her kittens in a tank filled with alcohol—I haven't stopped launching the arrow of torments against myself. Today, under the impression of wounds that my body received in various circumstances—either by the fatality of my birth or by the fact of my own fault—overwhelmed by the consequences of my moral decline (some things have been completed; who will forecast the others?); impassive spectator of monstrosities, acquired or natural, which decorate the aponeuroses and intellect of he who speaks, I throw a long look of satisfaction on the duality which forms me... and I find myself beautiful! As beautiful as the vice of congenital conformity in the sexual organs of Man, comprising the relatively short canal of the urethra and the division or absence of its lower wall, in such a way that this canal opens at a variable distance from the glans and below the penis; or, more so, like the fleshy wattle, conical in form, furrowed by fairly deep transverse wrinkles, which rises from the bottom of the upper beak of the turkey; or rather like the following truth: "The system of scales, modes and their harmonic sequence, is not founded on the invariable natural laws but is, on the contrary, the result of

æsthetic principles which have changed with the progressive development of humanity and which will change again"; and, above all, like an armored corvette with turrets! Yes, I stick to the precision of my assertion. I have no presumptuous delusion—I boast about it—and I've found no benefit in lying; therefore, you should show no hesitation at all in believing what I've said. Because, why would I draw my inspiration from horror in the face of the glowing testimonies that emerge from my conscience? I don't envy the Creator anything; but let Him allow me to flow down the river of my destiny through a growing series of glorious crimes. If not, raising a look annoyed by every obstacle level with His forehead, I will make Him understand that He isn't the only master of the universe—that there are several phenomena directly relevant to a more profound knowledge of the nature of things, giving evidence in favour of the contrary opinion and opposing a formal denial of the viability of the unity of power. In fact we're contemplating each other's eye-lashes, you see... and you know that the victory banzai has reverberated more than once from my lipless mouth. Farewell, illustrious warrior; Your courage through misfortune inspires respect in Your fiercest foes; but Maldoror will soon find You again to contest the prey called Mervyn. In this way will be realized the rooster's prophecy, when it had foreseen the future deep down in the candelabra. Would to Heaven that the turtle crab rejoins the pilgrims' caravan in time and apprises them in a few words of the narrative of the ragpicker of Clignancourt!

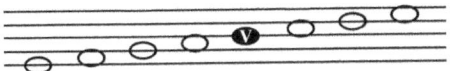

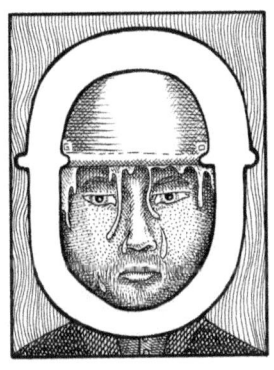

N A BENCH at the Palais-Royal, on the left side and not far from the ornamental pond, an individual leaving the Rue de Rivoli came to sit down. He has unkempt hair and his clothes reveal the corrosive action of prolonged destitution. He dug a hole in the soil with a pointed piece of wood and filled the hollow of his hand with earth. He brought this food to his mouth and quickly spat it out. He got up and, pressing his head against the bench, he aimed his legs upwards. But as this grotesque position is outside of the laws of weight governing the centre of gravity, he has fallen back clumsily onto the ground, arms hanging, his cap half-obscuring his face and legs beating against the gravel in an act of precarious balance less and less reassuring. He remains in that position for a considerable time. Near the adjoining northern entrance, beside the rotunda containing a coffee house, our hero's arm is resting against the railing. His view travels over the rectangular area in a manner that lets none of the perspective escape. His eyes refocus after the completion of this investigation and he perceives in the middle of the garden a man who performs staggering gymnastics with a bench on which he tries to stabilise himself while executing miracles of strength and skill. But what can the best intention bring to the aid of a just cause — against the disorders of insanity? He moved towards the madman to kindly help him restore his dignity to a normal state — he held out his hand to him and sat beside him. He notices that the madness is only intermittent; the attack has passed; his interlocutor replies logically to all questions. Is it necessary to report the sense of his words? Why reopen the volume of human miseries, on any page, with blasphemous eagerness? There is no education more fruitful. Even if I might have no real event for you to hear, I will concoct imaginary accounts to transfer into your brain. But the sufferer hasn't become this way for his own pleasure; and the sincerity of his replies combines marvellously with the reader's credulity. "My father was a carpenter in the Rue de la Verrerie… May the deaths of the three Marguerites fall on his head, and may the canary's beak gnaw perpetually at the axis of his eyeball! He had developed the habit of getting soused; at the times when he would return to the house after frequenting night clubs, his fury became almost limitless and he would indiscriminately strike any objects appearing to his sight. But soon, confronted by reproaches from his friends, he cured himself completely and took on a taciturn mood. Nobody could get close to him, not even our mother. He harboured a secret resentment against the idea of duty that hindered his behaving as he pleased. I had purchased a canary for my three sisters; it was for my three sisters that I had purchased a canary. They placed it in a cage above the door and passers-by would always stop to listen to the bird's songs, to admire its ephemeral grace and to study its clever manners. More than once my father had ordered that the cage and its contents be removed because he suspected the canary was mocking him by throwing him the bouquet of ærial cavatinas with its vocal skill. He had gone to detach the cage from its nail and had slipped from the chair, blinded with rage. A slight graze on the knee had been the trophy for his venture. After staying a few moments to press the swollen part with a wood-shard, he had lowered his trouser-leg, frowning — had taken better precautions, put the cage under his arm and gone towards the rear of his workshop. There, despite the cries and pleas of his family (we were very attached to this bird, who was like the household genie to us), he had crushed the wicker box with his iron heels, while a wood-plane whirling around his head kept his audience at bay.

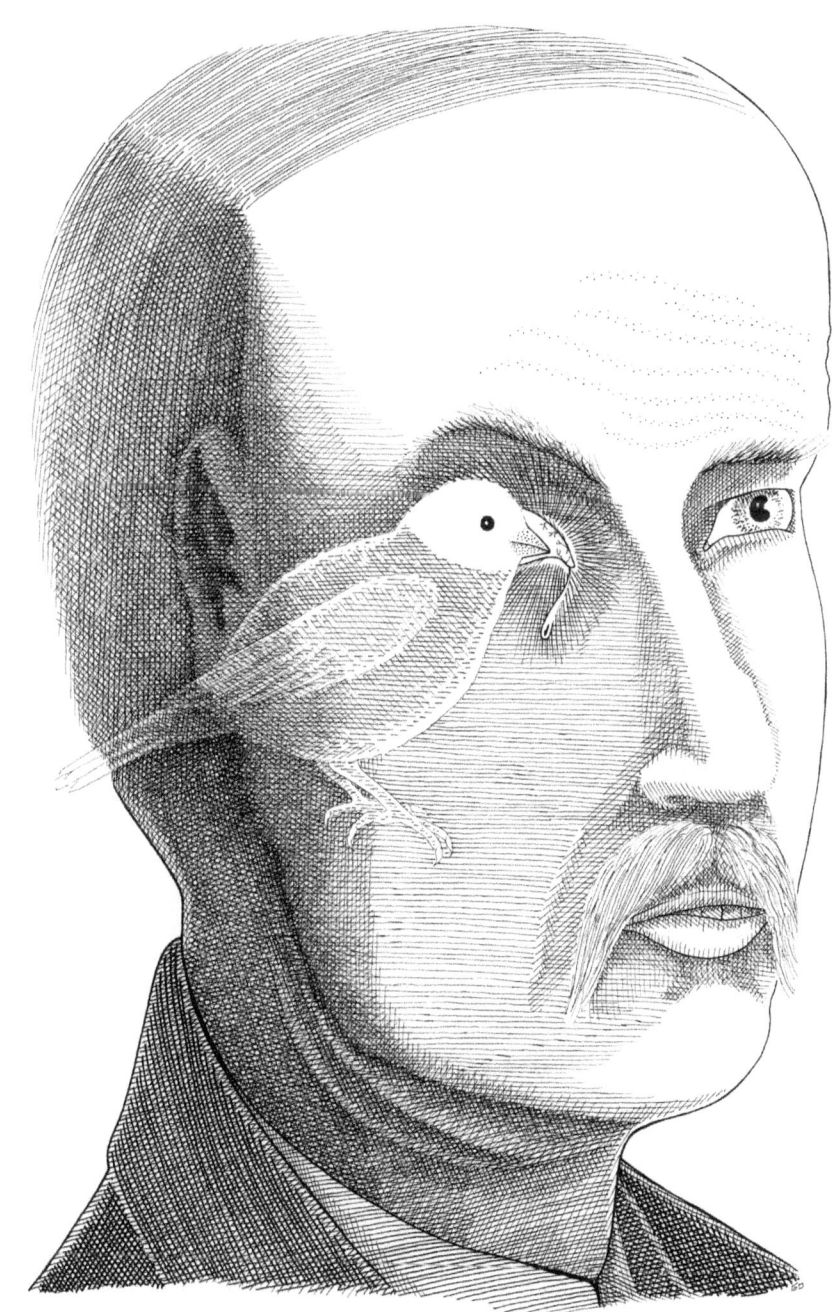

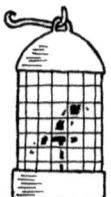

By chance the canary hadn't immediately died; despite the bloody spotting, this flock of feathers was still living. The carpenter had withdrawn and closed the door with a bang. My mother and I strove to sustain the bird's life, which was ready to flee; it achieved its aim, and the movement of its wings manifested no more than the mirror of ultimate death-agony. Meanwhile the three Marguerites, when they saw that all hope had been lost, joined hands with common accord, and the living chain went to squat behind the staircase next to our bitch's kennel, after pushing a barrel of grease a few feet away. My mother wasn't ceasing her task, and took the canary between her fingers in order to warm it with her breath. *I* was running distraught through all the rooms, bumping into furniture and tools. From time to time one of my sisters would show her head at the foot of the staircase in order to inquire about the fate of the unfortunate bird, and would withdraw it sadly. The bitch left its kennel and, as if it had understood the extent of our loss, it was licking the dresses of the three Marguerites with the tongue of pointless comfort. The canary hadn't more than moments to live. In her turn, one of my sisters (the youngest) had shown her head in the penumbra formed by the rarefaction of the light. She had seen my mother grow pale and the bird—after having in a flash raised its neck at the final protest of its nervous system—fall again between her fingers, motionless forever. She had broken the news to her sisters. They hadn't made the slightest rustle of complaint, nor any murmur. Silence reigned in the workshop. We only discerned the staccato creaking of the cage fragments which, according to the elasticity of wood, were partly recovering the original state of their construction. The three Marguerites weren't letting a tear fall and their faces didn't lose their crimson bloom; no... they were just staying still. They dragged themselves into the interior of the kennel and lay beside each other on the straw, as the bitch, passive witness to their move, watched them go with astonishment. My mother had called to them many times; they didn't make any sound of reply. Exhausted by their earlier emotions, they were probably sleeping! She had searched every corner of the house without glimpsing them. She followed the bitch, who was pulling her by the dress, towards the kennel. This woman had knelt and placed her head at the opening. According to my mental reckoning, the scene she'd been given to witness, quite apart from the unhealthy excesses of maternal fear, could only have been harrowing. I had lit a candle and given it to her; in that way no detail would escape her. She had drawn her head, covered with strands of straw, from the premature tomb and told me: "The three Marguerites are dead." As we couldn't get them out of that place—because bear in mind they were tightly linked together—I had gone to look in the workshop for a hammer to break open the canine domicile. I had immediately started on the demolition work and passers-by would have thought, if only they'd had the imagination, that labour wasn't idle in our home. My mother, impatient at these delays which were nevertheless necessary, was breaking her fingernails against the boards. Finally the adverse rescue operation had ended—the split kennel was broken open on all sides and we had removed the carpenter's daughters, one after the other, from the rubble, after having separated them with difficulty. My mother had left the country. I never saw my father again. As for me, they say that I'm crazy, and I beg for public charity. What I do know is that the canary sings no more." The listener inwardly approves of this new lesson backing up his disgusting theories. As though, because of one man once sozzled by wine, one would be right to accuse all humanity. At least such is the paradoxical reflection he is looking to inject into his mind, but it can't drive away the important lessons of solemn experience. He consoles the madman with feigned compassion and wipes his tears away with his own handkerchief. He leads him into a restaurant and they eat at the same table. They go to a swank tailor and the protégé is fitted-out like a prince. They knock for the concierge at a grand house on the Rue Saint-Honoré, and the madman is settled into a luxurious apartment on the third floor. The bandit forces him to accept his money, and taking the chamber-pot from beneath the bed he puts it on Aghone's head. "I crown you 'King of Intellects,'" he exclaims, with deliberate emphasis. "I will scurry at your least request; take from my coffers with both hands; I belong to you, body and soul. At night you will return the alabaster crown to its rightful place, at your leave to use it; but in the day, once dawn illuminates the cities, place it back there on your forehead as the symbol of your power. The three Marguerites will live again in me, not counting that I will be your mother." Then the lunatic drew back a few steps, as if he were the victim of a confronting nightmare; lines of happiness were painted on his face wrinkled by sorrows; filled with humiliation, he knelt down at the feet of his protector. Like a poison, gratitude had entered the heart of the crowned madman! He had wanted to speak, and his tongue came to a stop. He had leaned his body forward and had fallen back onto the floor. The man with the bronze lips takes off. What was his aim? To acquire a foolproof friend innocent enough to obey the least of his commands. He couldn't have met better and chance had favoured him. The one whom he'd found lying on the bench no longer knows, since an event in his youth, how to recognize good from evil. It's this very Aghone whom he needs.

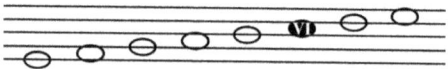

HE OMNIPOTENT HAD sent one of His archangels to earth to save the young man from certain death. He Himself will be forced to descend! However, we haven't reached that part of our story yet, and I feel compelled to shut my mouth because I can't tell everything at once—each gimmick will therefore appear in its place when the plot of this fiction deems it convenient. In order to not be recognized, the archangel had taken the form of a turtle crab as large as a vicuña. It held on to the point of a reef in the middle of the sea and waited for the favourable moment in the tide to facilitate its raid on the beach. The man with lips of jasper, hidden behind a curve of the beach, was watching the animal, a stick in his hand. Who would have wanted to read the thoughts of these two beings? The first one didn't conceal that it had a difficult mission to accomplish: "And how to succeed there," it exclaimed, while the breakers were beating its temporary refuge, "where more than once my master has seen His strength and courage founder? *I* am only a limited substance, while the other—nobody knows where he comes from and what his final aim is. At his name the heavenly armies shake; and in the regions I've left, more than one recounts that Satan himself—Satan, the personification of evil—is not as ruthless." The second being made the following remarks: they found an echo up in the azure bowl they'd soiled: "It reeks of inexperience—I will settle its account swiftly. No doubt it comes from Heaven, sent by the One who fears so much to

come Himself! We'll see in the deed if it is as imperious as it seems; this is not an inhabitant of the terrestrial apricot; it betrays its seraphic origin by its straying and hesitant eyes." The turtle crab, which had been scanning a particular area of the shore for some time now, caught sight of our hero (this one had then risen up to his full Herculean height) and apostrophized him with the following words: "Do not attempt combat, and surrender yourself. I am sent by Someone who is superior to us both, to place you in chains and make it impossible for both your limbs to move complicit with your thoughts. To grasp knives and daggers between your fingers must henceforth be forbidden you, believe me, in the best interests of yourself and others. Dead or alive, I'll have you; I have orders to bring you alive. Don't force me to resort to the power that was granted me. I will behave with delicacy; as for you, don't offer me any resistance. It is thus that I will know, eagerly and joyfully, that you've made the first step towards repentance." When our hero heard this harangue, marked by such profoundly comical wit, he had trouble preserving seriousness on the roughness of his tanned features. But, well, nobody will be surprised if I were to add that he ended up by laughing out loud. This was too much for him! There was no ill intent there! He certainly didn't want to attract the reproaches of the turtle crab! What efforts did he not make to drive off mirth! How many times did he not zip his lips so as not to appear to offend his astonished interlocutor! Unfortunately, his character shared humanity's nature and he laughed like sheep do! Finally he ceased! It was time! He had almost choked! The wind carried this response to the archangel on the reef: "When your Master no longer sends me snails and crayfish to sort out His affairs, and when He deigns to negotiate personally with me, I'm sure we'll find a way of coming to terms—since I am inferior to He who has sent you, as you've so rightly said. Until then, thoughts of reconciliation appear premature to me and they are apt to produce only a mixed result. I'm very far from misunderstanding what is supposed in each of your syllables, and as we would exhaust our voices pointlessly by making them cover a three-kilometre distance, it seems to me that you would act wisely if you came down from your impregnable fortress and gained *terra firma* by swimming—we will more conveniently discuss conditions of a surrender which, as legitimate as it may be, nevertheless has an ultimately unfavourable aspect for me." The archangel, who wasn't expecting this good will, poked its head up a notch from the depths of the crevice and replied: "O Maldoror, has the day finally arrived when your abominable habits will see extinguished the torch of unjustifiable pride leading them to eternal damnation? It will then be *I* who'll first recount this laudable transformation to the ranks of cherubim, happy to find one of their own once more. *You* know, and haven't forgotten, that there was a time when you had your premier place among us. Your name flew from mouth to mouth; you are actually the subject of our *tête-à-têtes*. Come, then... come to make a lasting peace with your old Master; He will receive you like a lost son and he will never glimpse the mass of guilt, like a mountain of moose antlers raised by Native Americans, that you've heaped upon your heart." It had spoken—and it withdraws every part of its body from the bottom of the dark opening. It appears atop the reef, radiant like a priest when he is assured of retrieving a stray sheep. It is about to dive into the water in order to swim towards the pardoned one. But the man with the sapphire lips has calculated a treacherous strike a long time in advance. His stick is thrown with force; after many rebounds on the waves it strikes the head of the do-gooder archangel. The crab, mortally wounded, falls into the water. The tide carries the floating flotsam towards the shore. It *had* been waiting for the tide in order to carry out its raid more easily. Oh well, the tide has come; it has lulled it with its lullabies and softly deposited it on the beach: isn't the crab content? What more must it do for it? And Maldoror, bending down towards the sand on the beach, receives two friends in his arms, inseparably reunited, by chance, by the wave: the corpse of the turtle crab and the killer stick! "I haven't lost my skill yet," he exclaims to himself. "It just requires practice; my arms retain their power and my eye its accuracy." He regards the inanimate animal. He fears that he might be held accountable for the bloodshed. Where will he hide the archangel? And at the same time he wonders whether death had been immediate. He has put an anvil and a corpse on his back; he heads towards a large ornamental lake whose banks are completely covered, and seemingly walled-in, by a tangled mess of high reeds. Initially he wanted to take a hammer, but it is too lightweight a tool, while with a heavier object, if the corpse should show signs of life, he will place it on the ground and pulverize it with blows from the anvil. It's not vigour that his arm lacks—come off it! That's the least of his worries. Arriving in view of the lake, he sees it populated by swans. He tells himself that this is a sanctuary for him; by means of

a metamorphosis—without giving up his cargo—he mingles with the group of other birds. Note there the hand of Providence where we were tempted to find it absent, and take advantage of the miracle of which I'm going to speak. As black as the wing of a crow, thrice he swam among the sownder of dazzlingly-white palmipeds; thrice he had retained that distinctive colour that made him resemble a block of coal. This is how God, through His justice, never allowed his ploy capable of deceiving even a lamentation of swans.[29] In such a way that he had remained conspicuously in the middle of the lake—but all had kept their distance and not one bird approached his shameful plumage to keep him company. And so he had circumscribed his dives to an excluded bay at the far end of the ornamental lake, alone among the avians—as he was alone among men! This is the way he introduced the incredible event at the Place Vendôme!

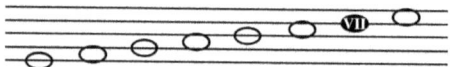

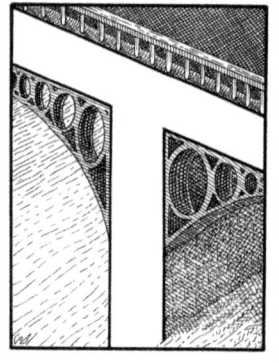

HE PIRATE WITH the golden hair received Mervyn's reply. In that singular page he follows the trail of intellectual anxieties of the one who'd written it, surrendering to the weak powers of his own suggestion. The young man would have done better to have consulted his parents before responding to the stranger's friendship. Absolutely no good would come to him by getting caught up as the main player in this equivocal drama. But, in the end, he wanted it. At the appointed time Mervyn headed straight out of the door of his house, following the Boulevard Sébastopol up to the Saint-Michel Fountain. He takes the Quai des Grands-Augustins and crosses the Quai de Conti; just as he passes over the Quai Malaquais, he sees on the Quai du Louvre, parallel to his own path, an individual carrying a sack under his arm and who appears to examine him carefully. The morning mists have dissipated. The two pedestrians emerge at the same time on each side of the Pont du Carrousel. Although they had never seen one another before, they recognized each other! It was truly touching to see these two beings, divided by age, bring their souls closer through the grandeur of their feelings. At least, that would have been the opinion of those who might have paused before this sight—which more than one person, even with a mathematical mind, would have found moving. With a teary face Mervyn was reflecting that he was meeting, at the start of life as it were, a precious supporter in future adversities. Be assured that the other said nothing. Here is what he'd done: he had unfolded the sack he was carrying, freed the opening, and, seizing the young man by his head, he'd shoved his whole body into the canvas shroud. He had tied the open end with his handkerchief. As Mervyn was shouting shrilly, he had carried off the sack like a bundle of linen and bashed it repeatedly against the parapet of the bridge. Then the casualty, becoming aware of the cracking of his bones, had gone quiet. Unique scene—which no novelist will encounter again! A butcher was passing, astride the meat on his cart. An individual runs up to him, implores him to stop, and tells him: "There's a dog trapped in that sack—it's got the mange: slaughter it quick smart." The addressed man proves to be compliant. The interrupter, while departing, sees a young girl in rags holding her hand out to him. How far, then, does the height of impudence and impiety go? He gives her alms! Tell me if you would like me to lead you, a few hours from now, through the door of a remote abattoir. The butcher returned and said to his colleagues, while throwing a burden to the ground: "Let's hurry up and slaughter this mangy dog." There are four of them, and each grabs his customary hammer. And yet they were hesitating—because the sack was moving forcefully. "What emotion takes hold of me?" cried one of them while slowly lowering his arm. "This dog moans with pain like a baby," said another. "One would think it knows the fate awaiting it." "It's their habit," replied a third. "Even when they aren't sick, as is the case here, it's enough when their master is away from home for a few days to start them making howls that are really hard to bear." "Stop!...halt!..." cried the fourth, before every arm had risen rhythmically to bash—decisively this time—the sack. "Stop, I tell you—there's a fact escaping us here. Who told you this sack contains a dog? I want to make sure." Then, despite his companions' gibes, he had untied the sack and extricated, one after the other, Mervyn's limbs! He was almost choked by the discomfort of this position. Seeing the light again, he fainted. A few moments later he gave the unmistakable signs of life. The saviour said: "Learn, once more, to show prudence—including in your trade. You've failed to note,

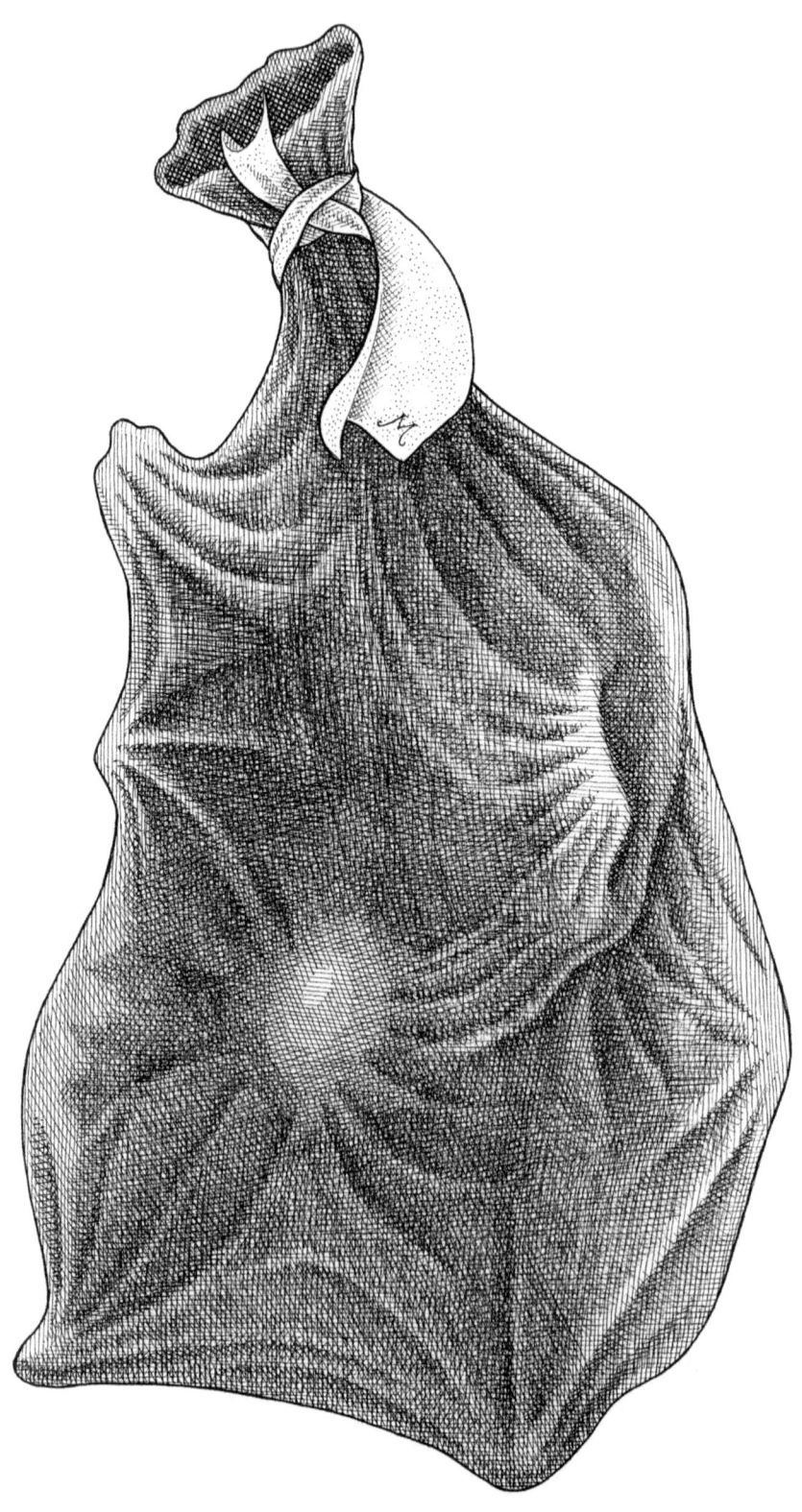

for yourselves, that it's useless to practise non-compliance with this law." The butchers had fled. Mervyn, heart aggrieved and full of grim forebodings, returns home and shuts himself in his room. Do I need to press the point about this stanza? Well! Who *wouldn't* deplore the events consummated there! Let's wait for the end in order to deliver an even more severe verdict. The *dénouement* is going to dash; and in tales of this kind—where passion (whatever type it may be) is given, the latter not fearing any hurdle in order to clear its path—there is no reason to dilute four hundred mundane pages in a mug of shellac. It is necessary to say what can be said in half a dozen stanzas, and then be silent.

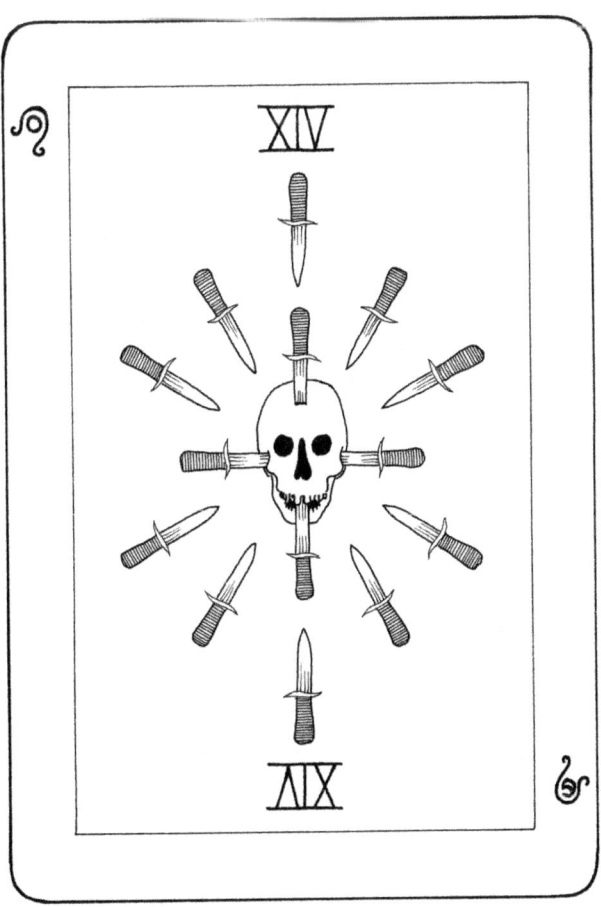

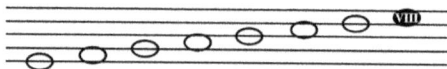

**N ORDER TO** put together mechanically the brain of a somnolent story, it's not enough to dissect trifles and to strongly stupefy the reader's intellect with renewed doses so as to render his faculties paralyzed for the rest of his life by the infallible law of fatigue; in addition, it is necessary to ingeniously place him, by means of good mesmeric fluid, into somnambulistic immobility while forcing his eyes to blur, against his nature, through the fixity of yours. I want to say—in order not to make myself easier to understand but only to develop my thinking, which interests and irks simultaneously with a most penetrating harmony—that I don't believe it's necessary, in order to reach the bottom line that one proposes, to invent a poetry entirely outside of Nature's normal course and whose pernicious exhalation seems to upset even absolute truths; but to achieve such a result (conforming moreover to æsthetic rules, if one were to consider it properly)—that's not as easy as one might think: *that's* what I wanted to say. This is why I will make every effort to attain it! If death halts the fantastic meagreness of my shoulders' two long arms, employed in the lugubrious crushing of my literary gypsum, I at least want the grieving reader to be able to soliloquize: "Justice must be done him. He has cretinized me muchly. What might he *not* have done if he'd been able to live longer! This is the best teacher of hypnotism I know!" These few moving words will be engraved on the marble of my tomb and my ancestors' spirits will be satisfied!—

I would continue! There was a fish-tail wriggling beside a worn-out boot at the bottom of a hole. It wasn't natural to wonder: "Where is the fish? I only see the wriggling tail." For considering that one had, in a precise way, confessed implicitly to having not seen the fish, it wasn't really there. The rain had left some drops of water at the bottom of this crater bored into the sand. As for the decrepit boot, some

people have since thought that it originated from some voluntary abandonment. The turtle crab was to be revived by divine power from its resolved atoms. He withdrew the fish-tail from the well and promised to reattach it to its lost body if it would announce to the Creator His envoy's impotence to control the raging waves of the maldororian ocean. He had lent it two albatross wings and the fish-tail had taken flight. But it had flown towards the renegade's domicile in order to report what was happening and to betray the turtle crab. The latter had guessed the spy's plan and, before the end of the third day, it had transfixed the fish-tail with a poisoned arrow. The spy's throat managed a weak exclamation, delivering the final sigh before landing. Then a secular girder, placed on the peak of a castle, had recovered its full height by jumping up on itself and had demanded revenge with great cries. But the Omnipotent, transformed into a rhinoceros, apprised it that this death was deserved. The girder had been appeased, it had gone to place itself at the foot of the manor, it had resumed its horizontal position and had called back the scared-off spiders so that they might resume weaving their webs in the corners. The man with the sulphur lips had discovered his ally's weakness; that is why he had ordered the crowned madman to burn the girder and reduce it to ashes. Aghone had executed this extreme order. "Since, according to you, the moment has come," he'd exclaimed, "I've retrieved the ring that I buried beneath the stone and I've attached it to one end of a cable. Here's the bundle." And he had proffered a coiled-up hawser, sixty metres long. His master had asked him what the fourteen daggers were doing. He had replied that they remained loyal and stood ready for any event, if it were necessary. The convict had nodded as a sign of satisfaction. He had shown surprise, and even concern, when Aghone had added that he'd seen a rooster cleave a candelabra in two with its beak, alternately glancing between each part and crowing while flapping its wings with frantic movement: "There isn't as much distance as one would think between the Rue de la Paix and the Place du Panthéon. We'll soon see the lamentable proof!" The turtle crab, mounted on a feisty charger, was racing flat out in the direction of the reef: the witness to the hurling of the stick by a tattooed arm, and its asylum from the first day of its descent onto the earth. A caravan of pilgrims was journeying to visit that place henceforth consecrated by an august death. The crab was hoping to reach it in order to ask the caravan for urgent aid against the intrigue about to happen, and of which it had knowledge. Aided by my glacial silence, you'll see a few lines down that the crab hadn't arrive in time to tell them what had been reported to it—by a ragpicker hidden behind the scaffolding next to a house under construction—on the day when the Pont du Carrousel, still tinged with night dew, glimpsed with horror the horizon of its thought enlarged confusingly by concentric circles at the morning vision of the rhythmic massaging of an icosahedron sack against its limestone parapet! Before it may stimulate their pity with remembrance of this episode, they will do well to extinguish the seed of hope within them… In order to break your lethargy, put the resources of good will to use, walk beside me, and don't lose sight of that madman, head crowned with a chamber pot, hand armed with a stick, who shoves before him the very one you would have trouble recognizing if I wasn't taking the trouble to inform you and reminding your ear of the word pronounced "Mervyn." How changed he is! Hands bound behind his back, he walks forward as though marching to the scaffold—and yet he's not guilty of any crime. They have arrived in the circular compound of the Place Vendôme. On the entablature of the massive column, leaning against the square balustrade more than fifty metres above the ground, a man has thrown and rolled out a rope which falls down to the ground a few feet from Aghone. One does a thing quickly with habit—but I can say that the latter didn't take very long to tie Mervyn's feet to the end of the rope. The rhinoceros had learned what was going to happen. Covered in sweat, it had shown up, breathless, at the corner of the Rue Castiglione. It hadn't even had the satisfaction of undertaking combat. The person who was surveying the surrounding area from the top of the

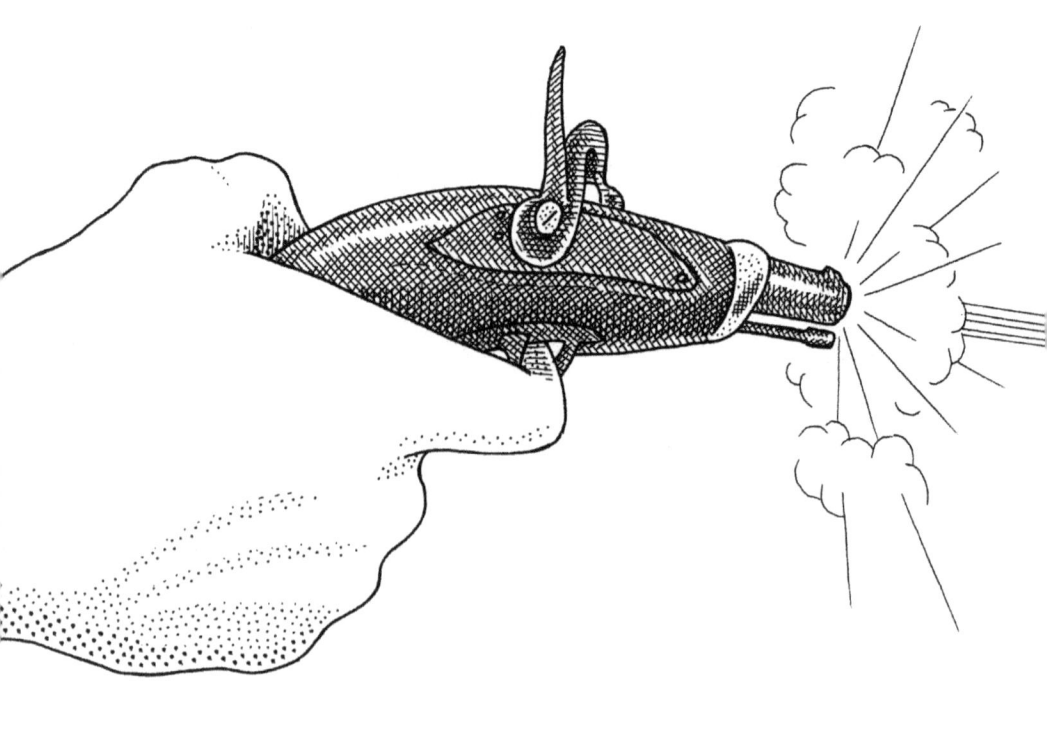

column had cocked his revolver, aimed carefully, and pulled the trigger. The commodore—who had been begging in the streets ever since the day when his son's suspected insanity had started—and the mother—the one called *the snow maiden* because of her extreme pallor—had carried their chests forward in order to protect the rhinoceros. Futile charge! The bullet had penetrated its hide like a corkscrew; one might have believed, with seeming logic, that death must inevitably ensue. But we knew that the essence of the Lord had been inserted into this pachyderm. It had withdrawn with chagrin. If it hadn't been so well proven that He was too kind regarding one of His creations, I would pity the man on the column! With a flick of his wrist, the latter reels in the rope thus weighted. Positioned abnormally, its oscillations swing Mervyn whose head is facing down. With his hands he quickly seizes a long festoon of evergreens that had connected two consecutive corners of the base—against which he bangs his forehead. He carries into the air with him what wasn't a fixed point. After piling up a large part of the rope (in the form of stacked ellipses) at his feet, so that Mervyn remains hanging mid-way up the bronze obelisk, the escaped convict, with his right hand, causes the young man to undertake an accelerated motion of uniform rotation in a plane parallel to the column's axis, and with his left hand he draws in the serpentine windings of rope lying at his feet. The sling whistles in space; Mervyn's body follows suit, always distanced from the centre by the centrifugal force, always keeping its mobile and equidistant position in an ærial circumference independent of matter. Little by little the civilized savage releases, up to the other end which he reins in with a firm metacarpus, what mistakenly resembles a steel bar. He begins running around the balustrade while holding onto the bannister with one hand. This manœuvre has the effect of transforming the original plane of the rope's revolution and increasing its already substantial tensile strength. Henceforth it turns majestically in a horizontal plane after having passed successively, in an imperceptible course, through several oblique planes. The right angle formed by

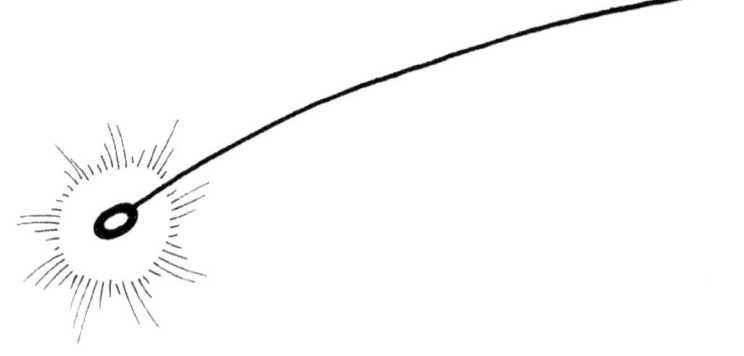

the column and the vegetal thread has equal sides! The renegade's arm and the deadly instrument are merged in linear unity, like the atomistic elements of a beam of light penetrating a dark room. Mechanical theorems allow me to speak in this way—alas! we know that one force added to another force generates a result composed of the two original forces! Who would dare claim that the linear rope might have already broken if it hadn't been for the athlete's vigour or the good quality of the hemp? The golden-haired privateer suddenly and simultaneously arrests his acquired speed, opens his hand and releases the cable. The rebound from this operation, so contrary to the previous ones, causes the balustrade to creak in its joints. Mervyn, following the rope, resembles a comet trailing its flaming tail behind it. The iron ring in the slip-knot, sparkling in the rays of the sun, is itself

enlisted to complete the illusion. In the course of his parabola the ill-fated man cuts through the atmosphere up to the Left Bank, goes past it (by virtue of what I assume is an infinite momentum) — and his body strikes the dome of the Panthéon while the rope partly embraces, with its windings, the upper face of the immense dome. It is on its spherical and convex surface, resembling only an orange in terms of shape, that can be seen, all day long, a desiccated skeleton remaining suspended. When the wind swings it, they say that the students of the Latin Quarter, fearing a similar fate, say a short prayer: these are insignificant rumours which aren't worth taking seriously and only fit for frightening small children. Between its clenched hands it holds what appears to be a large ribbon of old yellow flowers. One must take into account the distance, and nobody can swear, despite the evidence of their good eyesight, that these might actually be the evergreens I told you about, and which an unequal battle waged near the new Opéra had seen detached from a grandiose pedestal. It is none the less true that the hangings in the shape of the crescent moon no longer receive the expression of their final symmetry in the quaternary number: if you don't believe me, go and see for yourself.

END OF THE SIXTH DIRGE

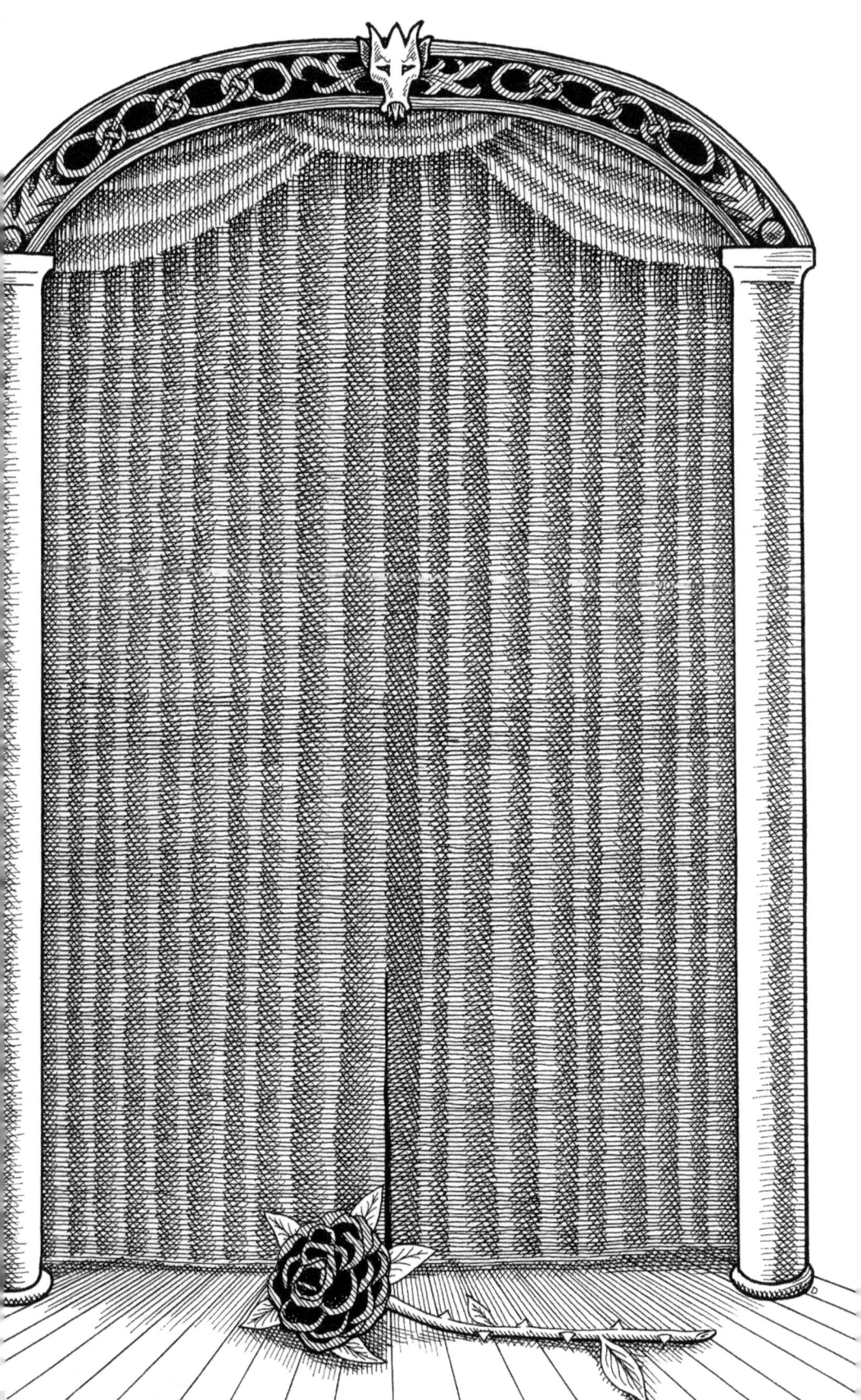

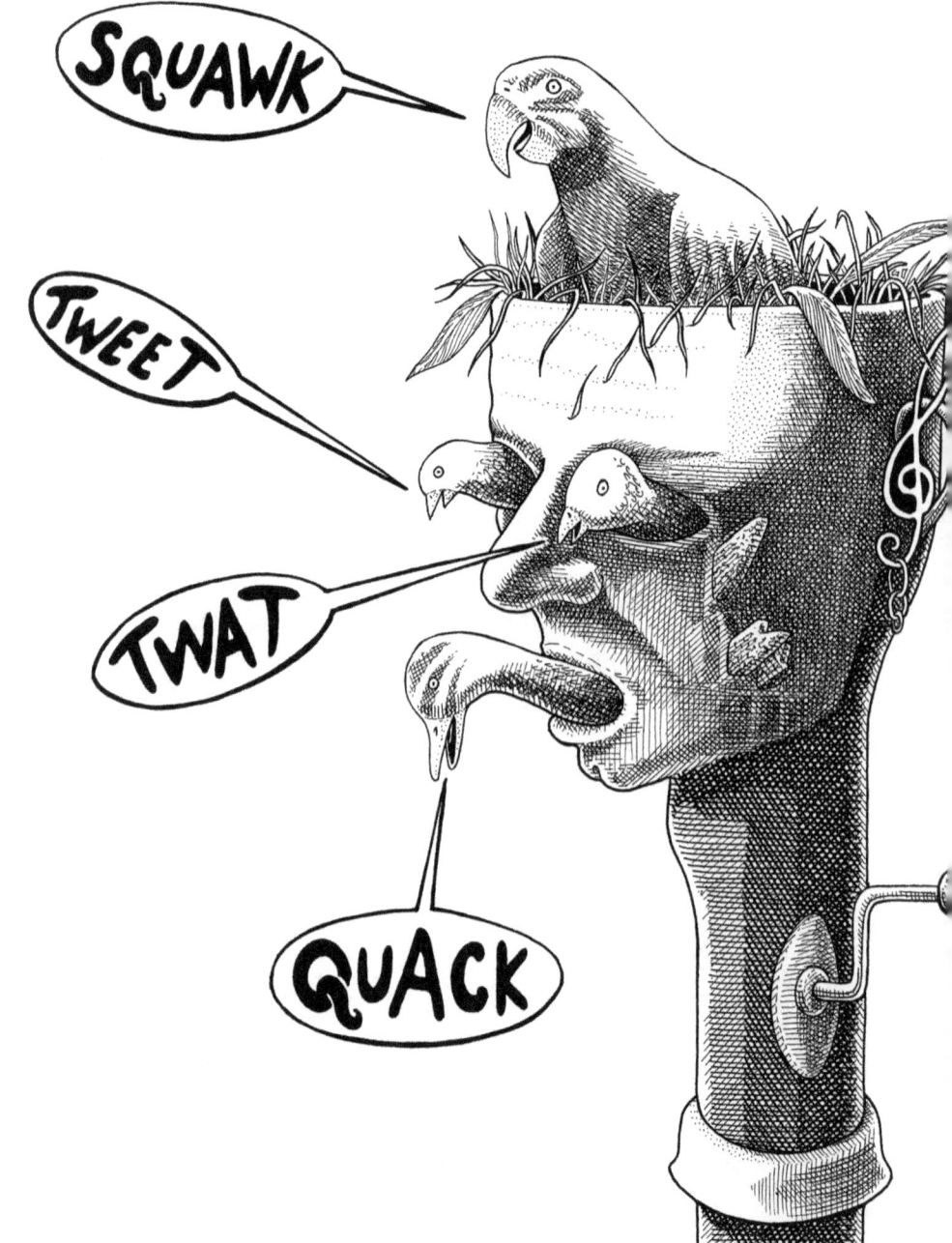

End Notes

1. "habitants des sphères": literally "inhabitants of the spheres," but I have extrapolated the more concise and modern term "extraterrestrials."

2. "un ver luisant": literally "a glowing worm" (ie., a glow-worm). The insects indicated are beetles in the Lampyridae family, comprising numerous species including fireflies.

3. The original text reads: "contre les feux, qui paraissent aux mâts des navires invisibles..."
   Although "the fires" referred to here can be interpreted and translated in various ways, the regular appearance of ships on stormy seas in *Maldoror* suggests that this is a prime candidate for the phenomenon of luminous plasma formed by ionization during thunderstorms, and which has historically been observed on the masts of ships at sea.
   St. Elmo was the patron saint of sailors, and mariners sometimes considered the appearance of St. Elmo's fire as a good omen in bad weather.

4. The original text reads: "l'ours marin de l'océan Boréal," or "the sea-bear of the Boreal ocean." Early accounts of the Northern fur seal referred to it as a "sea-bear," which is reflected in its scientific name *Callorhinus ursinus*.

5. "acarus sarcopte," otherwise *Sarcoptes scabiei*, the itch-mite that causes scabies.

6. "les crampes," here used colloquially to indicate the Common torpedo or Eyed electric ray (*Torpedo torpedo*). This species of electric ray has also been called the crampfish or cramp ray. There is subtle wordplay here, with the added suggestion of muscular cramps ("the bends") from deep-sea diving.

7. In the original text, Ducasse gives the scientific name "acantophorus serraticornis" (actually *Acanthophorus serraticornis*), a species in the Cerambycidae family of beetles, whose members are known variously as longhorn, long-horned, or longicorn beetles.

8. "nègre" is commonly translated into English as "negro," but I have chosen to use its other meaning: "ghostwriter." This may be seen as an oblique reference to the role of the pseudonymous author (or even the translator).

9. The illusion created by refraction.

10. "panoccos" in the original text. In *Lautréamont's Imagery: A Stylistic Approach* (Librairie Droz, Geneva, 1969, p.23, n.5) Peter W. Nesselroth notes the oddity of this word as it appears in the original published version of *Maldoror*, and he assumes a misspelling of "panococo," a name for *Swartzia panacoco*, a tree in the bean family also known as Brazilian ebony.

11. "l'anarnak groënlandais," otherwise *Anarnacus Grœnlandicus*, or Greenland Anarnak. This was later found to be the same species as the Northern bottlenose whale *Hyperoodon ampullatus* in the genus Hyperoodon; this species is found in the North Atlantic Ocean.

12. "le scorpène-horrible," otherwise *Scorpæna horrida*. The Scorpionfish family, Scorpænidæ, includes the stonefish, lionfish, turkeyfish and dragonfish. These fish are extremely venomous.

13. "... d'en élargir encore les frontières;" — literally translated as "... of extending the boundaries further," I have chosen to use the late-20th century equivalent idiom.

14. "une baleine" can be translated generically as "a whale," but also refers to "whalebone," the horny plates found in the upper mouthparts of baleen whales; hence this latter type of whale is indicated here, especially regarding its method of feeding which fuels the simile in this passage. Baleen whales open their mouths while swimming, taking in large volumes of water and filtering plankton (their main source of food) from it; this act of feeding causes the baleen whale's mouth to distend enormously.

15. "deux jumeaux, mon frère et moi, parurent à la lumière." The obvious thrust here is that the twins were born, ie. they "appeared to the light." However, "lumière" can also be translated as "lumen," a general anatomical term for the interior of a tubular formation, such as the female genital tract (including the urinary tract).

16. A "murmuration" is the collective noun for starlings.

17. "rotifères," ie., microscopic organisms of the phylum Rotifera. Also known as "wheel animals." Tardigrades are tiny eight-legged animals of the phylum Tardigrades, also known as "water bears." Rotifers and tardigrades live in water.

18. The Pelecaniformes order (as per R. B. Sharpe's classification of 1891) now includes the following families:

    Pelecanidæ (pelicans)
    Ardeidæ (egrets, bitterns, herons)
    Balaenicipitidæ (shoebills)
    Scopidæ (hamerkops)
    Threskiornithidæ (spoonbills)

    The booby, cormorant and frigate-bird thus belong to the Sulliformes order, with their families being respectively Sulidæ, Phalacrocoracidæ and Fregatidæ.

19. "onguiculée" — otherwise "unguiculate," a technical term used to describe animals which have a nail or claw on each digit, or plants with petals displaying small tabs. Derived from the Latin "unguiculus," pertaining to a claw or nail.

20. "le vautour des agneaux" — *Gypaetus barbatus*, the Bearded vulture, otherwise known as the lammergeier or ossifrage. This species is found throughout Europe, Asia and Africa. "le grand-duc de Virginie" — *Bubo virginianus*, the Great horned owl, a North American bird.

21. "un système de coloration diamentée" — literally translatable as "a system of diamonded colouration," which doesn't smoothly convey the striking play of prismatic light I believe is intended here. A "brilliant" is a finely cut diamond.

22. "serpentaire reptilivore," ie. *Sagittarius serpentarius*, a large bird of the family Sagittariidae, native to Africa. Though their diet may include reptiles such as snakes, their reputation as being primarily snake-eaters appears to have been exaggerated.

23. "l'atonie encéphalique" is highly suggestive of *encephalitis lethargica*, otherwise known as "sleepy sickness" or "sleeping sickness" (the latter term is shared with a completely different disease caused by the bite of the tsetse fly). This is a form of encephalitis first described by Constantin von Economo in 1917; its other scientific name is von Economo Disease.

24. "two lustra" indicates ten years. A lustrum is a period of five years, derived from the ritual ceremony performed in ancient Rome every five years.

25. "le fondement de la construction" may otherwise be translated as "the basis of the construction," but the alternative meaning of "le fondement" as "buttocks" or "anus" suggests a more tongue-in-cheek implication.

26. "victimes toutes préparées" — literally "victims all prepared," I have instead used the expression "sitting ducks." This not only equates to the intended meaning of an easy target, but also neatly relates to the Ducassian aviary.

27. "l'engoulevent de la Caroline," called the Chuck-will's-widow in English; its scientific name is *Caprimulgus carolinensis*. This bird in the nightjar family is found in the Americas and the West Indies.

28. "à perfectionner le dessin de votre style" — literally "to refine the design of your style." I have instead used the expression whose nautical provenance is in keeping with the commodore's career.

29. "Sownder" and "lamentation" are among many collective nouns for swans.

Outro

Gavin L. O'Keefe

Lautréamont's Aviary

In his collection of essays exploring the symbolism of *Les Chants of Maldoror*[1] Gaston Bachelard devotes a chapter to 'Lautréamont's Bestiary' and examines the extensive inclusion of fauna within *Maldoror* and the importance of animal imagery in the work. Bachelard estimates "185 animals in the Ducasse Bestiary" and finds "the most prominent as the dog, horse, crab, spider, and toad."[2] These five animals do figure prominently throughout the text, but to my mind the most conspicuous animal in *Maldoror* is the bird.

By my reckoning there are over fifty distinct bird species referred to in the text. This suggests that birds held a particular fascination for Ducasse and that by referencing them, in action or within simile, the author evoked the peculiar natures of each species to suit his context. The following list shows the variety of bird types.

albatross	chicken (hen)	frigate-bird
Andean condor	Chuck-will's-widow	Great horned owl
Bearded vulture	Cochinchinese chicken	greenfinch
'bird of passage'	cockatoo	grouse
'bird of prey'	cormorant	heron
blackbird	crane	hummingbird
booby	crow	kite
buzzard	curlew	lark
canary	duck	'night bird'
cassowary	eagle	nightingale
chickadee	eider	osprey
chicken (rooster)	flamingo	ostrich

---

1. Gaston Bachelard, *Lautréamont*, trans. Robert S. Dupree (The Dallas Institute Publications, Dallas, Texas, second printing 2012).
2. Ibid., pg.13.

owl	'sea-bird'	swallow
palmiped	sea eagle	swan
pelican	seagull	turkey
petrel	secretary bird	turtledove
Philippine cockatoo	skua	vulture
raptor	sparrow	warbler
red kite	sparrowhawk	woodpecker
robin	starling	
screech owl	stork	

Molluscs also feature in *Les Chants de Maldoror*, and although only three types are mentioned—the octopus, snail, and slug—the author clearly found the nature of these creatures well-suited to some of his scenarios. The octopus easily predominates, appearing as a central character several times and inspiring Ducasse to wax lyrical on the animal's attributes. Most memorable are a poetic account of a romantic liaison between a man and an octopus, and a scene where Maldoror metamorphoses into an octopus so large that it is able to attack God. One memoir mentions Ducasse's fascination with natural history,[3] so that his interest in the animal kingdom and the use of its 'characters' in *Maldoror* should come as no surprise. What is noteworthy is the author's allusion to specific animal species, and not only birds and molluscs. Various exotic species of mammal, sea creature, insect and microbe make appearances throughout the work and become part of the surreal weave of the text.

---

3. Paul Lespès and Isidore Ducasse were school-mates at the Pau Lycée in 1864. In an interview with François Alicot published in *Mercure de France*, 1 January 1928, Lespès remembers Ducasse's fascination with natural history and recounts an occasion when Ducasse was absorbed in studying a beetle in the school grounds.

   At another time Ducasse asked Lespès and another school-mate, Georges Minvielle (both of whom were amateur hunters) about the behaviour of Pyrenean birds. This rare memoir supports my point that Ducasse had a particular interest in birds, as reflected in the text of *Maldoror*.

   The Lespès/Alicot interview is provided in translation by Alexis Lykiard in *Maldoror & The Complete Works of the Comte de Lautréamont* (Exact Change, Cambridge USA, 1994), p.270. Lykiard's English translations of Ducasse's works are generally considered the finest and are highly recommended.

Translator's Note

An English translation of *Les Chants de Maldoror* is a good introduction to the work, but I recommend that readers wishing to fully engage with *Maldoror* turn to the original French text. There is much subtlety in Ducasse's original that defies translation into English.

I have aimed in my rendering to convey the spirit of the original text via the English idiom while also trying to present a translation that speaks to a 21st century readership conversant with English expressions (including some modernisms) from the present day.

My first encounter with *Maldoror* was when I read Alexis Lykiard's English translation in the mid-1980s. At that time I was inspired to draw several illustrations for the work, and one of these illustrations was published in an Australian poetry journal.[4] Almost thirty years later I returned to *Maldoror* afresh and was able to devote my time and energies to completing the version you now hold in your hands.

The primary source for my translation has been the 'Pocket Classiques' edition of *Les Chants de Maldoror* (Paris, 1999). Reference has also been made to the edition of the book published by Editions «La Boétie».[5] The latter edition featured illustrations by René Magritte, and these have been an inspiration to me—as have the illustrations Salvador Dalí completed for an edition of the book.[6]

The illustration on page [52] is a treatment of page 36 of the «La Boétie» edition of *Les Chants de Maldoror*, in the style of English artist Tom Phillips. The resulting text suggests a new English subtext.

---

4. *Scarp*, Issue 11, ed. Ron Pretty (University of Wollongong Union Writers' Club, October 1987). pg.54.
5. *Les Chants de Maldoror* (Editions «La Boétie», Brussels, 1948). With 77 illustrations by René Magritte.
6. *Les Chants de Maldoror* (Albert Skira, Paris, 1934). With 44 illustrations from engravings by Salvador Dalí.

My work on this translation has been as great a challenge as creating the illustrations, and I wish to thank all the individuals — too many to list here, but each knows the part they've played — who provided assistance and encouragement.

I am especially grateful to my family and friends, without whom this book would not have come into being.

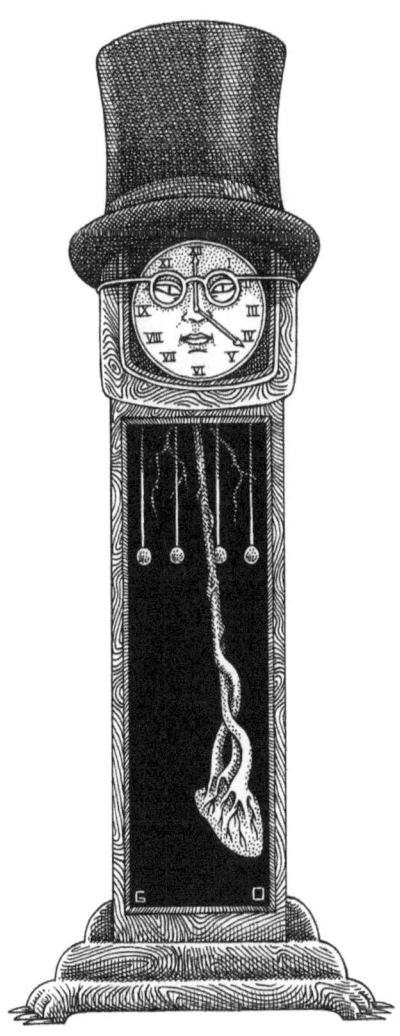

Toutes les bonnes choses prennent du temps

Isidore-Lucien Ducasse & Gavin L. O'Keefe

Isidore-Lucien Ducasse was born in 1846 in Montevideo, Uruguay. He attended high school in France in 1859, and eventually settled in Paris in 1867. In 1868 the first 'chant' of *Les Chants de Maldoror* was published anonymously, and the following year the full work was published under Ducasse's pseudonym, Le Comte de Lautréamont. His next work, *Poésies*, remained unfinished at the time of his death in Paris in 1870.

Gavin L. O'Keefe was born in 1965 in Melbourne, Australia. Since 1985 he has worked as an illustrator, designer, musician and writer. He has illustrated Lewis Carroll's *Alice* and *Snark* books, and L. Frank Baum's *The Wonderful Wizard of Oz*. *The Dirges of Maldoror* is his first translation.

List of Books
IN
BELLES LETTRES
PUBLISHED BY
RAMBLE HOUSE

RAMBLE HOUSE's
HARRY STEPHEN KEELER WEBWORK MYSTERIES
(RH) indicates the title is available ONLY in the RAMBLE HOUSE edition

The Ace of Spades Murder
The Affair of the Bottled Deuce (RH)
The Amazing Web
The Barking Clock
Behind That Mask
The Book with the Orange Leaves
The Bottle with the Green Wax Seal
The Box from Japan
The Case of the Canny Killer
The Case of the Crazy Corpse (RH)
The Case of the Flying Hands (RH)
The Case of the Ivory Arrow
The Case of the Jeweled Ragpicker
The Case of the Lavender Gripsack
The Case of the Mysterious Moll
The Case of the 16 Beans
The Case of the Transparent Nude (RH)
The Case of the Transposed Legs
The Case of the Two-Headed Idiot (RH)
The Case of the Two Strange Ladies
The Circus Stealers (RH)
Cleopatra's Tears
A Copy of Beowulf (RH)
The Crimson Cube (RH)
The Face of the Man From Saturn
Find the Clock
The Five Silver Buddhas
The 4th King
The Gallows Waits, My Lord! (RH)
The Green Jade Hand
Finger! Finger!
Hangman's Nights (RH)
I, Chameleon (RH)
I Killed Lincoln at 10:13! (RH)
The Iron Ring
The Man Who Changed His Skin (RH)
The Man with the Crimson Box
The Man with the Magic Eardrums
The Man with the Wooden Spectacles
The Marceau Case
The Matilda Hunter Murder

The Monocled Monster
The Murder of London Lew
The Murdered Mathematician
The Mysterious Card (RH)
The Mysterious Ivory Ball of Wong Shing Li (RH)
The Mystery of the Fiddling Cracks-man
The Peacock Fan
The Photo of Lady X (RH)
The Portrait of Jirjohn Cobb
Report on Vanessa Hewstone (RH)
Riddle of the Travelling Skull
Riddle of the Wooden Parrakeet (RH)
The Scarlet Mummy (RH)
The Search for X-Y-Z
The Sharkskin Book
Sing Sing Nights
The Six From Nowhere (RH)
The Skull of the Waltzing Clown
The Spectacles of Mr. Cagliostro
Stand By—London Calling!
The Steeltown Strangler
The Stolen Gravestone (RH)
Strange Journey (RH)
The Strange Will
The Straw Hat Murders (RH)
The Street of 1000 Eyes (RH)
Thieves' Nights
Three Novellos (RH)
The Tiger Snake
The Trap (RH)
Vagabond Nights (Defrauded Yeggman)
Vagabond Nights 2 (10 Hours)
The Vanishing Gold Truck
The Voice of the Seven Sparrows
The Washington Square Enigma
When Thief Meets Thief
The White Circle (RH)
The Wonderful Scheme of Mr. Christopher Thorne
X. Jones—of Scotland Yard
Y. Cheung, Business Detective

Keeler Related Works

A To Izzard: A Harry Stephen Keeler Companion by Fender Tucker—Articles and stories about Harry, by Harry, and in his style. Included is a compleat bibliography.

Wild About Harry: Reviews of Keeler Novels—Edited by Richard Polt & Fender Tucker—22 reviews of works by Harry Stephen Keeler from Keeler News. A perfect introduction to the author.

The Keeler Keyhole Collection: Annotated newsletter rants from Harry Stephen Keeler, edited by Francis M. Nevins. Over 400 pages of incredibly personal Keeleriana.

Fakealoo—Pastiches of the style of Harry Stephen Keeler by selected demented members of the HSK Society. Updated every year with the new winner.

Strands of the Web: Short Stories of Harry Stephen Keeler—29 stories, just about all that Keeler wrote, are edited and introduced by Fred Cleaver.

RAMBLE HOUSE'S LOON SANCTUARY

A Clear Path to Cross—Sharon Knowles short mystery stories by Ed Lynskey.

A Corpse Walks in Brooklyn and Other Stories—Volume 5 in the Day Keene in the Detective Pulps series.

A Fair Californian—Novel by Olive Harper about a young woman's quest for gold — a quest that turns into something completely unexpected.

A Jimmy Starr Omnibus—Three 40s novels by Jimmy Starr.

A Niche in Time and Other Stories—Classic SF by William F. Temple.

A Shot Rang Out—Three decades of reviews and articles by today's Anthony Boucher, Jon Breen. An essential book for any mystery lover's library.

A Snark Selection—Lewis Carroll's *The Hunting of the Snark* with two Snarkian chapters by Harry Stephen Keeler—Illustrated by Gavin L. O'Keefe.

A Young Man's Heart—A forgotten early classic by Cornell Woolrich.

Alexander Laing Novels—*The Motives of Nicholas Holtz* and *Dr. Scarlett*, stories of medical mayhem and intrigue from the 30s.

An Angel in the Street—Modern hardboiled noir by Peter Genovese.

Automaton—Brilliant treatise on robotics: 1928-style! By H. Stafford Hatfield.

Away From the Here and Now—Clare Winger Harris stories, collected by Richard A. Lupoff

Beast or Man?—A 1930 novel of racism and horror by Sean M'Guire. Introduced by John Pelan.

Black Beadle—A 1939 thriller by E.C.R. Lorac.

Black Hogan Strikes Again—Australia's Peter Renwick pens a tale of the 30s outback.

Black River Falls—Suspense from the master, Ed Gorman.

Blondy's Boy Friend—A snappy 1930 story by Philip Wylie, writing as Leatrice Homesley.

Blood in a Snap—The *Finnegan's Wake* of the 21st century, by Jim Weiler.

Blood Moon—The first of the Robert Payne series by Ed Gorman.

Bogart '48—Hollywood action with Bogie by John Stanley and Kenn Davis

Butterfly Man—1930s novel by Lew Levenson about a dancer who must come to terms with his homosexuality.

Calling Lou Largo!—Two Lou Largo novels by William Ard.

Cathedral of Horror—First volume of collected stories by weird fiction writer Arthur J. Burks.

Chalk Face—Curious supernatural murder thriller by Waldo Frank.

Circus-Show—Joseph Delmont's 1931 epic tale of circus life and murder.

Cornucopia of Crime—Francis M. Nevins assembled this huge collection of his writings about crime literature and the people who write it. Essential for any serious mystery library.

Corpse Without Flesh—Strange novel of forensics by George Bruce

Crimson Clown Novels—By Johnston McCulley, author of the Zorro novels, *The Crimson Clown* and *The Crimson Clown Again*.

Dago Red—22 tales of dark suspense by Bill Pronzini.

Dark Sanctuary—Weird Menace story by H. B. Gregory.

David Hume Novels—*Corpses Never Argue, Cemetery First Stop, Make Way for the Mourners, Eternity Here I Come*. 1930s British hardboiled fiction with an attitude.

David&Son: Peregrine Parentus and other tales—Collection of tales and memoirs by Avram Davidson and Ethan Davidson, some published for the first time. Introduced by Grania Davidson Davis.

Dead Man Talks Too Much—Hollywood boozer by Weed Dickenson.
Death in a Bowl—1930's murder mystery by Raoul Whitfield.
Death March of the Dancing Dolls and Other Stories—Volume Three in the Day Keene in the Detective Pulps series. Introduced by Bill Crider.
Deep Space and other Stories—A collection of SF gems by Richard A. Lupoff.
Detective Duff Unravels It—Episodic mysteries by Harvey O'Higgins.
Devil's Planet—Locked room mystery set on the planet Mars, by Manly Wade Wellman.
Dime Novels: Ramble House's 10-Cent Books—*Knife in the Dark* by Robert Leslie Bellem, *Hot Lead* and *Song of Death* by Ed Earl Repp, *A Hashish House in New York* by H.H. Kane, and five more.
Doctor Arnoldi—Tiffany Thayer's story of the death of death.
Don Diablo: Book of a Lost Film—Two-volume treatment of a western by Paul Landres, with diagrams. Intro by Francis M. Nevins.
Dope and Swastikas—Two strange novels from 1922 by Edmund Snell
Dope Tales #1—Two dope-riddled classics; *Dope Runners* by Gerald Grantham and *Death Takes the Joystick* by Phillip Condé.
Dope Tales #2—Two more narco-classics; *The Invisible Hand* by Rex Dark and *The Smokers of Hashish* by Norman Berrow.
Dope Tales #3—Two enchanting novels of opium by the master, Sax Rohmer. *Dope* and *The Yellow Claw*.
Double Hot & Double Sex—Two combos of '60s softcore sex novels by Morris Hershman.
Dr. Odin—Douglas Newton's 1933 racial potboiler comes back to life.
E. Charles Vivian—*Evidence in Blue, Accessory After* and *The Lady of the Terraces.*
E.C.R. Lorac—*Black Beadle, The Case in the Clinic, The Devil and the C.I.D.* and *Slippery Staircase.*
E. R. Punshon novels—*Information Received, Crossword Mystery, Dictator's Way, Diabolic Candelabra, Music Tells All, Helen Passes By, The House of Godwinsson, The Golden Dagger, The Attending Truth, Strange Ending, Brought to Light, Dark is the Clue, Triple Quest,* and *Six Were Present*: featuring Bobby Owen.
Ed "Strangler" Lewis: Facts within a Myth—Authoritative illustrated biography of the famous American wrestler Ed Lewis, by noted historian Steve Yohe.
Evangelical Cockroach—Jack Woodford writes about writing.
Fatal Accident—1936 murder-by-automobile mystery by Cecil M. Wills.
Fighting Mad—Todd Robbins' 1922 novel about boxing and life
Five Million in Cash—Gangster thriller by Tiffany Thayer writing as O. B. King.
Food for the Fungus Lady—Collection of weird stories by Ralston Shields, edited and introduced by John Pelan.
Francis M. Nevins—Three omnibus volumes of novels: *Publish and Perish / Corrupt and Ensnare, Into the Same River Twice / Beneficiaries' Requiem* and *The 120-Hour Clock / The Ninety Million Dollar Mouse.*
Freaks and Fantasies—Eerie tales by Tod Robbins, collaborator of Tod Browning on the film FREAKS.
Gadsby—A lipogram (a novel without the letter E). Ernest Vincent Wright's last work, published in 1939 right before his death.
Gelett Burgess Novels—*The Master of Mysteries, The White Cat, Two O'Clock Courage, Ladies in Boxes, Find the Woman, The Heart Line, The Picaroons* and *Lady Mechante*. Recently added is *A Gelett Burgess Sampler*, edited by Alfred Jan. All are introduced by Richard A. Lupoff.

Geronimo—S. M. Barrett's 1905 autobiography of a noble American.
Gordon Eklund—*Second Creation*, *Retro Man* and *Stalking the Sun*: three volumes of the author's best short stories.
Go Forth and Multiply—Anthology of science fiction tales of repopulation, edited by Gordon Van Gelder.
Hake Talbot Novels—*Rim of the Pit*, *The Hangman's Handyman*. Classic locked room mysteries, with mapback covers by Gavin O'Keefe.
Hands Out of Hell and Other Stories—John H. Knox's eerie hallucinations
Hell is a City—William Ard's masterpiece.
Hollywood Dreams—A novel of Tinsel Town and the Depression by Richard O'Brien.
Homicide House—#6 in the Day Keene in the Detective Pulps series.
Hostesses in Hell and Other Stories—Russell Gray's most graphic stories
House of the Restless Dead—Strange and ominous tales by Hugh B. Cave
Inclination to Murder—1966 thriller by New Zealand's Harriet Hunter.
Invaders from the Dark—Classic werewolf tale from Greye La Spina.
J. Poindexter, Colored—Classic satirical black novel by Irvin S. Cobb.
Jack Mann Novels—Strange murder in the English countryside. *Gees' First Case*, *Nightmare Farm*, *Grey Shapes*, *The Ninth Life*, *The Glass Too Many*, *Her Ways Are Death*, *The Kleinert Case* and *Maker of Shadows*.
Jake Hardy—A lusty western tale from Wesley Tallant.
James Corbett—*Vampire of the Skies*, *The Ghost Plane*, *Murder Begets Murder* and *The Air Killer* – strange thriller novels from this singular British author.
Jim Harmon Double Novels—*Vixen Hollow/Celluloid Scandal*, *The Man Who Made Maniacs/Silent Siren*, *Ape Rape/Wanton Witch*, *Sex Burns Like Fire/Twist Session*, *Sudden Lust/Passion Strip*, *Sin Unlimited/Harlot Master*, *Twilight Girls/Sex Institution*. Written in the early 60s and never reprinted until now.
Joel Townsley Rogers Novels and Short Stories—By the author of *The Red Right Hand*: *Once In a Red Moon*, *Lady With the Dice*, *The Stopped Clock*, *Never Leave My Bed*. Also two short story collections: *Night of Horror* and *Killing Time*.
John Carstairs, Space Detective—Arboreal Sci-fi by Frank Belknap Long
John G. Brandon—*The Case of the Withered Hand*, *Finger-Prints Never Lie*, and *Death on Delivery*: crime thrillers by Australian author John G. Brandon.
John S. Glasby—Two collections of Glasby's Lovecraftian stories: *The Brooding City* and *Beyond the Rim*. Introduced by John Pelan.
Joseph Shallit Novels—*The Case of the Billion Dollar Body*, *Lady Don't Die on My Doorstep*, *Kiss the Killer*, *Yell Bloody Murder*, *Take Your Last Look*. One of America's best 50's authors and a favorite of author Bill Pronzini.
Keller Memento—45 short stories of the amazing and weird by Dr. David Keller.
Killer's Caress—Cary Moran's 1936 hardboiled thriller.
Knight Asrael and Other Stories—Collection of fourteen fantasy tales by Una Ashworth Taylor
Knowing the Unknowable: Putting Psi to Work—Damien Broderick, PhD puts forward the valid case for evidence of Psi.
Lady of the Yellow Death and Other Stories—More stories by Wyatt Blassingame.
Laughing Death—1932 Yellow Peril thriller by Walter C. Brown.
League of the Grateful Dead and Other Stories—Volume One in the Day Keene in the Detective Pulps series.

Library of Death—Ghastly tale by Ronald S. L. Harding, introduced by John Pelan

Lords of the Earth—A novel of meddling dabblers in the occult invoking the ancient powers of Atlantis. J.M.A. Mills' sequel to *The Tomb of the Dark Ones*.

Mad-Doctor Merciful—Collin Brooks' unsettling novel of medical experimentation with supernatural forces.

Malcolm Jameson Novels and Short Stories—*Astonishing! Astounding!*, *Tarnished Bomb*, *The Alien Envoy and Other Stories* and *The Chariots of San Fernando and Other Stories*. All introduced and edited by John Pelan or Richard A. Lupoff.

Man Out of Hell and Other Stories—Volume II of the John H. Knox weird pulps collection.

Marblehead: A Novel of H.P. Lovecraft—A long-lost masterpiece from Richard A. Lupoff. This is the "director's cut", the long version that has never been published before.

Mark of the Laughing Death and Other Stories—Shockers from the pulps by Francis James, introduced by John Pelan.

Mark Hansom Novels—*Master of Souls*, *The Ghost of Gaston Revere*, *The Madman*, *The Shadow on the House*, *Sorcerer's Chessmen* & *The Wizard of Berner's Abbey*.

Max Afford Novels—*Owl of Darkness*, *Death's Mannikins*, *Blood on His Hands*, *The Dead Are Blind*, *The Sheep and the Wolves*, *Sinners in Paradise* and *Two Locked Room Mysteries and a Ripping Yarn* by one of Australia's finest mystery novelists.

Miles Burton novels — *A Smell of Smoke*, *Death Leaves No Card*, *Situation Vacant* and *Death Paints a Picture*.

Mistress of Terror—Fourth volume of the collected weird tales of Wyatt Blassingame.

Molly and her Man of War— Romantic novel with a difference, by Arabella Kenealy.

Money Brawl—Two books about the writing business by Jack Woodford and H. Bedford-Jones. Introduced by Richard A. Lupoff.

More Secret Adventures of Sherlock Holmes—Gary Lovisi's second collection of tales about the unknown sides of the great detective.

Muddled Mind: Complete Works of Ed Wood, Jr.—David Hayes and Hayden Davis deconstruct the life and works of the mad, but canny, genius.

Murder among the Nudists—1934 mystery by Peter Hunt, featuring a naked Detective-Inspector going undercover in a nudist colony.

Murder in Black and White—1931 classic tennis whodunit by Evelyn Elder.

Murder in Shawnee—Two novels of the Alleghenies by John Douglas: *Shawnee Alley Fire* and *Haunts*.

Murder in Suffolk—A 1938 murder mystery novel by the mysterious 'A. Fielding.'

My Deadly Angel—1955 Cold War drama by John Chelton.

My First Time: The One Experience You Never Forget—Michael Birchwood—64 true first-person narratives of how they lost it.

My Touch Brings Death—Second volume of collected stories by Russell Gray.

Mysterious Martin, the Master of Murder—Two versions of a strange 1912 novel by Tod Robbins about a man who writes books that can kill.

Norman Berrow Novels—*The Bishop's Sword*, *Ghost House*, *Don't Go Out After Dark*, *Claws of the Cougar*, *The Smokers of Hashish*, *The Secret Dancer*, *Don't Jump Mr. Boland!*, *The Footprints of Satan*, *Fingers for Ransom*, *The*

Three Tiers of Fantasy, The Spaniard's Thumb, The Eleventh Plague, Words Have Wings, One Thrilling Night, The Lady's in Danger, It Howls at Night, The Terror in the Fog, Oil Under the Window, Murder in the Melody, The Singing Room. This is the complete Norman Berrow library of locked-room mysteries, several of which are masterpieces.

Old Faithful and Other Stories—SF classic tales by Raymond Z. Gallun

Old Times' Sake—Short stories by James Reasoner from Mike Shayne Magazine.

One Dreadful Night—A classic mystery by Ronald S. L. Harding

Pair O' Jacks—A mystery novel and a diatribe about publishing by Jack Woodford

Pawns of Destiny—Psychological drama by Kay Seaton.

Perfect .38—Two early Timothy Dane novels by William Ard. More to come.

Prince Pax—Devilish intrigue by George Sylvester Viereck and Philip Eldridge

Prose Bowl—Futuristic satire of a world where hack writing has replaced football as our national obsession, by Bill Pronzini and Barry N. Malzberg.

Ralph Trevor—*Murder in Silk, Easy for the Crook, Front Page Murder, The Deputy Avenger* and *The Phantom Raider.*

Red Light—The history of legal prostitution in Shreveport Louisiana by Eric Brock. Includes wonderful photos of the houses and the ladies.

Researching American-Made Toy Soldiers—A 276-page collection of a lifetime of articles by toy soldier expert Richard O'Brien.

Reunion in Hell—Volume One of the John H. Knox series of weird stories from the pulps. Introduced by horror expert John Pelan.

Ripped from the Headlines!—The Jack the Ripper story as told in the newspaper articles in the *New York* and *London Times.*

Rough Cut & New, Improved Murder—Ed Gorman's first two novels.

R. R. Ryan Novels — *Freak Museum, The Subjugated Beast, Death of a Sadist, Echo of a Curse, Devil's Shelter* and *No Escape.* Introduced by John Pelan.

Roland Daniel Novels — *Ruby of a Thousand Dreams, The Girl in the Dark,* and *A Roland Daniel Double: The Signal and The Return of Wu Fang.*

Ruled By Radio — 1925 futuristic novel by Robert L. Hadfield & Frank E. Farncombe.

Rupert Penny Novels — *Policeman's Holiday, Policeman's Evidence, Lucky Policeman, Policeman in Armour, Sealed Room Murder, Sweet Poison, The Talkative Policeman, She had to Have Gas* and *Cut and Run* (by Martin Tanner.) Rupert Penny is the pseudonym of Australian Charles Thornett, a master of the locked room, impossible crime plot.

Sacred Locomotive Flies — Richard A. Lupoff's psychedelic SF story.

Sam — Early gay novel by Lonnie Coleman.

Sand's Game — Spectacular hardboiled noir from Ennis Willie, edited by Lynn Myers and Stephen Mertz, with contributions from Max Allan Collins, Bill Crider, Wayne Dundee, Bill Pronzini, Gary Lovisi and James Reasoner.

Sand's War — More violent fiction from the typewriter of Ennis Willie

Satan's Den Exposed — True crime in Truth or Consequences New Mexico — Award-winning journalism by the *Desert Journal.*

Satan's Secret and Selected Stories — Barnard Stacey's only novel with a selection of his best short stories.

Satans of Saturn — Novellas from the pulps by Otis Adelbert Kline and E. H. Price

Satan's Sin House and Other Stories — Horrific gore by Wayne Rogers

Secrets of a Teenage Superhero — Graphic lit by Jonathan Sweet

Sex Slave — Potboiler of lust in the days of Cleopatra by Dion Leclerq, 1966.

Slammer Days — Two full-length prison memoirs: *Men into Beasts* (1952) by George Sylvester Viereck and *Home Away From Home* (1962) by Jack Woodford.

Star Griffin — Michael Kurland's 1987 masterpiece of SF drollery is back.

Stakeout on Millennium Drive — Award-winning Indianapolis Noir by Ian Woollen.

Strands of the Web: Short Stories of Harry Stephen Keeler — Edited and Introduced by Fred Cleaver.

Summer Camp for Corpses and Other Stories — Weird Menace tales from Arthur Leo Zagat; introduced by John Pelan.

Suzy — A collection of comic strips by Richard O'Brien and Bob Vojtko from 1970.

Tail of the Lizard King / Kaliwood — Two novellas by Adam Mudman Bezecny paying homage to the sleaze genre.

Tales of the Macabre and Ordinary — Modern twisted horror by Chris Mikul, author of the *Bizarrism* series.

Tales of Terror and Torment Vols. #1 & #2 — John Pelan selects and introduces these samplers of weird menace tales from the pulps.

Tenebrae — Ernest G. Henham's 1898 horror tale brought back.

The Alice Books — Lewis Carroll's classics *Alice's Adventures in Wonderland* and *Through the Looking-Glass* together in one volume, with new illustrations by O'Keefe.

The Amorous Intrigues & Adventures of Aaron Burr — by Anonymous. Hot historical action about the man who almost became Emperor of Mexico.

The Anthony Boucher Chronicles — edited by Francis M. Nevins. Book reviews by Anthony Boucher written for the *San Francisco Chronicle*, 1942 – 1947. Essential and fascinating reading by the best book reviewer there ever was.

The Barclay Catalogs — Two essential books about toy soldier collecting by Richard O'Brien

The Basil Wells Omnibus — A collection of Wells' stories by Richard A. Lupoff

The Beautiful Dead and Other Stories — Dreadful tales from Donald Dale

The Best of 10-Story Book — edited by Chris Mikul, over 35 stories from the literary magazine Harry Stephen Keeler edited.

The Bitch Wall — Novel about American soldiers in the Vietnam War, based on Dennis Lane's experiences.

The Black Dark Murders — Vintage 50s college murder yarn by Milt Ozaki, writing as Robert O. Saber.

The Book of Time — The classic novel by H.G. Wells is joined by sequels by Wells himself and three stories by Richard A. Lupoff. Illustrated by Gavin L. O'Keefe.

The Broken Fang and Other Experiences of a Specialist in Spooks — Eerie mystery tales by Uel Key.

The Strange Case of the Antlered Man — A mystery of superstition by Edwy Searles Brooks.

The Case of the Bearded Bride — #4 in the Day Keene in the Detective Pulps series.

The Case of the Little Green Men — Mack Reynolds wrote this love song to sci-fi fans back in 1951 and it's now back in print.

The Charlie Chaplin Murder Mystery — A 2004 tribute by noted film scholar, Wes D. Gehring.

The Cloudbuilders and Other Stories — SF tales from Colin Kapp.

The Collected Writings — Collection of science fiction stories, memoirs and poetry by Carol Carr. Introduction by Karen Haber.

The Compleat Calhoon — All of Fender Tucker's works: Includes *Totah Six-Pack, Weed, Women and Song* and *Tales from the Tower,* plus a CD of all of his songs.

The Compleat Ova Hamlet — Parodies of SF authors by Richard A. Lupoff. This is a brand new edition with more stories and more illustrations by Trina Robbins.

The Contested Earth and Other SF Stories — A never-before published space opera and seven short stories by Jim Harmon.

The Corpse Factory — More horror stories by Arthur Leo Zagat.

The Crackpot and Other Twisted Tales of Greedy Fans and Collectors — The first retrospective collection of the whacky stories of John E. Stockman. Edited by Dwight R. Decker.

The Crimson Butterfly — Early novel by Edmund Snell involving superstition and aberrant Lepidoptera in Borneo.

The Crimson Query — A 1929 thriller from Arlton Eadie. A perfect way to get introduced.

The Daymakers, City of the Tiger & Perchance to Wake — Three volumes of stories taken from the influential British science fiction magazine *Science Fantasy*. Compiled by John Boston & Damien Broderick.

The Devil Drives — An odd prison and lost treasure novel from 1932 by Virgil Markham.

The Devil of Pei-Ling — Herbert Asbury's 1929 tale of the occult.

The Devil's Mistress — A 1915 Scottish gothic tale by J. W. Brodie-Innes, a member of Aleister Crowley's Golden Dawn.

The Devil's Nightclub and Other Stories — John Pelan introduces some gruesome tales by Nat Schachner.

The Disentanglers — Episodic intrigue at the turn of last century by Andrew Lang

The Dog Poker Code — A spoof of *The Da Vinci Code* by D. B. Smithee.

The Dumpling — Political murder from 1907 by Coulson Kernahan.

The End of It All and Other Stories — Ed Gorman selected his favorite short stories for this huge collection.

The Evil of Li-Sin — A Gerald Verner double, combining *The Menace of Li-Sin* and *The Vengeance of Li-Sin*, together with an introduction by John Pelan and an afterword and bibliography by Chris Verner.

The Fangs of Suet Pudding — A 1944 novel of the German invasion by Adams Farr

The Finger of Destiny and Other Stories — Edmund Snell's superb collection of weird stories of Borneo.

The Gold Star Line — Seaboard adventure from L.T. Reade and Robert Eustace.

The Great Orme Terror — Horror stories by Garnett Radcliffe from the pulps

The Hairbreadth Escapes of Major Mendax — Francis Blake Crofton's 1889 boys' book.

The House That Time Forgot and Other Stories — Insane pulpitude by Robert F. Young

The House of the Vampire — 1907 poetic thriller by George S. Viereck.

The Illustrious Corpse — Murder hijinx from Tiffany Thayer

The Incredible Adventures of Rowland Hern — Intriguing 1928 impossible crimes by Nicholas Olde.

The John Dickson Carr Companion — Comprehensive reference work compiled by James E. Keirans. Indispensable resource for the Carr *aficionado*.

The Julius Caesar Murder Case — A 1935 retelling of the assassination by Wallace Irwin that's more fun than Shakespeare's version.

The Kid Was a Killer — Caryl Chessman's only novel, based on his own experiences.

The Koky Comics — A collection of all of the 1978-1981 Sunday and daily comic strips by Richard O'Brien and Mort Gerberg, in two volumes.

The Lady of the Fjords — Barnard Balogh's novel of Norse gods and heroes, reincarnation, and a love affair transcending mortality.

The Lord of Terror — 1925 mystery with master-criminal, Fantômas.

The Man who was Murdered Twice — Intriguing murder mystery by Robert H. Leitfred.

The Melamare Mystery — A classic 1929 Arsene Lupin mystery by Maurice Leblanc

The Man Who Was Secrett — Epic SF stories from John Brunner

The Man Without a Planet — Science fiction tales by Richard Wilson

The N. R. De Mexico Novels — Robert Bragg, the real N.R. de Mexico, presents *Marijuana Girl, Madman on a Drum, Private Chauffeur* in one volume.

The Night Remembers — A 1991 Jack Walsh mystery from Ed Gorman.

The One After Snelling — Kickass modern noir from Richard O'Brien.

The Organ Reader — A huge compilation of just about everything published in the 1971-1972 radical bay-area newspaper, *THE ORGAN*. A coffee table book that points out the shallowness of the coffee table mindset.

The Place of Hairy Death — Collected weird horror tales by Anthony M. Rud.

The Poker Club — Three in one! Ed Gorman's ground-breaking novel, the short story it was based upon, and the screenplay of the film made from it.

The Private Journal & Diary of John H. Surratt — The memoirs of the man who conspired to assassinate President Lincoln.

The Ramble House Coloring Book — Twenty illustrations to color in, each adapted from one of Gavin L. O'Keefe's cover designs.

The Ramble House Mapbacks — Recently revised book by Gavin L. O'Keefe with color pictures of all the Ramble House books with mapbacks.

The Secret Adventures of Sherlock Holmes — Three Sherlockian pastiches by the Brooklyn author/publisher, Gary Lovisi.

The Secret of the Morgue — Frederick G. Eberhard's 1932 mystery involving murder and forensic science with an undercurrent of the malaise that's driven by Prohibition.

The Sign of the Scorpion — A 1935 Edmund Snell tale of oriental evil.

The Silent Terror of Chu-Sheng — Yellow Peril suspense novel by Eugene Thomas.

The Singular Problem of the Stygian House-Boat — Two classic tales by John Kendrick Bangs about the denizens of Hades.

The Smiling Corpse — Philip Wylie and Bernard Bergman's odd 1935 novel.

The Sorcery Club — Classic supernatural novel by Elliott O'Donnell.

The Spider: Satan's Murder Machines — A thesis about Iron Man.

The Stench of Death: An Odoriferous Omnibus by Jack Moskovitz — Two complete novels and two novellas from 60's sleaze author, Jack Moskovitz.

The Story Writer and Other Stories — Classic SF from Richard Wilson

The Strange Thirteen — Richard B. Gamon's odd stories about Raj India.
The Technique of the Mystery Story — Carolyn Wells' tips about writing.
The Tell-Tale Soul — Two novellas by Bram Stoker Award-winning author Christopher Conlon. Introduction by John Pelan.
The Threat of Nostalgia — A collection of his most obscure stories by Jon Breen
The Time Armada — Fox B. Holden's 1953 SF gem.
The Tomb of the Dark Ones — Adventure in Egypt where ancient forces are roused from æons of slumber. A J. M. A. Mills novel from 1937.
The Tongueless Horror and Other Stories — Volume One of the series of short stories from the weird pulps by Wyatt Blassingame.
The Town from Planet Five — From Richard Wilson, two SF classics, *And Then the Town Took Off* and *The Girls from Planet 5*
The Tracer of Lost Persons — From 1906, an episodic novel that became a hit radio series in the 30s. Introduced by Richard A. Lupoff.
The Trail of the Cloven Hoof — Diabolical horror from 1935 by Arlton Eadie. Introduced by John Pelan.
The Triune Man — Mindscrambling science fiction from Richard A. Lupoff.
The Unholy Goddess and Other Stories — Wyatt Blassingame's first DTP compilation
The Universal Holmes — Richard A. Lupoff's 2007 collection of five Holmesian pastiches and a recipe for giant rat stew.
The Werewolf vs the Vampire Woman — Hard to believe ultraviolence by either Arthur M. Scarm or Arthur M. Scram.
The Whistling Ancestors — A 1936 classic of weirdness by Richard E. Goddard and introduced by John Pelan.
The White Owl — A vintage thriller from Edmund Snell
The White Peril in the Far East — Sidney Lewis Gulick's 1905 indictment of the West and assurance that Japan would never attack the U.S.
The Wonderful Wizard of Oz — by L. Frank Baum and illustrated by Gavin L. O'Keefe.
The Yu-Chi Stone — Novel of intrigue and superstition set in Borneo, by Edmund Snell.
They Called the Shots — Collection of authoritative articles by Francis M. Nevins exploring the action movie directors of the late silents through to the late 1960s.
Time Line — Ramble House artist Gavin O'Keefe selects his most evocative art inspired by the twisted literature he reads and designs.
Tiresias — Psychotic modern horror novel by Jonathan M. Sweet.
Tortures and Towers — Two novellas of terror by Dexter Dayle.
Totah Six-Pack — Fender Tucker's six tales about Farmington in one sleek volume.
Tree of Life, Book of Death — Grania Davis' book of her life.
Trail of the Spirit Warrior — Roger Haley's saga of life in the Indian Territories.
Twelve Who Were Damned — Collection of weird menace tales by Paul Ernst.
Two Kinds of Bad — Two 50s novels by William Ard about Danny Fontaine
Two Suns of Morcali and Other Stories — Evelyn E. Smith's SF tour-de-force
Two-Timers — Time travel double: *The Man Who Mastered Time* by Ray Cummings and *Time Column* and *Taa the Terrible* by Malcolm Jameson. Introduced by Richard A. Lupoff.
Ultra-Boiled — 23 gut-wrenching tales by our Man in Brooklyn, Gary Lovisi.

Up Front From Behind — A 2011 satire of Wall Street by James B. Kobak.

Victims & Villains — Intriguing Sherlockiana from Derham Groves.

Wade Wright Novels — *Echo of Fear, Death At Nostalgia Street, It Leads to Murder* and *Shadows' Edge*, a double book featuring *Shadows Don't Bleed* and *The Sharp Edge*.

Walter S. Masterman Novels — *The Green Toad, The Flying Beast, The Yellow Mistletoe, The Wrong Verdict, The Perjured Alibi, The Border Line, The Bloodhounds Bay, The Curse of Cantire, The Baddington Horror* and *Death Turns Traitor*. Masterman wrote horror and mystery novels, some introduced by John Pelan.

We Are the Dead and Other Stories — Volume Two in the Day Keene in the Detective Pulps series, introduced by Ed Gorman. When done, there may be 11 in the series.

Welsh Rarebit Tales — Charming stories from 1902 by Harle Oren Cummins

West Texas War and Other Western Stories — Western hijinks by Gary Lovisi.

What Was That? — Ghostly murder mystery from 1920 by Katharine Haviland Taylor.

What If? Volume 3 — Richard A. Lupoff introduces SF short stories that should have won a Hugo, but didn't.

When the Bat Man Thirsts and Other Stories — Weird tales from Frederick C. Davis.

When the Dead Walk — Gary Lovisi takes us into the zombie-infested South.

Whip Dodge: Man Hunter — Wesley Tallant's saga of a bounty hunter of the old West.

Win, Place and Die! — The first new mystery by Milt Ozaki in decades. The ultimate novel of 70s Reno.

Writer, Volumes 1, 2 & 3 — A *magnus opus* from Richard A. Lupoff summing up his life as writer.

You'll Die Laughing — Bruce Elliott's 1945 novel of murder at a practical joker's English countryside manor.

You're Not Alone: 30 Science Fiction Stories from *Cosmos Magazine*, edited by Damien Broderick.

RAMBLE HOUSE

www.ramblehouse.com
flyingspiderster@gmail.com
10329 Sheephead Drive, Vancleave MS 39565 USA

www.ingramcontent.com/pod-product-compliance
Lightning Source LLC
Chambersburg PA
CBHW051035160426
43193CB00010B/953